The Never, *Um,* Ever Ending Story

LIFE, COUNTDOWN AND EVERYTHING IN BETWEEN

IAN MOLLY MELDRUM

with Jeff Jenkins

With special thanks to Lawrie Masterson

ALLEN&UNWIN
SYDNEY·MELBOURNE·AUCKLAND·LONDON

First published in 2014

Allen & Unwin
83 Alexander Street
Crows Nest NSW 2065
Australia
Phone: (61 2) 8425 0100
Email: info@allenandunwin.com
Web: www.allenandunwin.com

Cataloguing-in-Publication details are available
from the National Library of Australia
www.trove.nla.gov.au

ISBN 978 1 76011 205 9

Internal design by Deborah Parry Graphics
Endpapers (© Newspix)
Index by Puddingburn
Set in 11.5/16 pt Minister by Midland Typesetters, Australia
Printed and bound in Australia by Griffin Press

10 9 8 7 6 5 4 3 2 1

MIX
Paper from
responsible sources
FSC® C009448

The paper in this book is FSC certified.
FSC promotes environmentally responsible,
socially beneficial and economically viable
management of the world's forests.

Though I wasn't witness to his early antics, they have become industry legend. Long may he reign as our King, or Queen, of Pop 'n' Roll. Molly Meldrum is, in short, 'The Real Thing'.
Kylie Minogue

I must give Molly credit where credit is due—I know of no one else who can write so much about so little and take up so much space saying it.
Stan Rofe, *Go-Set* magazine, 19 June, 1971

Molly is at a club in Regent Street, London, at a party for the Royal Command screening of *Titanic*, when he feels a tap on the shoulder.

'Excuse me, Molly, I'm sorry to interrupt you, but there are a lot of people here and I might miss you later and this is my chance to say hello and tell you how much I loved *Countdown* and how much I admire you.'

It is Geoffrey Rush, Australia's Academy Award-winning actor.

Molly smiles. 'Thank you very much, Geoffrey. I haven't had the honour of meeting you until now, but I want to congratulate you on winning your Academy Award for your excellent performance in *The Piano*. I just thought it was so good, and the odds were against you . . .'

As Molly waffles on, he's struck by a dreadful realisation.

'Geoffrey, I'm so sorry. I said *The Piano*, but, of course, it wasn't *The Piano*. You played a piano in it, but it was *Shine*. I'm so sorry.'

'That's all right.'

'No, it's not. It's inexcusable. I am so sorry.'

'Look,' Geoffrey says, placing his hand gently on Molly's shoulder, 'that's what I'm trying to say, Molly—that's why we love you so much.'

CONTENTS

About a decade after I got my 'Molly' tattoo on my left arm, I returned to The Tattoo Shop on Sunset Boulevard to get it re-coloured.

'Hey,' beamed the tattooist, 'the boss must have done this one all those years ago! Would you like the name changed?'

'Um, no.'

'So you're still with the same girl?!'

'Um, yeah.'

'That's great! Hey, everyone, check this out—this guy is still with the same lady after more than 10 years!'

Then he whispered to me, 'How do you do it? I'm having some problems with my lady right now . . .'

Over the following minutes, I dispensed some vague relationship advice—as I hoped and prayed that no one from Australia walked in and said, 'Hey, Molly!'

But I guess the tattooist was right. Molly and I have been together for a very long time.

FOREWORD

By John Farnham

I once had a bath with Ian, so I know he's been clean at least once in the 40-odd years I've known him!

I'm writing this without having read the book, so at the moment my imagination is running wild, with the 'volume' knob on 11 and the 'outrageous' knob falling off! As always with Ian, it's hard not to go straight to the outrageous. His sense of drama—and, believe me, we're talking a highly developed sense of drama—I am sure will entertain as you rip (figuratively) through the pages to follow.

Jill, Rob, James and I don't see a lot of Ian nowadays, which is good—absence makes the heart grow fonder! And we're all very fond of him at this time . . .

All jokes aside, though, the man's a passionate crusader, not only for the Australian music industry, but the music industry as a whole. If I had to sum him up in a few words, I couldn't. That's why you've had to read all this drivel.

I know one thing for sure—if you're interested in the ins-and-outs and the comings-and-goings in the world of popular music and its exponents, then you just made a pretty good investment.

As the great lady herself said:

'Fasten your seat belt, you're in for a bumpy ride . . .'

John Farnham was the only artist to perform on the first and last Countdown.

INTRODUCTION
By Michael Gudinski

Molly and I didn't become really close until *Countdown* started broadcasting in 1974. A year or so before that, I had started the fledgling independent record label Mushroom Records. We were all putting our heart and soul into it, and had some success with a couple of minor hits and a gold album, but we almost went under.

Finally, one of our acts, Skyhooks, who I was also managing at the time, was embraced by the Australian public. This five-piece band was made up of brazen lads sporting make-up, bizarre costumes and, most importantly, writing and performing fantastic songs featuring risqué double-entendre lyrics delivered by a cheeky young chippie with surfie good looks and a killer voice—the late great Graeme 'Shirley' Strachan.

Skyhooks were an ideal act in the early '70s when *Countdown* began. At that time, colour TV burst into our lounge-rooms and the perfect entertainment storm had arrived. Molly developed the show and put his stamp all over it. His key role when the show began broadcasting was talent coordinator, until 1975, when he finally agreed to host a weekly news segment that John Paul Young nicknamed 'Humdrum'. *Countdown* was Molly and Molly was *Countdown*.

The Australian public can thank one Ian Molly Meldrum for introducing them to a plethora of Australian and international artists during this segment: to name-drop a couple of prime international examples, ABBA and Madonna, who no one had ever heard of before Molly championed them. Ultimately, they charted in Australia before they enjoyed success in their own countries.

As for Mushroom Records and *Countdown*, every week we would meet, talk and argue about which Mushroom artists would perform, have their video played and/or be reviewed by Molly. If it wasn't me, it would be one of the other Mushroom staff who would go around to his house to try to convince Molly to give our artists an airing on national TV.

During all the years that *Countdown* broadcast on the ABC every Sunday at 6 p.m., it was rare for a week to go by that one of our Mushroom label artists wasn't performing, or a clip played or the album spoken about by Molly. Thank you, Molly.

Molly always listened to the music he was presented with and was often the first one to call to say either how much he loved the act or, alternatively, to ask me what the hell I was thinking. A classic example of this was Split Enz. We had released four albums with minor success, but I really believed in them and wasn't ready to give up. It came down to the last straw and Molly begged me to let them go, but this was one occasion where I was stubborn. The smash hit 'I Got You' from the mighty *True Colours* album—their fifth—finally broke them big-time in the Australian and international marketplace. To be fair, Molly and the *Countdown* team once more got right behind them.

Molly has always had faith in Australian artists—even if they didn't want to perform on the show, he still supported them. He believed in developing the careers of young up-and-coming artists from all over the world, but was particularly proud of talent nurtured in our own backyard. Some seriously successful careers were aided and abetted by the support of Ian Alexander 'Molly' Meldrum and *Countdown*.

It was a sad evening, truly the end of an amazing era, when *Countdown* finished up in 1987. It was around this time that Molly and I went into business together with his label Melodian. Mushroom had been pretty successful with pop acts, but pop wasn't really my thing. Molly had a great ear for it, and I trusted his judgment to sign pop artists to the label. He found Indecent Obsession, who became hugely popular internationally, and

Peter Andre, who gave Mushroom UK their first number 1 with the single 'Mysterious Girl'. The song was originally titled 'Mysterious Man' but Molly insisted that it was far better changed. And he was resolute that he not be credited, for that and for many other behind-the-scenes creative decisions.

Molly and I started talking about a way of introducing the *Countdown* era to young music fans who were still asking if the show would ever return to TV. We discussed doing a live concert tour featuring some of the artists who appeared on *Countdown* and had gone on to great success.

It took some time but it led to the launch of the Countdown Spectacular tours in 2006 and 2007, which re-invented many musicians and put them back in the spotlight. Molly was co-director of the tour with me, and he co-hosted the concert with John Paul Young, who also performed. We had Gavin 'the voice-over man' Wood, Sherbet reformed and it was a sold-out tour. There was a cast of hundreds, an even bigger crew and it was a blast from the past for all those dedicated *Countdown* fans. Spectacular indeed—and that was just Molly's segment.

To this day, nobody has had a more positive or powerful role in bringing contemporary music, especially Australian music, to our attention. It could be said that Molly has certainly 'done his bit' to stitch together the fabric of our society.

I love you, mate. You are like a brother (not a sister!), and are very much a part of both the Gudinski and Mushroom Group family. Thank you for your passion and your belief in Australian music. I look forward to our next argument and many many more shared occasions.

With love and respect,
Michael G

To my Grandma, my mother Isobel and my father Robert,
Nanna Peele and Michael Fox—
and Ronnie Burns' parents, Aunty Edna and Uncle Bob,
who took me into their home for nine years and gave me a new life.

I would also like to dedicate this book to a girl I loved as
my dear friend—
Jan Pickett. She made me laugh and she made me cry.
Crystal, Morgan and myself miss you so much.

PREFACE

As I fell from the roof on that fateful day just before Christmas 2011, I could see my life flash before my eyes:

My childhood in Quambatook, being thrown out of The Beatles' concert, working for Apple Records in London, producing 'The Real Thing', *Countdown*, *Hey Hey It's Saturday*, seeing Melbourne Storm win four premierships, fainting before St Kilda won their only flag . . .

That would have been a poetic start to this book. But if truth be told, I can't remember a thing about my accident. All I know is I am incredibly lucky to still be here, telling these stories.

Life can change in the blink of an eye. Or, in my case, a fall from a ladder. As you all know, I've been out on the tiles a number of times. But never like this. One minute, I was getting ready for a Christmas party; the next, I was in intensive care at The Alfred Hospital.

A wonderful team of doctors and nurses put me back together. My brother Brian tells me that things were grim for a few days. When I was being transferred from The Alfred to the Epworth, I was wheeled through the morgue, to avoid the photographers camped at the front of the hospital. Fortunately, we didn't stop. My wonderful assistant, Yael, tells me I was so out of it, I thought I was walking the red carpet at an awards show. I kept tapping the nurse on the arm, asking, 'Who's been nominated?'

A near-death experience teaches you many things. The biggest lesson: life is short.

It was time to finish this book.

You could probably write a book about the writing of this book. When the book started, Michael Jackson was at number one with 'Don't Stop 'Til You Get Enough'. Madonna had just landed a job with the Patrick ('Born To Be Alive') Hernandez Revue. Malcolm Fraser was Prime Minister, and Daniel Johns from Silverchair was yet to celebrate his first birthday.

And I wasn't wearing a hat.

Under the headline, 'Molly Tells Almost All', there it was in print, in Melbourne's *The Herald* on New Year's Eve, 1979:

> Ian 'Molly' Meldrum is being recorded. It's a book about the *Countdown* compere's famous friends, which looks like being called 'Most Of My Best Friends Aren't . . .'
>
> 'It's like a fairytale except it's all true,' Meldrum's personal manager, Mr Brian de Courcy, said today.
>
> 'Molly's got up every Sunday morning and just gushed for hours into a tape recorder. No sentences, no commas, no punctuation—just Molly raving on.
>
> 'If anyone can make any sense of it, we should have a book out by April.'

The working title for the book was actually 'Some Of My Best Friends Aren't'. (I remember my dear friend Jim Keays revealed the title to a journalist mate, who said, 'What a great name for a book: "The Son Of My Best Friend's Aunt!"' Jim loved it—I think he thought it was psychedelic.)

That was a line I dropped when interviewed by *60 Minutes*' George Negus. The intrepid reporter decided he wasn't going to be as delicate as *Playboy* magazine, which, in an earlier profile, had referred to my sexual preferences as 'Melbourne's worst-kept secret'.

George, after taking his production team into the St Kilda

Football Club and the Croxton Park Hotel where I DJ-ed, put the most bent of all straight questions: 'Are you a homosexual or not?' or, at least, words to that effect. My response was lightning fast. Placing my hand on George's knee, I said, 'A lot of people would say, "Some of my best friends are." In my case, George, some of my best friends *aren't*.'

The interview was conducted while we sat on the couch in the tiny lounge room of my cluttered house in Alfred Street, Prahran. While George did his 'noddies'—those intelligent looks and understanding nods of assent you see when an interview goes to air—I raced into my bedroom, donned a rather colourful bathrobe, grabbed a vacuum cleaner, put a tea towel around my waist like a skirt, and rushed back into the lounge room.

'George!' I screeched in mock surprise as I wedged between camera and interviewer. 'Are you still here?'

For a brief period during the '80s, we were calling the book 'An Attempt At The Story So Far'. I loved 'Some Of My Best Friends Aren't', but then I thought there was a more appropriate title. My life—and this book—really has been the never-ending story. Fortunately, not even a little fall from a roof has been able to stop it.

I was overwhelmed by the love and support I received after my accident. Famous friends, such as Elton John and Julia Gillard, rang to see if I was okay. Duran Duran dedicated a show to me. I got bags of cards from people I'd never met. Ted Baillieu, the then Premier of Victoria, dropped in to say hello. 'You're a national treasure, Molly,' he said.

'No, I'm not,' I replied, 'I'm just an idiot.'

A lucky idiot.

Writing these pages has made me realise just how fortunate I have been. After his near-death experience, my mate Kerry Packer famously said, 'I've been to the other side and let me tell you, son, there's fucking nothing there.' I had no such revelation, but I do know that it's great to be alive.

Every day is a new adventure. As Sherbet said, *Life . . . is for living*.

It really has been a remarkable life. Thanks to all of you for being a part of it.

'Bloody hell, that's the cunt we need.'

As Robbie Weekes stares out the window of the Botanical Hotel in South Yarra, he has a revelation. A white Celica, with a hole in the driver's door, is racing down Domain Road. It does a crazy U-turn, between two trams, and mounts the footpath. Out leaps a guy who runs into the hotel's bottle shop.

'Which particular cunt is that?' Robbie's ABC colleague Michael Shrimpton asks.

But Robbie is already out the door, dragging the driver from the bottle shop to the main part of the hotel. Holding a bottle of Johnnie Walker in a paper bag in one hand, the guy is introduced: 'Michael Shrimpton, this is Ian Meldrum.'

Michael points to the Celica on the footpath. 'Why did you do that?'

'Um, er, because there was nowhere else to park.'

'And what do you do for a living, Ian?' Michael asks.

'Um, I'm a record producer and I write a rock column, and, oh yeah, at the moment I host a children's show on Channel Seven. It's called *Anything Can Happen*.'

Michael says nothing, but thinks, 'God help the country.'

'Um, I need a drink,' Molly says. 'Do you want one?'

Both Michael and Robbie decline. As Molly goes to the bar, Michael leans across the table and says to Robbie: 'For God's sake, the man can't put two sentences together.'

1: I SHOULD BE SO LUCKY

1974: I get a new job—I owe it all to drinking—Shrimpton and
Weekes, the new men in my life—*Countdown* to blast off!

*Growing up in Brisbane in the 1970s, the local hero was
Joh Bjelke-Petersen, a stuttering, incoherent icon. But suddenly
in 1974 along came a challenge from the south.*
Ellen Fanning, *60 Minutes* reporter, 1999

It was August 1974, a cold day in Melbourne, and unbeknownst
to me, Michael Shrimpton and Robbie Weekes—two of the
ABC's rising stars—were having a drink to discuss plans for a
music show.

My life was about to change forever.

A couple of months earlier, Ken Watts, the ABC's director of
television, had come into Michael's Ripponlea office and said,
'You know, the ABC's audience is ageing something shocking.
Most of them are my age [about 50] and this is the death of
the organisation. We get them until they're ten and then they
don't come back to us until they're about to die. Do something
about it.'

Michael had started at the ABC in 1957, under the
network's specialist trainee system. By the time he ended up
in the entertainment department, he had worked in all areas

of the organisation, including four years in Perth. When he landed in Melbourne, he found himself working alongside a blond beanpole, who would introduce himself as, 'I'm Robbie Weekes, I've recently been retrenched from the 0–10 Network.'

Both highly theatrical, Shrimpton and Weekes became kindred spirits, and after his chat with Ken Watts, Michael went to Robbie and said, 'Mate, I've got a problem. Watts has come into my office and dumped this time bomb in my lap. We need to talk.'

I knew Robbie from the 0–10 Network, where he had directed both the *Happening* series and *Kommotion*. Robbie made the amazing clip for Russell Morris' 'The Real Thing', inserting exploding bombs and archival footage from Nazi Germany. It helped the song become a huge hit.

Robbie convinced Michael that a music show was the way to keep young viewers watching the ABC.

I had been campaigning for a national music show in the pages of *Go-Set*. In July 1973, I wrote:

> When I tried to persuade my colleagues who write television pages for the dailies and the Sunday papers to put editorial pressure on the television stations, they did point out to me that the budget to stage such a show would be astronomical and the time-slot ratings wouldn't justify the cost. They did, however, say that they thought the ABC should at least give an hour a week to such a program. Well, I ask you, who do you go to to convince the ABC? Oh, yes, they could afford to present a pop show because, after all, it's our money they're using.

Two months later, my good friend Ed Nimmervoll wrote a *Go-Set* editorial, headed 'The Lost Music'. 'It is frustrating to realise the existence of talent that has no way of reaching an audience. Television, though, might be the answer to many of the music business's ills.'

The only pop show in prime time was *GTK*, which ran for a few minutes on weeknights on the ABC. I was outraged when that show's axing was announced at the end of 1973.

'Well, that's the last straw,' I furiously wrote, 'Australian television has finally hammered in the last nail. Australian artists desperately need a television outlet.' I started a petition—'We consider the show the one vital contribution to the youth culture aired on television'—which saved the show.

Robbie and Michael decided they would do a show combining local and international acts, with high production values, so the local acts wouldn't suffer in comparison to the overseas artists. They didn't want viewers saying, 'Gee, that David Bowie's terrific, but who's this lot?' They also refused to accept the view that because the show was aimed at kids they could skimp on production values. Robbie and Michael were TV geniuses. They planned *Countdown* like you would plan a drama, fighting to get the best people—the best directors, the best camera people and the best set designers—working on the show.

Robbie and Michael later told me that as they sat drinking pots of beer at the Botanical, they came across a stumbling block: who would select the acts to appear on the show?

'Do you want to go out and look for the bands?' Robbie asked Michael.

'Oh, heavens no,' replied Michael, 'What about you?'

'Certainly not.'

Musically, even though I was 30ish, I would rather sit under a willow tree listening to Sarah Vaughan than any of the people who ended up on *Countdown*. I had no interest in it and neither did Michael. To be absolutely frank, neither of us was really equipped to be able to know if they were good or not.

Robbie Weekes, *Countdown* co-creator

And then I drove up. Robbie remembered me from our days together on *Kommotion* and the *Happening* series. He knew I'd just finished on *Go-Set* and that I'd produced records for Russell Morris and Colleen Hewett.

> I knew he had a good ear. And also he wasn't aligned with any record company. We didn't want anyone with a vested interest.
>
> **Robbie Weekes**

On that fateful day at the Botanical Hotel, I became the talent coordinator for the as-yet unnamed music show.

Michael later revealed he had his doubts, but Robbie assured him I was the right man for the job.

At the end of our Botanical encounter, Michael asked when we could catch up again.

'Well, we can always meet at my place, at No. 1 Alexandra Avenue, South Yarra—it's just around the corner.'

'God,' thought Michael, 'the maniac lives two doors from me.'

The next task was pitching the concept to Ken Watts. Michael instructed me: '*You* sell it to him.'

I was aghast. Here was this man, who looked and talked like Sir John Gielgud, and he wanted *me* to sell the concept? He had to be joking.

But a week later, I was at the ABC, pitching the show.

It was daunting, because I had never dealt with such hierarchy before. I stumbled and bumbled in front of a bureaucrat with grey hair in a suit. I just spat out what I thought about television and the need for music shows and I walked out thinking, 'Well, that was fucked, I don't know what that was all about.'

Me, too. I didn't understand a word Molly had said. Ken called me and said, 'Where did you find *that?*' I lied and told him that *he* found *us*. And that there was something there, so why didn't he give us a chance? He asked me what I wanted. And completely off the top of my head, for no particular reason, I said, 'Give us six half-hours.' I guess I knew we wouldn't get it right first up. And this was the sort of bloke he was. Extraordinary faith and he loved young people. 'Okay, you've got six,' Ken replied.

Michael Shrimpton, *Countdown* co-creator

We had our show; we now had to come up with a name.

We toyed with the title 'Six O'Clock Still Rocks', as a reference to the great Johnny O'Keefe's pioneering rock show *Six O'Clock Rock*, which started in the late '50s. Then we came up with the name 'Countdown', because the show would be counting down to the week's number one song. It was a great name. It also had people thinking of the space race. Even though it was five years since the moon landing, people were still fascinated by space exploration, with *Lost In Space* a hit show on Australian television.

As we counted down to the start of *Countdown*, I wrote about the show in 'The Meldrum Beat', my column in *Listener In-TV*. You could tell I was excited. 'For this show the audience will be asked to join in with the groups by dancing around and becoming a general part of the show,' I told the readers.

The birth of *Countdown* coincided with the arrival of colour television in Australia. At the end of 1974, each network had a limited licence to test colour transmission. When I first went to meetings at the ABC, I was surprised to see a team of German people. The ABC had bought the PAL colour TV system—a German system—and the Germans sent Boeings of experts to teach us how to use it. They told the drama people, 'Less is more', so when *Bellbird* first appeared in colour, it was in deep mourning. There wasn't a primary colour to be seen; everyone was wearing beige. (Michael had a wonderful way with words. He described the colour TV experts as 'dour house-bricks in suits'.)

> Robbie and I knew that the way to go was to throw up all over them. Let *Bellbird* do Monday to Thursday in the same time slot and we'll appear on the Friday and just go *'Chuck!'*
>
> **Michael Shrimpton**

When I got the *Countdown* gig, I was still doing my children's show *Anything Can Happen* on Channel Seven, five days a week for two hours from 4 p.m. to 6 p.m., and four hours on a Saturday morning. As much as it was good fun and I was able to have musical guests on the show, it wasn't exactly what I envisaged doing for the next few years.

But I didn't think *Countdown* was my future. When Robbie and Michael told me we'd been given six weeks, I thought, 'Well, that's nice, but that will be it. Don't give up your day job.'

I booked the acts for the first show. The line-up was all Australian: Johnny Farnham (singing 'One Minute Every Hour'), Sherbet ('Silvery Moon'), Daryl Braithwaite ('You're My World'), Linda George ('Mama's Little Girl') and Skyhooks ('Living In The 70's'). And we presented Sherbet with a gold record.

Skyhooks songwriter and bass player Greg Macainsh missed the show. He had hepatitis and was in the infectious diseases ward at Fairfield Hospital. Greg never got to see the Hooks' performance—there were no VCRs or Foxtel iQ back in 1974.

Greg's place on the first *Countdown* was taken by Red Symons' girlfriend, Jenny Keath, who dressed up like Greg. No one seemed to notice.

A great trivia question: *Who hosted the first* Countdown?

Most people think I was the host, but I was nowhere to be

seen on camera during that first show. The *Countdown* premiere was hosted by Grant Goldman, who hosted the 3UZ breakfast show at the time.

It was my feeling that because music had been the providence of radio until this point, we had to bring DJs in because they had the audience. Hitch them to your wagon and they would talk about you and themselves for a week. And they did.

Michael Shrimpton

Three radio DJs auditioned for Michael and Robbie: Grant Goldman; 3XY's Ric Melbourne; and John O'Donnell. Grant— who started in radio at the age of fourteen at 2TM in his home town of Tamworth—had some TV experience in Brisbane, hosting *Jukebox Jury* and a *Young Talent Time*-like show called *It's A Small World*, as well as introducing cartoons on Channel Seven.

He was a natural.

I knew that *Countdown* was going to be a special show because Michael and Robbie were like two-week-old puppies—they were very excited. When they sold it to me, they said, 'This is going to be the biggest thing!'

Grant Goldman, radio host

Grant was paid $140 for the gig.

Believe it or not, I never intended to have an on-camera role on *Countdown*.

Part of the reason he [Molly] went on air was because someone failed to turn up. He was like our standby compere. He was hopeless, but people seemed to like him.

Robbie Weekes

Another great trivia question: *What time and day did the first* Countdown *go to air?*

Even though the show became forever linked with the Sunday 6 p.m. timeslot, the first *Countdown* went to air on a Friday at 6.30 p.m.

I'll never forget Friday, 8 November, 1974.

As usual, I was sitting in the Channel Seven studios between 4 p.m. and 6 p.m. hosting my live show. I was a little anxious because I knew that *Countdown* was about to go to air.

All I could think was, 'I wonder what people will think of it?'

Grant Goldman hired a colour TV for the weekend and watched the show with 3UZ's programmer Bill Gates, a radio legend who helped inspire the Bee Gees' name (when he was on Brisbane's 4BH, Bill would open his show, 'Hi, this is BG on BH').

> What I learned that day was that wearing a striped shirt wasn't a good idea. None of us knew anything about colour TV; my shirt made it look like I was moving all the time. And, yes, I had the '70s mo and long hair—I looked like I was a member of the Village People.
>
> **Grant Goldman**

At one minute to six, I said goodbye to our viewers with the parting line, 'I'll see you tomorrow morning.' I then dashed up to the office of Gordon French, Channel Seven's chief programmer, to watch the show because he had one of the few colour television sets in the country.

And there it was—*Countdown* in living colour.

'Wow,' I thought, 'this is really happening.'

Michael and Robbie were a mile away, in the city at Myer, standing alongside hundreds of curious people in the TV department, checking out the new technology. It was black and white until 6.30 p.m.

Then *Countdown* started.

Michael and Robbie stood at the back of the room with tears running down their faces. They knew they had struck a nerve.

When Molly and I worked together at Channel Seven, it was a running joke that I wouldn't let him look in my magic bag. Years later, Molly was in the control room at Studio 31 at the ABC, where I was doing a show called *The Magic Bag*. They were running a tape of the show in the control room and Molly thought I was live in the studio. He pressed the intercom and said, 'Look out, Buckland, I'm coming to look in your bag', not knowing that this was broadcast across the 7 o'clock news!

Ian Buckland, TV presenter/magician

2: I REMEMBER WHEN I WAS YOUNG

1942–1974: Good golly, it's Molly—Stan is The Man—The Mallee Boy—The darkness before the Dawn—The Greatest Show On Earth—Bright lights, big city—I join the *Go-Set*—Quite a *Kommotion*—Meet The Beatles!—Molly the Monster—Just do it.

Humility is Ian's greatest asset and I'm sure he doesn't know it. All right, so he's a loud mouth and suffers constantly from foot-in-mouth disease, but beneath all that, he's got a peculiar warmth, which comes through no matter how noisy and rude he might get. The Americans coined a beautiful word for it: 'Charisma'.
Stan Rofe, *Go-Set* magazine, 1971

So how did a man named Molly end up on the ABC?

And I guess you're also wondering, how did a country boy named Ian become known as Molly?

Well, my first media idol was a DJ named Stan Rofe. I loved his radio show. He was the first DJ to play Johnny O'Keefe, and he was instrumental in the careers of Normie Rowe, Russell Morris, Johnny Chester, The Masters Apprentices, Ronnie Burns and countless others.

Hi-de-hi, Victoria, yours truly Stan the Man, Melbourne's rocky jockey—winning, chinning and grinning. Welcome to our swingin' soiree . . .

In 1966, I got my first job in journalism, writing for the pop paper *Go-Set*. My column was called 'Ian Meldrum Listens Thru Keyholes'; Stan's column was 'Stan Rofe's Tonic'. Stan and I had a wonderfully bitchy rivalry in the pages of *Go-Set*. Some readers thought we hated each other, but it was pure theatre. Usually.

> **Stan Rofe:** The last time I saw a mouth like Meldrum's, there was a fish hook in it . . . I even heard Ronnie Burns say the other day that Ian Meldrum is so silly he thinks that a blueprint is a dirty picture.
>
> **Ian Meldrum:** I must say that Stanley Rofe has got a cheek. How dare he criticise me for not wearing shoes to certain receptions. I mean, who's Stan Rofe to talk—it's much better than the pantyhose that he gets around in.

On a Tuesday in 1967 in his 3UZ office on Bourke Street, Stan was pondering what he would write in his column in that week's *Go-Set*. As he paced around the room, Ian Buckland, who also worked at 3UZ, was sitting at the typewriter. Next to him was the office boy, Frank Howson, cousin of celebrity John-Michael 'Hollywood' Howson.

Stan was reading my column in *Go-Set*'s latest edition. 'Look at what he's said about me this week!' he bellowed, throwing the paper on the desk next to Ian. 'How can I get him back?'

After a few suggestions, Frankie said, 'Why not give him a girl's name, something that goes with Meldrum?'

'Terrific,' Stan smiled, 'that'll get right up his nose!'

Stan dictated the column as Ian typed. When Stan came to my name, he said, 'Let's call him Mildred.' But for some reason, Ian typed 'Molly' instead.

And people have called me 'Molly' ever since. The name has not been without some drama. When I first went to London, *The Sun*'s music writer cheekily said that Ian *and* Molly Meldrum were off to visit the Queen. My mother called me, distraught. 'Oh Ian,' she cried, 'how could you get married and not tell us?'

In the 1980s, I would often tell reporters that I was born on a boat off Cairo, saying, 'I'm a bit of an Arab.' But I was actually born in Orbost in East Gippsland, Victoria. At the age of two or three, we moved to Quambatook, a small farming community in the Mallee in north-western Victoria. Quambatook is an Aboriginal name meaning 'resting place beside a river'.

I also spent a lot of time living with my grandmother in Orbost, because my family was quite dysfunctional. My grandma looked after me and became the absolute love of my life. I remember she would read the Bible to me at night. We'd also often visit Lake Tyers, where there was a vibrant Aboriginal community. The Aborigines became like family to me. In fact, I would lie in the sun, trying to get a darker tan, so I could look like them.

The Mallee has always been a part of me. I remember catching up with the Red Hot Chili Peppers in the '90s. 'You guys look great,' I said. 'You look as fit as Mallee Bulls.' They looked at me strangely. 'What,' singer Anthony Kiedis said, 'we're as fit as *Molly's balls*?'

In Quambatook, my nicknames were 'Mallee Chick' and 'Mallee Root'.

The smell of the Mallee comes back to me at times. I loved my bike—riding around, smelling the wheat, the heat and the mud of the Avoca River. I remember the use of water coolers instead of fridges, with the slight taste of hessian in the water. Whenever I hear the ABC news theme, I can still hear my father's voice. 'Quiet! This is news time.' And my mum, a deeply religious woman, was addicted to the radio serial *Blue Hills*.

I was brought up to dislike Catholics. I can remember throwing stones at Catholic houses in Quambatook.

One day, I was playing in Minister Holloway's garden at the Anglican Church. I was a little mischievous and I pulled up all of his tomatoes. He gave me a frightful belting. When it came time for church the following Sunday, I told Mum I was not going.

'Why?' she asked.

'Because God doesn't like me.'

My father, Robert, who had just returned from World War II (including a stint in Cairo in Egypt), worked in the hardware section at Quamby's general store. Dad would wear a dust jacket and always have a pencil behind his ear. I spent a lot of time at the local milk bar, which was run by Mr Tinkler. The Tinklers owned a gramophone. I would listen to 78s with their daughter, Beverley, who looked after me like an older sister. She would tell me that I needed to spend as much time listening to my teacher at school as I did listening to records.

When we were kids, Quambatook was booming—some of the best wheat country in Victoria. But the bitumen roads came and killed the town. Swan Hill is 37 miles away, and Kerang 26 miles. That used to be a big drive. It's not anymore.

Quambatook's biggest musical export is John 'True Blue' Williamson, 'The Mallee Boy'.

Molly's family and mine go back a long way. His mother, who had a beautiful mezzo-soprano voice, and my dad played the leading roles in *The Mikado*. No, not on Broadway, but in the Quambatook Town Hall. Quamby had an extraordinarily strong musical society, considering our town's district population was about 600. My mother also sang. Now, it was always a source of embarrassment to see your parents perform, but I remember Mrs Meldrum. She was a very good-looking, dark-haired woman.

Even though Molly was just a child, he was always a part of the concerts. He didn't have to be asked to provide an item. It would always be a surprise and we were never disappointed. We all remember Molly, teeth blacked out, singing 'All I Want For Christmas Is My Two Front Teeth', spitting all over my grandma in the front row. And I won't forget him performing 'Bicycle Built For Two' with 'Freddo' Cameron. And who played the part of the bride? Wrong! It was Freddo. Molly loved to make us laugh, and Freddo—who became a carpenter in Quamby—was the ugliest bride I have ever seen. The shows were always a huge success. It's the locals watching the locals making idiots of themselves. Footballers as girls, all that sort of stuff. You can't beat it. Actually, I was surprised Molly didn't end up in the Comedy Theatre. He was always far more flamboyant than any other kid I knew. Or anyone else in Quamby for that matter.

John Williamson

John's cousin, Dawn Williamson, was my first girlfriend. Our relationship started when we were six, and lasted until I moved to Kyabram. We would leave notes for each other under a stone between our houses.

We lived across the road from Dawn's family. Dawn and I bonded because we were 'townies', whereas most of the other kids at Quambatook Primary School lived on farms and caught the bus to school. We walked to school together and then played after school, playing dress-ups and re-enacting scenes from the movies we would see on Friday nights, when the town hall became a picture theatre. Our stage was an old trailer in the yard next to Dawn's house.

Next to Dawn's house was another family of kids, but they were never allowed to perform in our productions. They had to be the audience.

I loved going to Dawn's house because they always had a tin of Akta-Vite, a beautiful powdered chocolate drink, which our family couldn't afford. We would also go to the Tinkler's milk bar and listen to Paul Anka on the Tarax jukebox.

And Dawn would watch me perform at the Quamby concerts and talent quests.

He sang 'Mad Dogs And Englishmen' and that absolutely brought the house down. Another time he did 'Lazybones'. Ian would always win hands-down. He just didn't seem to get shy like the other kids. They would lose their nerve once they got on stage, but Ian never did. He was always the entertainer, but that side got him into trouble in the classroom. He never knew when to shut up. I remember being really upset because he couldn't see that all he had to do to stay out of trouble was to keep quiet.

Dawn Williamson

I loved Dawn, even though she would get angry at me because I would mispronounce words, particularly 'chimney' and 'film' (I would say 'chim-ley' and 'fill-um').

An old tyre hung from a tree on the banks of the river. In summer, we'd swing from the tyre into the river, getting leeches all over us.

Ian was always a bit theatrical about getting a leech on him. He never missed an opportunity to perform. He wouldn't just brush it off, he had to make a song and dance about it.

Dawn Williamson

Quambatook was a big sporting town. Jim Wallis from St Kilda went there to coach after his VFL career ended.

But my memories of Ian aren't of sport. We would walk home and have long talks about families and what we were going to do. He was always going to Orbost in the school holidays to see his grandmother, his mother's mum. He was very fond of his grandmother, she was a special person to him.

Dawn Williamson

I have a memory of being driven to Kerang and put on an Ansett plane to go to Essendon Airport, where I caught another plane to Sale. My aunty and uncle picked me up there and took me to my grandmother's house in Orbost. I had no idea why this was happening. I was a little boy sitting all alone at Essendon Airport. I saw a photo years later of The Beatles' fill-in drummer Jimmy Nicol sitting all alone at Essendon Airport and I thought, 'That's exactly what I was like.' It was my first plane ride ever. I can remember taking off from Kerang and the hostess gave me a piece of barley sugar and said, 'Chew this, it will help your ears.' I was nine years old. I can still hear that voice in my head whenever I eat on a plane: 'Chew this, it will help your ears.'

We stayed in Quambatook for about eight years, before moving to Kyabram in Victoria's Goulburn Valley. But I was sent to stay with my Uncle Doug and Aunty Mary in nearby Shepparton, where they were both teachers at the local high school. Aunty Mary tried to teach me French, but the lessons were not successful.

When I was twelve, 'The Greatest Show On Earth' came to town. I was fascinated by the circus, and I ran away with them, pretending to be one of the crew. But after five days, they found out and sent me home.

In Kyabram, I was an altar boy at St Andrew's Anglican Church. My academic record was not outstanding, though I do recall winning a competition run by the Rechabites, a temperance society. I was a school leader against drinking, a fact worthy of *Ripley's Believe It Or Not!*

At Shepparton High, Aunty Mary wrote her name on the board, explaining, 'This is my name—Mrs Meldrum.' She then got every member of the class to repeat it. When it was my turn, I called her Aunty Mary.

I was kicked out of class.

In a separate class, another teacher wrote a word on the board and asked me how it was pronounced. I had no idea. The boy next to me whispered: 'It's pronounced *fuck*.'

'It's pronounced "fuck",' I said, proudly.

I was kicked out of school.

In 1986, it was reported that Kyabram was considering erecting a statue of me in the town's main street. Either me or a giant kangaroo. When the press alerted me to the plan, I said: 'What?! No, no, no. I think we can do a lot better than put me up there.'

I don't want my childhood romanticised with statues or fanciful stories. My memories of that time are simple: I was always a storyteller, and I was always dreaming stories, thinking about what I could be. I just wanted to be accepted. And I wanted to be part of a family. I just wanted to be *something*. And I knew I was nothing at the time.

> I think everyone in Quamby is proud of Molly in a way. But I don't think they've ever been too sure about him. I remember one old guy in the town said to me, 'But he wasn't a real boy.'

> Quamby, like most country towns, was a great place for a kid, a terrible place for a teenager. I went to boarding school in Melbourne, and I remember running into Molly, who had just started at university. He had a top hat and a cane. He was a real dandy. I remember he told me about his flat, with leopard-skin couches.

> **John Williamson**

I moved to Melbourne to finish my high-school education, staying with a couple of aunties above a milk bar in Elwood.

But I also discovered Melbourne's music scene, becoming a regular at jazz clubs such as Ormond Hall. I remember getting my first pair of blue jeans with red stitching—I felt like a king. My aunties didn't like me staying out late—they thought I was partying too much and studying too little.

One day, I lost a textbook on the Barkly Street bus. I'd noticed a young guy on the bus. I knew he lived across the road from the milk bar, but I had no idea what his name was. In fact, we'd never even had a conversation. That night, I knocked on his door and asked if he'd seen my book.

'My name's Ian,' I mentioned, after he offered to make me a cup of tea. 'I live with my aunts above the milk bar over the road and I need to get away from them for a while . . . would it be possible to stay with you for a couple of weeks?'

Nine years later, I was still living with Ronnie Burns and his family.

The book was lost forever, but I had found my Melbourne family. The Burns' home, at 3/98 Barkly Street, Elwood, became the centre of my new life in the big city. Ronnie's mum, who I called Aunty Edna, and his dad, Uncle Bob, took me in as if I were another son.

Aunty Edna—who had beehive hair like Marge Simpson— loved vaudeville and the theatre. She encouraged me to make my first TV appearance. Wearing a top hat and scarf, I entered a talent segment, miming Noel Coward's 'Mad Dogs and Englishmen' on the piano on *In Melbourne Tonight* with Graham Kennedy and Bert Newton.

I was gonged.

At the end of 1963, I was using lemon juice to try to turn my hair blond as I was learning to surf with a group called the

Suicide Savages at Point Leo. I'll never forget my first time on a surfboard. I was all over the place because I had it the wrong way round. My mates on the beach were cracking up as they yelled, 'It's the other way round, Ian!'

Then it happened. Sitting in the Point Leo sand dunes, listening to Malcolm Searle on 3AK.

He plays a song called 'She Loves You'. As the sound leaps out of the transistor, I think, 'I want to be a part of that.'

The world was changing, and I was part of it.

Years later, I interviewed Keith Richards.

Molly: You obviously love rock 'n' roll to the hilt.
Keith: I do.
Molly: Why?
Keith: You know, that's one of the things I ask myself occasionally. But I don't know. One minute it wasn't there, you know, living in England, [the] BBC. One minute it was 'How Much Is That Doggie In The Window?' then you give me 'Heartbreak Hotel', baby, and I know what I like. It's a feeling more than anything to me. Take me away!

One of the Suicide Savages was English and his cousin had sent him the first Beatles album, *Please Please Me*, so we went back to his place in Seaford to listen to it. It was like an explosion in my mind. As a kid, I would listen to composers—Mahler is my favourite—and I'd want to be the conductor. Now I wanted to be a record producer. I'd go to sleep and hear these sounds in my head.

Little did I know that as I was sitting on the beach at Point Leo, a promoter named Kenn Brodziak was finalising a deal to bring The Beatles to Australia. I camped outside Myer in Lonsdale Street for two days to pay 37 shillings for my Beatles tickets. And when they arrived in Melbourne, on Sunday,

14 June, 1964, Ronnie and I were at the Southern Cross Hotel to greet them—with 20,000 other screaming fans.

We would do anything to catch a glimpse of them. I later saw the Channel Nine news, with reporter Michael Charlton saying, 'Mothers, if your child is out there, you should be ashamed. You should take a very good lesson from this. The stupidity of letting their children come to something like this.'

I rushed for the cars when they arrived, pretending to be part of the security team. The ploy worked, except one of the cars ran over my foot. And then I realised they were decoy cars—the real cars were sneaking in via the hotel's back entrance.

The following day, Ronnie and I hid in the Southern Cross car park. Our friend Bruce Rose pinched his dad's car and we hid on the floor. We parked there from 8.30 a.m. to 5 p.m., sending one of our party out for meat pies. Then the lift door opened and George Harrison stepped out. But just as we leapt out of the car, we were spotted by the security guards. I was shattered—I would have given anything to meet The Beatles.

The Beatles did six 35-minute shows at Festival Hall, at 6 p.m. and 8.45 p.m. on June 15, 16 and 17. I saw the 6 p.m. show on the first night; well, at least part of it.

I will never forget the thrill of seeing the support band Sounds Incorporated's bass drum sign being peeled away after the interval, and there it was—the famous Beatles drum sign. And then the band walked onstage.

'There's Paul!'

'There's John!'

It was unbelievable excitement. Festival Hall seemed like the biggest place in the world. It was like being in a sea with massive waves containing millions of people. In actual fact, there were only about 6000 people there.

Everyone was screaming, especially the girls. Ronnie says I was like a girl. I was hysterical. A St John's Ambulance guy apparently came up to me and asked: 'Are you all right? Can I take you out of here?' But I was oblivious to anything apart from The Beatles.

Ronnie tells me he told the guy, 'Don't worry, I'll look after him.' He tried to get me to calm down and sit down, but I just couldn't.

Apparently, the next thing that happened was I jumped up and screamed, 'John, I love you . . . Paul, I love you!', and I accidentally grabbed the long hair of a girl sitting in front of me, who then proceeded to scream as well. The St John's guy appeared again, this time with security. 'He has *got* to come out of there.'

Ronnie stood up and said, 'Look, he'll be okay.' But as he did so he inadvertently clenched his fists and three bouncers pounced on him and me. They dragged us through the crowd and threw us out the door and slammed it shut. For me, hysteria took on a new meaning. I could hear, over the screaming inside, Paul starting to sing 'Long Tall Sally', my favourite.

I fell down, sobbing. Utter devastation. As they carried me away, I gave one last boot to the Festival Hall door. I think my scratch marks are still there today.

I became known as 'Beatle' to my surfer mates. Surfing and music were my two passions. In fact, I often slept with my surfboard in my Elwood bedroom. The tiny room, at the front of the Burns' flat, was decorated with posters of my surfing heroes, Midget Farrelly and Nat Young, as well as countless photos of the Fab Four.

I also loved footy and became a member of the St Kilda cheer squad, which was led by a striking blonde girl named Sandy Breen, who became my girlfriend. I even asked Sandy to marry me, but she said, 'I don't think so, I think we're having too much fun.'

It was the last thing on my mind. But for years, my mum would say to me, 'I wonder what your life would have been like if you'd married Ian?' And I'd say, 'Mum, if I'd married Ian, it would've lasted a year. Tops. And we probably would have ended up enemies.' The way it's worked out we're best friends for life.

Sandy Breen

By the mid-'60s, Ronnie Burns was a pop star. In 1964, he answered an ad to join a Beatles-inspired band called The Flies. After several singles, including 'Doin' The Mod', The Flies scored the support slot on The Rolling Stones' first Australian tour. I dreamed of becoming a record producer, but one day I bumped into *Go-Set*'s owner Phillip Frazer, who asked if I could organise a photo shoot with Ronnie Burns. I wrote the words accompanying the picture, at the bottom of page 15 in *Go-Set* on July 20, 1966, under the headline 'Ronnie Meets The Barrett Brothers':

Ronnie Burns went backstage of the Princess Theatre show *Robert and Elizabeth* to meet some of his old friends who are taking the part of the Barrett Brothers in the show. The Brothers are by no means square to the Top 40 world as Evan Dunstan used to manage the pop group The Flies and Rod Anderson was a singer on *Bandstand*. Paul Thompson was an original member of The Cherokees, whilst Andrew Guild played the Artful Dodger in the hit musical *Oliver!* Ronnie also met the principals of the show, June Bronhill, Denis Quilley, and last, but not least, Frank Thring. Could it be that Ronnie Burns is thinking of turning to the stage?

That was my journalism debut. My first pay cheque was $10, which I deposited at the ANZ Bank across the road from the *Go-Set* office in Charnwood Crescent, St Kilda.

My first bylined story was page one of *Go-Set*'s next issue: 'Twilights Take National Title. Ex-Adelaide Group Win Hoadley's Battle Of The Sounds. By *Go-Set*'s Roving Reporter Ian Meldrum'. ('"Whoopee-ee-ee" was the reaction of Glenn [Twilights lead singer] on winning the National Battle of the Sounds, watched by a crowd of thousands of screaming teenagers,' I wrote. I also claimed the atmosphere at Festival Hall was 'the best since the Beatles'.)

The hottest teen show in Melbourne at the time was *Kommotion*, 5.30 p.m. weekdays on Channel O. The *Kommotion* team—including Grant Rule and Denise Drysdale—would mime the hits of the day. It was a primitive form of music video, and it was a smash hit. There was even a *Kommotion* icy pole.

> It's quite bizarre when you look back at it, but things were different back then. It was just ten years after TV started, and no one knew what the real performers looked liked, so it didn't matter. It was very popular.
>
> **Tony Healey, *Kommotion***

In August 1966, there was a *Kommotion* coup. When producer David Joseph was sacked, most of the cast quit and formed a breakaway group. I covered the story for *Go-Set*, interviewing the new producer, Al Maricic, who suggested I should audition for the new cast. I laughed and said I had no interest in a television career. But when I mentioned the offer to Phillip Frazer back at the *Go-Set* office, he said: 'You should audition, it'd be good for the paper if you were on TV.'

A few days later, I became a *Kommotion* mimer, alongside my friends Tony Healey and Keith Millar, Denise Drysdale, Chantal Contouri (then known as Maryanne), Maggie Stewart (who would later marry Ronnie Burns) and Bob Pritchard.

Lily Brett kindly reviewed my performances in *Go-Set*: 'What else can we say? This loveable boy brings just the right touch of the old vaudeville into *Kommotion*.'

As a viewer, I thought *Kommotion* had a big budget and big sets. I discovered it had a tiny budget and was shot in a small studio in Nunawading. Every Saturday, the cast taped five half-hour shows and one weekend special, working from 7.30 a.m. to 6 p.m. The Tuesday and Thursday shows were shot in the morning, with one set, while the Monday, Wednesday and Friday shows were done in the afternoon, with another set. Having two sets and shooting the shows out of order gave the impression that the show was live every day with a different set.

Ah, the magic of television!

I was paid $35 a week. It was great fun, and I felt like one of The Beatles when I signed my first autograph when the *Kommotion* cast did an appearance at Myer. The downside was that the Saturday shooting schedule meant I couldn't go to St Kilda football games.

My television career almost came to an end a month after it started. St Kilda were playing Collingwood in the Grand Final on September 24, 1966. I was required on set all day for the *Kommotion* taping. But I left at 11 a.m., to go to the game.

The director said, 'Son, you will never work in TV again.'

'I don't care,' I replied.

That director was Robbie Weekes.

With a minute to go in the game, the scores were level, when Barry Breen grabbed the ball. His kick wobbled through for a behind. The Saints were in front! The crowd went up—and I went down. The excitement of the day was too much for me: I fainted.

When the final siren sounded, I was unconscious. To this day, it is St Kilda's one and only premiership, so I have never actually 'seen' them win a Grand Final. The two biggest things in my life—The Beatles' concert and St Kilda's flag—and I missed the climax of both.

Soon after joining the *Kommotion* cast, *Sebastians* magazine featured a profile of me.

Musical education: Six years piano and stage experience.

Hobbies: Surfing, snow and water skiing, cricket.

Favourite singers: Barbra Streisand, Petula Clark and The Beatles.

Favourite actors: Peter O'Toole and Rex Harrison.

Favourite actresses: Julie Christie.

Favourite style of music: Musical comedy, pop classics.

Favourite food: Irish stew.

Favourite drink: Milk.

Ideal girl: Intelligent, sophisticated, moral, and a sense of humour.

Professional ambition: Be successful and make money.

Pet aversion: Insincere people.

Favourite TV show: *Peyton Place.*

Relaxation: Sport.

Has Kommotion changed your pattern of life?: No. My pattern of life has been rather irregular and has stayed that way.

Do you intend to be a singer? No.

Can you believe that milk was my favourite drink?

I became a regular at Melbourne's clubs, including Sebastians, Berties and The Thumpin' Tum. A *Go-Set* ad for Berties and Sebastians called me 'the swingingest guy on the scene'.

One of my big *Kommotion* songs was 'Winchester Cathedral', a number one hit in 1966 for The New Vaudeville Band. I did the song wearing a pinstripe suit, bowler hat, with a black umbrella. I also performed two of Sam The Sham and The Pharaohs' biggest hits—'Lil' Red Riding Hood' and 'The Hair

On My Chinny Chin Chin', as well as Peter and Gordon's 'Lady Godiva' and 'Knight In Rusty Armour'. And in Series 5, Episode 268, backed by four of the *Kommotion* girls, I did a song called 'Why Don't Women Like Me?'

I would rehearse at home, in front of the mirror, learning some basic dance routines, such as the Monkey and the Arrow, but I struggled to get them right. I was also not good at remembering lyrics.

Molly was given all the comedy songs to do. He would always send up the song. And he would always forget the words. It would infuriate the producers.

Keith Millar, *Kommotion*

Sadly, or perhaps fortunately, all of the *Kommotion* tapes were destroyed.

Adelaide band The Masters Apprentices once appeared on *Kommotion* to mime their debut single, 'Undecided'. I produced the Masters' third single, 'Living In A Child's Dream', which hit the Top 10 in Melbourne and Sydney, and won Song of the Year in the *Go-Set* Pop Poll.

Ian took a shine to us. He was very enthusiastic. He's actually a groupie, to be quite honest.

Ian was quite different in the studio. He doesn't know one knob from another. His production is something like, 'Can you make it sound more purple?' Somehow, miraculously, he would get what he wanted.

Jim Keays, The Masters Apprentices

My first record production was with a Melbourne band called Somebody's Image, who I saw supporting The Groop at the lifesaving club in Anglesea in January 1967. I thought the singer had genuine star potential. His name was Russell Morris.

Two years later, I would produce Russell's debut solo single, 'The Real Thing', and I was also his manager. But that's a book in itself . . . *Ooh ma ma ma mow.*

I wrote about The Beatles for the first time in *Go-Set* on 2 August, 1967, reviewing the *Sgt. Pepper's* album. 'Joy, utter wonderment, humour, sadness, melody are rolled into one,' I gushed, 'to make this piece of wax an experience.'

On 11 January, 1968, I went on my own magical mystery tour, boarding the *Castle Felice* at Station Pier in Port Melbourne. My friends The Groop had won Hoadley's Battle of the Sounds, and first prize was a trip to London. I tagged along as their roadie.

> I have to laugh at the description 'roadie'—I don't think Ian carried anything except drinks.
>
> **Brian Cadd, The Groop**

As we boarded the boat, Stan Rofe told me that Somebody's Image's version of 'Hush'—which I produced—had hit number one on the Melbourne charts. As we sailed through the heads, I felt like leaping on the bow of the boat and bellowing, 'I'm the king of the world!'

In London, I caught up with The Easybeats, who had relocated to the United Kingdom in 1966 and had a Top 10 hit with 'Friday On My Mind'. George Young introduced me to his older brother, Alex, who was the singer in a band called Grapefruit, one of the first signings to Apple. I became good friends with their manager, Terry Doran, who helped run the Apple empire.

During my first meeting with Terry, George Harrison walked in. I nervously stood up, but had to sit down because my legs started to shake. George said 'Hello'; all I could manage was a stutter.

Terry later showed me George's office. It was painted completely pink, with framed pictures of the Maharishi, the Krishna temple and numerous Indian gentlemen.

My second visit to Terry's office—to confirm the interview with Grapefruit—resulted in another Beatle encounter. Terry's secretary told me to wait on the couch outside Mr Doran's office and while I sat there, I could hear an argument going on in Terry's office. A guy was yelling at Terry about the Apple phone bill.

Then I recognised the voice—it was Paul McCartney!

Paul was yelling—really yelling—about the phone bill. I overheard him demanding, 'You'll have to write every phone call in a book.' Terry was furious. I remember thinking, 'My God, this is Paul McCartney, the richest man in the world [*well, he was to me*] and he's worried about the phone bill?'

I later met Paul at an Apple dinner. Again, nerves got the better of me. I went to shake his hand, forgetting that I still had a knife in my hand.

Soon after, I got to meet the Beatle I most idolised, John Lennon, but it was yet another little disaster. It was an EMI Records reception at Revolution, one of London's hip clubs. The party, for one of the company's new signings, was hailed as one of London's big events and the 'who's who' were in attendance. I arrived with my girlfriend Camilla Beach, who was the London correspondent for *Everybody's* magazine. We bumped into my old *Kommotion* castmate Chantal Contouri, who was working at Revolution as a waitress. I edged my way through the packed club, heading for the bar, when I spotted them . . .

'Stop!' I yelled to Camilla. 'Terry's here and he's with John and Ringo!'

It was one of my more 'uncool' moments. Camilla was furious with me for making her look silly. But we calmed down, had a couple of drinks and caught up with Chantal and Easybeats singer Stevie Wright. Terry later came over and said, 'Ah, my little Aussie Kangaroo [*that's what he often called me*], you have to meet John.'

I was sitting on the back of a chair when John appeared. As Terry said, 'John, this is one of your biggest fans', I went to shake his hand. But it was all too much for me. I fainted, and as my legs went, I dragged the chair down with me, and collapsed on a girl next to me, sending her scotch and coke flying. The drink went all over me—and John. Terry later told me that John had said: 'If that's one of my biggest fans, please don't ever introduce me to one of my enemies.'

It was very embarrassing. All I can remember is Little Stevie Wright laughing. And I broke up with Camilla soon after. I think she decided she couldn't continue going out with someone who was such an embarrassment.

Incidentally, I *did* get the Grapefruit interview for *Go-Set*. I gave them a big plug: 'And succeed they will,' I wrote, 'I can only rave, rave, rave.' The band's one and only hit, 'Dear Delilah'—produced by Doris Day's son, Terry Melcher—hit number 21 on the UK charts.

It was a strange time to be visiting the Apple office because The Beatles had just returned from their Indian sojourn. And as well as a record company, they had started a clothes shop, The Apple Boutique, in Baker Street, with Paul McCartney calling the venture 'Western communism'. George Harrison had obviously been inspired by the Indian trip because the shop was dominated by Indian clothes. Terry was so pleased with my Grapefruit story, he took me to the shop and said, 'Take anything you want.' I replied, 'I don't want any of it, thanks.'

I was one of the first journalists in the world to reveal that

John Lennon would divorce Cynthia and marry Yoko. In the July 10, 1968 edition of *Go-Set*, I quoted Terry Doran: 'It is true John and Cynthia are having marriage problems. It appears that John is very much in love with Yoko. Marriage between the two could be very likely.'

And then I inadvertently broke the story of The Beatles' break-up.

In 1969, I returned to London, sharing an EMI apartment with the Australian record producer David Mackay, next door to the Abbey Road Studios. And Terry offered me a job at Apple. This was a dream come true. Five years after I was thrown out of their Melbourne concert, I was working for the band and living next door to Abbey Road! My job was general office duties, helping out with publicity, though the plan was I would become a junior record producer. One day I even had to impersonate John Lennon. I had to get into bed with one of the secretaries, Dee, and pretend to be John and Yoko for a photo.

These were exciting times. In some ways, I even credit the Beatles with introducing me to drinking. Scotch and coke was the big drink at Apple, and it was a habit I soon picked up.

And then one day, John Lennon called me into the office and announced he wanted to do an interview with me. It was totally out of the blue because I hadn't requested any interviews. He called me 'cobber' as I sat down with him and Yoko.

John basically told me The Beatles were breaking up, that the marriage was over, and 'we are more married to our wives now'. But I was so in awe of him, I wasn't listening.

I sent the tapes back to *Go-Set*, and then I got an urgent call from the office: 'I can't believe The Beatles are breaking up.'

'What?' I was stunned.

'It's in your interview.'

My biggest scoop—and I missed it!

I have no idea why John picked me to drop this bombshell. Maybe it was his wry sense of humour: 'I'll give it to the Aussie mate of Terry's who works here.' I don't know. I guess I'll never know.

My interview ran in *Go-Set* at the start of 1970—more than four months before The Beatles officially disbanded.

My television career—if you can call it a career—continued whenever I was home in Melbourne. When *Kommotion* finished in September 1967, David Joseph asked me to join his new show, *Uptight*, a four-hour show on Saturdays from 8 a.m. to midday. It started on 28 October, 1967 on Channel O, hosted by Brisbane singer Ross D. Wyllie.

At the end of 1969, David Joseph went to London to manage The New Seekers. *Uptight*'s new producer was Kevin Lewis, who formed Lewis Young Productions with Johnny Young.

> What was Molly like as a TV presenter back then? Ah, just as bad. But he's got his own unique style, which apparently the kids identify with. He's never improved, but he's never gotten any worse either.
>
> **Kevin Lewis, *Uptight* producer**

Uptight evolved into *Happening '70*, which became *Happening '71* (hosted by Jeff Phillips), which became *Happening '72*.

In 1970, my old Quambatook mate John Williamson had a big hit with 'Old Man Emu'. 'I always knew the lad could drive a tractor, ride a horse and plant a crop,' I wrote in *Go-Set*, 'but to record a number one hit . . . well, that's another story. Good on yer, Johnno, for bringing a bit of the Aussie flavour into the charts. Must throw down a beer with ya one day.'

After the *Happening* series finished, my next TV gig was

as Molly The Monster. Seriously. I operated a puppet on a Channel Seven kids' show called *Do It*. Molly the puppet was made by Axel Axelrad, the same guy who made Ossie Ostrich.

> Axel came in with this thing and it was cute. But I didn't want cute, I wanted horrible. I wanted something ugly, but with pretensions to being pretty. But I got cute, with pearls and feathers. What can you do?
> **Ian Buckland, *Do It* host and magician**

Molly The Monster was a rival for Ossie Ostrich, and a foil for host Ian Buckland. I would often shriek when one of his magic tricks went wrong. 'Don't be stupid, Buckland,' I would say in a high-pitched voice, hiding under the desk. 'Isn't he silly, kids!'

If that wasn't enough, I was also a cow. The show was sponsored by Dairy Bell Ice Cream, so I also operated a puppet named Daisy the Dairy Cow. And Ian got me to play a grumpy cleaner named Curl.

In 1974, Skyhooks made their first television appearance on *Do It*. And it was my first drama with the band.

The music part of Saturday's show was recorded on Thursday and I wasn't there when Skyhooks did their four songs. All I can remember is Ian Buckland calling me, very upset, on Saturday, saying that the band had ruined his career. He had back-announced them as 'Skylights', but that wasn't his main concern. The band had played Red Symons' song 'Smut', which is about masturbating in a cinema—hardly the stuff for a children's program.

I advised the Hooks that they had better not pull a similar stunt on the upcoming *Countdown*. 'I will smack their bottoms if they do,' I warned.

'In your dreams, Molly,' Shirl replied.

The first telephone conversation I ever had with Molly went something like this . . .

Molly: How fucked am I?

Me: Pardon me?

Molly: How fucked am I?

Me: Um, I'm not sure. Who is this?

Molly: Ian.

Me: Ian?

Molly: Molly.

Me: Oh, Molly! Jeez, what's the matter?

I was sitting at my desk at the erstwhile evening daily newspaper, *The Herald*, basking in the glory of my page-one byline on a story about Graeme 'Shirley' Strachan, frontman of Australia's biggest band, Skyhooks, getting married secretly in London. I had quotes from his mum and everything. I am not sure where Molly was. I didn't even know him very well at the time, but I think he had just left the offices of *Truth*, the old bi-weekly scandal sheet where he'd signed a contract.

Unbeknownst to me, his first big *Truth* exclusive was to have been Shirley's wedding, but I had beaten him by a day, in the process causing *Truth* to totally revamp its front pages, turning Molly's name to crap as far as his editor was concerned.

I was blissfully ignorant to the background of the whole episode, as well. Molly had actually spoken to Shirley in London by phone the previous evening, confirming the wedding story and getting quotes. About the same time, Darryl Sambell, the Fagin lookalike who managed Johnny Farnham and lived downstairs from Molly in Alexandra Avenue in South Yarra, had shown himself in. Molly told

him about the wedding and some time later, when they'd had a disagreement about something (no doubt fuelled by a few drinks), Darryl threatened to call me the following morning and blab.

Molly didn't actually take him seriously, but that's exactly what he did.

Lawrie Masterson, journalist

3: LIVING IN THE '70S

1975–1979: A lesbian and a rabbit—I meet Caroline/Charles—The postman always rings twice—Rocked and docked—The Prahran Axe— I like it both ways—Rock at the Croc—Tweedledee & Tweedledum.

The '60s and the '70s had The Vibe. *And* The Vibe *requires lunacy. That's the one thing the '60s and '70s had—a certifiable bunch of nutters in reasonable control of things.*

Brian Cadd

People were eager for change and they were getting it. Melbourne *Age* journalist Martin Flanagan would later write:

> By the end of 1974, conservatives around Australia were saying the nation was in a state of chaos. A state of shock might have been more accurate. To some, the Whitlam years were the Great Awakening of the Australian Mind. Australian writers and artists suddenly found themselves in a land flowing with government funding . . . no one could doubt Australia was alive and kicking.

Australia was a country stretching out and looking at itself.

As John Watson would later write in *Rolling Stone*, it was a time of that most dangerous rejoinder . . . 'Why not?'

Britain might have had the Swinging Sixties; we swung in the '70s.

Carlton parties were full of people talking about something called 'cultural identity'. David Williamson was an emerging playwright. *Alvin Purple*, *Aunty Jack* and *Number 96* were confronting convention on TV. 'Gay' suddenly meant more than just 'happy'. People were wearing badges saying 'How Dare You Assume I'm Heterosexual'.

The Whitlam Government was appointing a minister to look after the environment. Clive James came home after thitreen years and found that Sydney had become a 'mini-Manhattan'. Patrick White won the Nobel Prize for 'introducing a new continent to literature'. Anne Summers wrote a 'herstory' of Australian feminism called *Damned Whores And God's Police*. Trade unionist Jack Mundey was imposing green bans to save historic buildings from demolition. A *Sydney Morning Herald* poll showed that 74 per cent of Australians thought the Government was 'trying to do too many things at once'. Alan Bond challenged for the America's Cup for the first time. People at parties were drinking rum and coke, doing The Bump, and saying things like 'Hi spunky' (yep, that's how we spoke back then). And the Whitlam Government spent $1.3 million to buy a painting, Jackson Pollock's *Blue Poles*.

It was into this climate that *Countdown* emerged.

A man called Molly talking to a guy called Shirley—on the ABC.

Yep, these were strange days, indeed.

People were eager for change, for things that were new. They were just kind of looking. For whatever was fresh and different.

Greg Macainsh, Skyhooks

When I think about all the shocks I've had in my life, one of the biggest came at the end of 1974 when Michael Shrimpton,

Countdown's executive producer, called me into his office. 'Sit down,' he said, 'I've got some news for you.'

When Michael spoke, you listened.

When *Countdown* started, we were given six shows. That was extended to eight, with the last two being one-hour shows. But by the end of 1974, I thought the show was over. We'd had our run. Then Michael said, 'It's rather good news—*Countdown* is going to become a series for a year.'

I was stunned.

It was a great time for a music show: 1975 was the year of Malcolm Fraser versus Gough Whitlam, and Skyhooks versus Sherbet. I tried to capture the mood in my 'Meldrum Beat' column in *Listener In-TV*, in a piece headed 'The Un-Civil War':

> In Australia over the past three months, two amazing armies have been building up for a confrontation which could make the American Civil War look like kindergarten playtime [*it wasn't like me to exaggerate*].
>
> It was only recently that it became evident that among thousands of pop fans in this country, especially on the female side, an incredible split has developed: you were either a hardcore Sherbet fan or a fanatical Skyhooks follower, and never the twain shall meet.

I was caught in the middle. I would get letters from outraged fans, accusing me of being a 'Skyhooks lackey' or a 'Sherbeteer'.

'In fact,' I wrote, 'it's got that way that I nearly die of a heart attack when a car backfires on the street.'

Skyhooks guitarist Red Symons fuelled the fire by telling journalists he'd slept with Sherbet's Garth Porter.

The truth was that, like The Beatles and The Rolling Stones, Skyhooks and Sherbet were actually good mates, particularly the singers, Shirley and Daryl, who had a lot in common. They both loved surfing, had both been tradesmen and were both Capricorns. My mate Michael Gudinski managed Skyhooks; later he would manage Daryl's solo career.

> Funnily enough, we got on really well with Sherbet. Roger Davies [Sherbet's manager] and I were already friends and we stayed good friends. People used to think, 'Oh, they hate each other' and the fans would be fighting. Yet Sherbet actually helped us out. The first gig we ever did in Sydney was at the Opera House with them, and we did quite a few shows together. But there'd be radio polls, where listeners would vote for their favourite, either Skyhooks or Sherbet. It was an exciting time, a great era for Australian music.
>
> **Michael Gudinski, Skyhooks manager**

Daryl Braithwaite's grandmother lived near me in Prahran. She would pop in, with freshly baked scones, and then tell me to play Sherbet more often.

I also got to know a lovely lady around the corner, who I called Nanna Peele. She was Paula Fox's mum, and the mother-in-law of the trucking magnate Lindsay Fox, who became one of my best mates. I loved having cups of tea with Nanna Peele, and after I moved to Richmond, I would often tap on her window if I'd had a big night at the nearby Chevron nightclub and was in no state to drive home. Nanna would let me in and I'd pass out in bed next to her. Lindsay loves telling people: 'Can you believe Molly slept with my mother-in-law?'

The first *Countdown* in 1975 was at midnight on 'C-Day'—the day colour TV was officially launched in Australia. After an introduction from Aunty Jack, *Countdown*, hosted by Johnny Farnham, was the first program to be shown nationwide in colour. It featured an all-Australian line-up—Skyhooks, Sherbet,

Denise Drysdale, Stevie Wright, AC/DC, Linda George, Hush, Debbie Byrne, Captain Matchbox, Ray Burgess and William Shakespeare.

The episode featured one of the first Australian 'film clips'— Skyhooks' 'Horror Movie', which the *Countdown* crew, headed by Robbie Weekes, shot at Luna Park in Melbourne. We were really proud of this clip. The ABC later entered the episode in an international television festival in Switzerland.

Countdown became my top priority in 1975. It was taking up so much of my time that I quit hosting my Channel Seven kids' show, *Anything Can Happen*, in April.

The most famous clip the *Countdown* crew made was AC/DC's 'It's A Long Way To The Top (If You Wanna Rock 'n' Roll)'.

Directed by Paul Drane, it's Melbourne's most watched music video—and it had a budget of $380. Paul, a *Countdown* producer, came up with the idea of putting Bon and the boys on the back of a flatbed truck travelling along the city's busiest street, Swanston Street, at lunchtime. The clip was shot on three cameras between Bourke Street and Flinders Street on Monday, 23 February, 1976. We told the police and the council and they didn't seem to mind—we didn't even have to shut the street. These days, a clip like that would take weeks to plan and you'd be forced to get a stack of permits.

By 1975, Skyhooks had become the biggest local band we'd ever seen. On Anzac Day they did a show at Festival Hall in Melbourne with AC/DC (Bon Scott dropped his pants on stage), Bob Hudson and 'New Zealand's top group', Split Enz (who were booed). Tickets cost $2.70. I raved about the reaction to the Hooks, in my *Listener In-TV* column:

Festival Hall was witnessing scenes of hysteria and adulation that have not been seen since the days of Beatlemania [*this time, I wasn't exaggerating*]. The crowd went absolutely out of their minds. Like in the early '60s, when a place called Liverpool turned the eyes and ears of the world with The Beatles, the '70s could very well see Melbourne become the city of the music world.

Born in England, Red Symons came to Australia on the same boat as the Bee Gees. He found fame as the guitarist in Skyhooks. Later, he was the grumpy judge on *Hey Hey It's Saturday*'s Red Faces. I remember Red once saying: 'I've just got very limited skills. They are the only two things I could ever really get together—being a huge pop star and television star.' He's now the breakfast presenter on ABC radio in Melbourne.

Skyhooks were always an exciting band to work with. They truly understood that television was a visual medium. For one *Countdown* appearance, Red used a stuffed fox instead of a guitar.

It didn't matter at all because we were a theatrical act. What it looked like clearly wasn't what it sounded like. They were separate things. That was a reality that we had a hold of before everybody else. You made the record, of course, but how you represented that record was up to you. It wasn't that you simply got up and mimed the record.

Red Symons, Skyhooks

We would tape *Countdown* on Saturday and then sit around watching it on Sunday night and learning how we could do things better. One of the things we learnt was to do things exactly how we did it in rehearsal because this makes it easier for the director and the cameramen. Also, we'd get stuck into the directors and say, 'Enough of these big wide shots, we want close-ups', because it made it more exciting and fun to look at. We found that television really works if you don't jump around too much. If you do, the camera people have to pull wider and wider. It was very different to being on stage where you'd run around.

Greg Macainsh, Skyhooks

Michael Gudinski, who was also the boss of the emerging Mushroom Records as well as managing Skyhooks, was immediately a *Countdown* fan and one of the show's biggest supporters.

I saw the vision of *Countdown* straight away. You didn't have to be a genius to work it out, but some people in the Australian record business couldn't understand it. I mean, it was based on *Top Of The Pops*, which was an institution in England, and it was going on the ABC, which goes to every nook and cranny in the country. And I had a visual band, when all the other bands were into jeans and faded shirts and long guitar solos. So that was my plan with Skyhooks—to do as much television as possible.

Michael Gudinski, Mushroom Records

Countdown helped Skyhooks become a success, and Skyhooks helped *Countdown* become a top-rater. But our relationship wasn't always smooth.

I recall a very frosty occasion in the control room of Studio 31, where the very opinionated Graeme Strachan committed the unpardonable crime of entering a control room without permission and criticising the shooting pattern, which was being directed by the equally outspoken Rob Weekes. The memory is kind, and I can't quite recall what happened except that it was noisy! I know that Robbie wasn't vastly impressed with Shirl's advice at the time.

Michael Shrimpton, *Countdown* executive producer

The band, particularly Greg, used to love confrontations. *Countdown* wanted to use smoke for one performance, but the band said, 'No smoke.' And you had the director saying, 'This is my show and they're doing it my way.' People would think, 'Hey, you're the manager, tell them what to do.' They didn't understand that this was the beginning of a different style of management. I would have an opinion, but I couldn't tell them, 'Jump, how high.' I remember going into their dressing room and saying, 'If we're really adamant about this, we're going to get thrown off the show.' I could see Greg really enjoying this, taking it to the point of us nearly getting thrown off, before saying, 'All right, we'll back off.' And that's how it used to be. Those sort of things actually worked for them because they left a mark on people's minds. They did things differently.

Michael Gudinski

As I said, this was an exciting time to be in the Australian music business. As well as *Countdown*, the ABC started a new radio station—2JJ, which went to air in Sydney on Sunday, 19 January. The first record on their turntable was Skyhooks' 'You Just Like Me Cos I'm Good In Bed'—one of six tracks on the band's debut album that the Federation of Australian Commercial Broadcasters had banned. Station boss Marius Webb said: 'Thumbing our noses? Oh, yeah, I suppose we were, in a small way. Yes, there's an anti-establishment sort of theme running through our thinking.'

In March 1975, the first issue of *RAM* (*Rock Australia Magazine*) appeared. Based in Sydney, it was the first rock journal to hit the newsstands since *Go-Set* folded in 1974. Their first cover featured Skyhooks. Two months later, a grinning Shirley Strachan graced the cover of another new rock paper, *Juke*, started by Ed Nimmervoll.

> Looking back, everything was geared towards making the '70s a very big era for rock 'n' roll—Australian rock 'n' roll. We might not have realised it then, but we were gearing up for a very big era.
>
> **Stan Rofe, DJ**

Because it was on the ABC, *Countdown* reached viewers who were not typically fans of pop and rock music.

> It was a fantastic family occasion, sitting around watching *Countdown*. There was no Eminem or soft porn going on, it was wholesome family entertainment. I'd sit down with Mum and Dad and have cheese on toast. Sure, Dad would say, 'That's not bloody music!', but it was wholesome entertainment.
>
> **Frankie J. Holden, Ol' 55**

The show's power took me by surprise. In mid-1975 we started playing a clip by a Scottish band named Pilot. The tape quality wasn't great, but the song, 'January', went from absolutely nowhere on the charts to number one. In America, 'January' peaked at number 87.

We didn't actually have many videos to play. This was pre-MTV—not many overseas artists were making videos. I think the first clip we played on *Countdown* was the Hues Corporation's 'Rock The Boat'.

Countdown quickly achieved what the ABC wanted—attracting younger viewers. And lots of them turned up to the studios in Elsternwick to see the show.

One of my favourite members of the *Countdown* crew was Paddy, the ABC's Irish security guard. In his sixties, Paddy became a bit of a mascot for the show. Only problem was the crew usually had to protect Paddy from the crowd.

One day, Paddy came running to Michael Shrimpton: 'I've got a woman who claims to be a friend of Ian's, perhaps you should come.'

Michael was confronted by a woman with a mop of lustrous black curls, wearing dark glasses and an army-grey coat, which she had dyed black. In one pocket was a bottle of black label Johnnie Walker, in the other pocket was a white rabbit. She introduced herself as 'Lenny'.

When Michael found me, he said, 'Who, pray tell, is Lenny?'

'Oh, don't worry,' I replied, 'that's Lenny The Lesbian, send her in.'

After the show, I got Lenny to show Michael her tattoo. She dropped her pants to reveal a cougar tattooed on her left bum cheek.

I have a suburban theory about all of this. Because the show burned so bright, it attracted people who would never have gone anywhere near the ABC, which was exactly what Ken Watts wanted, of course. They were moths about the flame. Extraordinary people. A kind of society no one knew existed—people like Lenny The Lesbian. In the '70s, rocks were turned over and people came running out.

Michael Shrimpton

It was an amazing time in Australia: The Swinging Seventies. It was post–Andy Warhol. It was fashionable to be interesting. And I loved being surrounded by fascinating characters.

Countdown was like the bad boy on the ABC block. It was a clash of cultures.

I think we were doing 'On The Prowl' for our very first *Countdown* appearance. We were in the dressing room, finishing a joint, as we often did, when the floor manager came in to say, 'We're ready for you.' We walked out of our dressing room and bumped into Malcolm Fraser, who was at the ABC for something else. His two burly bodyguards gave us a wink—they knew what we'd been up to.

Frankie J. Holden

The music industry was very different in the '70s. It was not as serious. It was a growing-up period for everyone.

In the early days of *Countdown*, I shared a house with Caroline, who was occasionally known as Charles. She ran a brothel, she'd had a sex change operation, and she had a terrible problem with heroin. But she was a beautiful person. As Michael Shrimpton once described her, she was a fey, wispy creature with a heart of gold and a fist of steel.

The ABC was very moral and conservative. Michael called me into the *Countdown* office—ironically in Horne Street, Elsternwick, next to the Daily Planet brothel and a business called S&M Furnishings—and told me: 'Meldrum, as much as we like Caroline and you're sharing a house with her, the fact is she is running a brothel and she has had a sex change. If this should get out, you understand that the ABC can't back you on this one.'

I walked out of the office and jumped in my battered old Celica. But about halfway home, I did a U-turn and returned to Michael's office. 'Look,' I told him, 'I'm not going to ask Caroline to leave. If I have to, I'll leave the show instead.'

And Michael did back me. 'God bless you,' he said. 'I thought you'd say that, and I love you for it.'

I took Caroline to the Logies and she got to know one of the international guests rather well. She came running in the next morning, all breathless. 'He thought I was heaven on a stick, he licked me all over.'

Happy days, indeed.

Caroline had had the perfect sex change operation. But whenever she took a guy home, she was always overcome with guilt and would say, 'You know I'm a man, don't you?' You'd see blokes, with their pants around their ankles, scurrying out the door.

She was a sensitive soul. In the '70s, I loved playing Truth Or Dare. One night, someone asked: *What would you do if you had a sex change operation?* My manager, Brian de Courcy, who was sitting on the lounge, reading a music magazine, suddenly piped up: 'Well, you know what I would do—I would crack a fat and root myself.' Caroline ran from the room, sobbing.

Caroline had a Maori drag-queen friend, who looked like Mick Jagger. We were doing a Rolling Stones special on *Countdown* and I wanted to have a party to show the videos to the press. Michael Shrimpton told me we didn't have any money, so I decided to have the party at my place.

Caroline brought her friend and, apparently, there was a drama in the kitchen: the friend had a drug-induced fit. Caroline didn't want me to know because I am so anti-drugs. My good friend Lawrie Masterson from *TV Week* later told me that Caroline was sitting at the kitchen table, patting her friend's hand. 'Don't tell Ian, will you? She's just had a little fit.' The friend was wedged under the table, with her dick and one boob hanging out.

Another day, two nuns knocked on the door, canvassing the neighbourhood for money and potential recruits. I came home to find the two 'girls' having cups of tea with the nuns. This was too much even for me—I turned around and went out again.

Caroline was a beautiful dreamer in a minefield. Drugs destroyed her. It was during these days that I developed an intense hatred of drugs, especially heroin. I could have been up for murder—if I'd found Caroline's dealer, I would have killed him. In the end, Caroline simply couldn't function properly. She'd spend an hour looking for her keys in her handbag, and she'd spend a fortune buying lollies at the milk bar.

She was like a child who needed looking after.

One day, she disappeared. I heard she was working on the streets in Sydney. Then she went home to Newcastle. I was told she died, but not from heroin.

While I was living with Caroline, I also got to know the postman. He was a big music fan and he'd always come in and have a chat to me when he delivered the mail. Only problem was he would only deliver the mail when I was home. I went overseas and we didn't get any mail for three weeks.

One morning I was lying in bed with my girlfriend at the time when I heard a rattling noise. I woke up to see the postman shaking the bed. 'Get up,' he ordered. 'We're going to Lorne.'

The side door was always open during summer and he had just walked in.

'What are you talking about?' I said.

Then he produced a knife, told me he'd just got a new car, and we were going to drive to Lorne, a coastal town about two hours away. He started taking gold records off the wall, saying, 'We'll take these with us.'

The phone rang and it was Ray Skinner from EMI Records. 'I've got Robbie Walker with me,' Ray said. 'He's just come over from New Zealand to work with us and I'd like you to meet him.'

'Come now,' I insisted.

'Oh no, we'll come over later.'

'Look,' I whispered, 'for God's sake come now. We've got this postman with a knife and he's got us holed up in the kitchen.'

The doorbell rang and the postman ushered Ray and Robbie into the kitchen. I said, 'How about I go to Lorne with you and we'll leave the others here?'

He agreed and I got into his car.

The road has a slight curve, so as the car slowed, I opened the door and rolled onto the footpath.

Fortunately, the postman's parents appeared soon after and took him away. We all went to lunch and had a laugh about it.

Later that day, we heard a crash at home and the postman was back. He started crying and they had to take him away again.

Eighteen months later, I was driving down Chapel Street in peak hour when I heard this cry, '*Molly! Molly!*' I looked around and it was the postman running towards me. As cars banked up with horns blowing, the postman yelled, 'I've got something for you!' He reached into his bag and pulled out a bundle of mail he hadn't delivered to me.

Fortunately, my life hasn't been filled with such incidents, but they do happen. One woman kept sending me crazy letters. She thought that Michael Hutchence and I were sending her messages through the personals section in *The Herald Sun*.

Another time, I picked up my phone to be greeted by, '*You're dead, Meldrum!*' It was a guy whose demo tape I didn't like.

As they say, with power comes great responsibility. I took my job seriously, trying to listen to everything that was sent to me. But we couldn't play everything on the show.

I also continued to pursue my dream of being a record producer. Being in the studio was a wonderful release from the pressures of dealing with record company reps, who all wanted their artists on *Countdown*.

In the mid-'70s, a young manager named Robbie Williams sent me a demo tape of a Perth band called Supernaut.

Molly encouraged us to head for Melbourne and he produced our first single. During those first months, before our record deal and *Countdown* appearances, we lived in a small, dark and depressing flat. When Molly came by the flat one day, he said we looked like The Children of The Damned. The name stuck.

Gary Twinn, Supernaut

Supernaut had a song called 'I Like It Both Ways'. It seemed to sum up the times.

The engineer for the Supernaut recording session was a young guy named Tony Cohen, who got a job at Armstrong Studios because his dad knew a friend of the owner, Bill Armstrong. Tony had a high-school band called Epitaph, but he thought he'd be a better studio engineer than drummer. He also got into trouble at school when he was busted smoking some not-so-legal tobacco. The studio environment was more suited to Tony's lifestyle.

Recording Supernaut was a funny time. They were a pretty bad band— they couldn't get in time or anything like that. In fact, on the take that was finally used—take number 90 or something—you can still hear the drums slowing down in certain sections. During another take, the phone rang in the studio, and Molly decided to leave it on the released version of 'I Like It Both Ways'.

Tony Cohen, recording engineer

Another major '70s act was Cheetah, featuring sisters Lyndsay and Chrissie Hammond, who the press called 'sex bombs with big hair'. The duo was managed by my manager, Brian de Courcy, and he got me to produce a Cheetah single, a cover of The Ronettes' song 'Walking In The Rain'.

I don't think there was a time when all four of us were in the studio together. There was always a fight going on and Ian would be saying, 'I'm not talking to those bitches!'

Brian de Courcy, manager

Apparently, I threatened to hit the sisters in the car park of a Bulleen hotel. We'd all been judging a heat of the *Countdown Saturday Night Fever* Dance Competition. At the end of the night, we couldn't agree on the winner, and I was out-voted by the sisters. The argument carried on into the car park, where one of the sisters said of my choice, 'You just fancied him.' I was furious, and Brian says he had to restrain me.

Molly was deeply apologetic. I used to live on Toorak Road, near Chapel Street, and one day Molly pulled up in his Celica. He jumped out and started yelling at me—stopping the traffic and the trams. Then he said, 'All right, I'm sorry—take these flowers!'

Lyndsay Hammond, Cheetah

'Walking In The Rain' was a hit in late 1978. The follow-up was 'Deeper Than Love'.

That recording session was an absolute nightmare. We used up all the board at AAV in Melbourne. Ian had this idea that we could run a coaxial cable from Melbourne to the 301 studios in Sydney. We would have had something like 72 tracks. We went to Sydney but the studios didn't match.

Brian De Courcy

In Sydney, where we were recording the song, I decided it would be great to have a pipe band play on the track. Fortunately, I was tipped off that Stephen Shrimpton, the boss of EMI Records and Michael's younger brother, was planning to pay us a visit, and we had time to hide the band.

When Stephen turned up at the studio, he asked me directly: 'Have you got a pipe band?'

'No,' I lied, 'we're just trying to get the effect of one.'

'Deeper Than Love' cost nearly $50,000 to produce. Brian was worried that EMI would refuse to pay the bill, so he went to see Stephen Shrimpton. 'Don't worry,' Stephen said, 'it's a record company. Money is paper to be pushed around a desk. It can be absorbed very quickly. It's not a problem.'

Ah, those were the days!

The Cheetah sessions did cause me some problems at *Countdown*. At the start of 1979, I had to fly back to Melbourne from Sydney, where we were recording the Cheetah sessions, to host one of the summer shows with Shirley Strachan. Driving to the ABC from the airport, I had a car accident at the Flemington Road roundabout. With steam billowing from my Celica, I finally pulled up at the ABC, where I was summoned to Michael Shrimpton's office.

'Your pay's docked,' he informed me. 'And Shirl's hosting the show, you can go home.'

It was much more than Meldrum being late. He was absent without leave for a week and he was working for someone else, in this case my brother. I got on the phone to Stephen and said, 'I hear a rumour you are employing Meldrum. Has it occurred to you that he's my talent?'

Stephen replied, 'You are fucking welcome to him!'
Michael Shrimpton, *Countdown* executive producer

'Deeper Than Love' flopped in Australia, but was a big hit in Germany.

Cheetah released just one album, *Rock 'n' Roll Women*, in 1982. In 1997, Lyndsay Hammond released a country album, *The Raven*, and Chrissie starred as Grizabella in *Cats* on the

West End. The singing sisters also appeared on *Countdown* doing backing vocals for Dame Edna Everage's 'Every Mother Wants A Boy Like Elton'.

At this time I was living in a house in Alfred Street, Prahran, and my home life was a little, er, chaotic. I moved to Alfred Street because I already knew a lot of people there—Dale Smedley (who we called Dame Delia), Barry Peters (Aunty Patsy), Brian Flaherty (Fay) and John Hoffman (Hoffa).

> Alfred Street was like a real family. I remember one Christmas, Molly bought this amazing collection of presents. Two weeks later, we were having a cup of tea in the kitchen. 'We've got to clean the kitchen, it stinks,' Molly said. I opened the oven door and the turkey was still in there, covered in maggots. Molly ran out of the house, screaming.
>
> **Brian Flaherty (Fay), neighbour**

On Sunday nights, Fay would cook a big bowl of spaghetti and we'd sit around and watch *Countdown*.

> It was always 'Fay and them' . . . Molly would come in on a Monday or Tuesday, full of what 'Fay and them' had to say about the previous show. 'Fay and them' had enormous sway.
>
> **Stephen Jones, *Countdown* producer**

Hoffa was the young, straight guy among all these mad queens. An electrician, he was a huge music fan, who would come to my house, drink my Kahlúa and bug me to play Bruce Springsteen on *Countdown*.

Hoffa and his best mate, Raggsy, were also aspiring rock stars. You'd always find Hoffa at parties, singing into broomsticks, doing Rod Stewart songs such as 'Maggie May' or 'Stay With Me'.

Hoffa and Raggsy created a magical, mythical band, The Prahran Axe. They would tell people that 'Prahran' was an

Aboriginal word for 'great rock 'n' roll band'. They would hire taxis, roll a joint, have a bottle of Cognac and Champagne and tell the driver to just drive around. They would even tell other bands about their band. Only problem was, they couldn't play a note.

One Sunday night in 1975, we all went to Isabella's in the city. Then it was a big gay venue with lots of transvestites; it later became a table-top dancing venue. I remember we were dancing to Ned Doheny's 'Get It Up For Love' when Raggsy jumped on a table and grabbed a chandelier and started swinging. Half the ceiling nearly came down as plaster rained on the dance floor.

The police were called and Raggsy was carted off to the Russell Street station.

Then Hoffa grabbed a rock and hurled it through the bottle-shop window. When asked what he was doing, he told the police: 'Just wanted to get a bottle of port.' As well as the window, the rock hit a prized painting, and Hoffa found himself up on charges of malicious damage.

It turns out that both Hoffa and Raggsy told the police they were out celebrating the fact that their band, The Prahran Axe, had just got a recording deal. The first I knew of this was when I was in the County Court getting ready to give character evidence for Hoffa. His lawyer said, 'Your Honour, my client is in a group called The Prahran Axe and they were celebrating signing a recording deal on the night of the incident.'

With my mouth wide open, I looked at Hoffa, who just nodded his head.

I started my evidence: 'There I was Your Honour doing this dance called The Bump . . .' And I went on and on.

The judge finally said, 'Mr Meldrum, we do appreciate your discourse on the disco scene in Melbourne . . . It sounds like the antics of Henry III are alive and well in Melbourne.'

Hoffa got off with a $500 fine, and the headline in the paper the next day was 'Rock Star Hi-Jinks Alive And Well In Melbourne'.

> We were living out our fantasies. I'm not sure if anyone behaves like that anymore. There were so many parties at that Alfred Street house. One night sticks in my mind: Raggsy was out the front, doing lines of speed on Molly's Rolls-Royce. He was saying, 'Look at this stuff! This stuff is so strong it's lifting the duco off the bonnet!'
>
> **John Hoffman**

Hoffa and Raggsy did actually end up doing a few gigs as The Prahran Axe.

> Molly would write about us in his *Truth* column. If we had've been able to get it together, we might have been the first punk band in Australia. But we weren't together enough to get it together.
>
> **John Hoffman, The Prahan Axe**

Raggsy got a job at a record company. But he developed a bad drug problem. He died of a heroin overdose in 1984.

The Prahran Axe wasn't the only axe in Alfred Street.

In 1981, a young guy tried to break down my front door with an axe. This incident later prompted one of the classic *Hey Hey* jokes—that the guy wasn't trying to get *in*, he was trying to get *out*.

I had met the guy at a gig and I think he got angry when he came to my place and found that I wasn't home. I spoke to the guy and his mother and decided not to press charges.

Those were crazy days. A journalist from Sydney came to

Melbourne to do a profile of me. The piece started: 'There was the usual retinue at Molly's place, including a person passed out in the toilet', namely Hoffa.

Hoffa made a hole in my fireplace so we could talk to each other without leaving our homes.

Molly used to have what we called 'The Treatment'. He would get a new single or new video and play it to death. It would always be, 'Just one more time.' Two songs in particular come to mind—Blondie's 'Heart of Glass' and Bonnie Tyler's 'It's A Heartache'. Another time, I remember this bloke had parked across the road. His wife was in The Alfred Hospital down the road. It was 10 o'clock in the morning and Molly was playing a new Jon English single for the twentieth time. The bloke said to me, 'What goes on in there?'

I said, 'Mate, you don't want to know.'

John Hoffman, The Prahan Axe

We were all having a gay old time. The female member of English act Haysi Fantayzee once chatted up Hoffa, saying: 'You're the only straight man I've met in Australia.' *Cleo* offered me several thousand dollars to appear nude in the *Cleo* centrefold; fortunately, I said no. My boyfriend at the time went through a Christianity phase and would preach the Bible to all of us. A would-be pop star arrived to audition for me—with his mother. Another guy came to the house and said he had Johnny O'Keefe's spirit. A man actually handcuffed himself to my fence for three days, wanting me to play his song on *Countdown*; Hoffa would give the guy a beer as he walked past.

George Negus also visited the Alfred Street house to prepare a profile of me for *60 Minutes*. We spent nearly a week together and had a great time. I took George to the MCG to see my beloved Saints play Richmond. We were sitting in a Richmond area and when I yelled, 'Carn the Saints!', a grumpy old woman turned around and told me to be quiet. Of course, I continued to barrack and the woman kept telling me off. 'You are a guest of the Richmond Football Club and you are not to barrack for St Kilda,' she ordered. After she told me to be quiet a third time, I leant forward and said, 'Would you quietly fuck off!'

After half-time, the woman and her two friends didn't return to their seats and I enjoyed the rest of the game—loudly barracking for St Kilda.

After the game, we attended a Richmond function. I introduced George to the Richmond president, Ian Wilson, who then said: 'Molly, I'd like you to meet my wife.' George went white, and I whispered in his ear: 'I think we better get out of here.'

I had told the president's wife to quietly fuck off. And her daughter—the esteemed football writer Caroline Wilson— never lets me forget it. Whenever I bump into Caroline, she takes great delight in saying, 'You told my mother to fuck off!'

Another sporting encounter around this time was a little less volatile. John McEnroe was known as the 'Superbrat', but he was actually a sweetheart. We did a milk ad together. It was quite an elaborate shoot, with filming at the Underground nightclub, in a taxi, and then in a hotel room at the Hilton. The original cut of the ad ended with John placing a 'Do Not Disturb' sign on his hotel-room door. I suggested to the director that we should remove that shot—it might not be good for John's reputation.

Away from the on-court tantrums, McEnroe was a sweet, caring guy. After the shoot, I said, 'I've gotta go, I've got a charity ball.' He said, 'I'll come with you.' And he did. He was the perfect guest—he even drew the raffle. I still enjoy catching up with John at the Australian Open, an event I proudly attend because I was one of the trustees who built the National Tennis Centre.

With *Countdown* and all these other commitments, I was incredibly busy. When a nightclub promoter friend, Paul Cross, arrived at my house one day, he could see that a life of partying and working was taking its toll. 'Ian,' he said, 'I think you need to take up squash.'

Instead of squash, I took on another job. My manager, Brian, got me a gig DJ-ing at the Croxton Park Hotel in Thornbury, a northern suburb of Melbourne. When Brian came to me and said he wanted me to DJ at a pub, I thought he was mad. I had no intention of doing it, but he convinced me.

My first night at the 'Croc' was not a success, with only about eighty people in the crowd. But the numbers swelled to a few hundred by the second week, and then we were getting crowds of more than a thousand people every Thursday night.

It became the place to be. The crowd was always wondering, 'Would Molly be there? What time would he turn up? What state would he be in?' But he always did a great gig. And he got to see what the public wanted and what they liked, not what the record company guys were feeding him. It kept him in touch with the street.

Brian de Courcy, Molly's manager

'Rock At The Croc On A Thursday Night' was a wild time. There used to be some terrible fights. One night, I looked into the crowd to see one guy drilling another guy's head—with a hand drill. Another night, I told one of the bouncers to go easy on one of the patrons. The bouncer came into the DJ box and head-butted me. Blood from my nose gushed onto the records as I tried to play them.

I also did a regular gig at a nightclub called Sweethearts in Parramatta in Sydney. The club was owned by Ross Visali, who became a great friend—even though he insisted on calling me 'Milly'.

All these years later, I'm still DJ-ing and I love it.

What DJ-ing taught me is that music snobbery is idiotic. I remember one night in Sydney, a group of guys in the crowd wanted to hear some Midnight Oil, but I didn't have any Oils records with me. I gave one guy $100 to go home and get an Oils album. I put it on and the guys went off. An hour later, I was playing 'Male Stripper' and these same guys were still dancing. 'Hey, aren't you Oils fans?' I said to them. 'Yeah, we are, but we love this song.' Music is music. It's ridiculous to limit yourself to just one or two styles.

Music is also meant to be fun. And, boy, did we have fun in the '70s. There to record the shenanigans was a rock reporter named Dave Dawson. In fact, Dave *created* a lot of the shenanigans.

Dave had played football for Warrnambool in the '60s. He would have been a nippy rover. He later looked like a country music version of a member of ZZ Top: long black beard and ample girth.

In the '70s, Dave was a reporter for the notorious *Truth* newspaper and Sydney's *Daily Mirror*. Despite having an editor who was dubbed 'The Undertaker' (because he knew how to kill and bury a good story), Dave always got a good run. His round was courts by day, showbiz by night.

They were wild days. There were just no inhibitions back then—people just did what they wanted to do. There was none of this political correctness. It was an exciting time. A lot of the music was awful, so the only way you could do anything for these artists was to write about their parties. And at a lot of those functions, Molly's mere presence made it more colourful. Wherever he went, controversy usually followed. One function after another, Molly was always in the middle of it.

Dave Dawson, journalist

Dave was there when Mushroom Records boss Michael Gudinski announced Skyhooks' overseas record deal at the Baron of Beef restaurant in the Dandenongs. On the day of the function, *The Truth* had run a front-page story stating that Ross Wilson was going to replace Shirley Strachan as the Skyhooks' singer.

We were shown to our tables, where there was a joint waiting for us. Molly got up on stage and held up a copy of *The Truth.* He said, 'I'm just about to prove that this story is wrong.' I stood on a chair and hit him on the head with a bread roll, which had been conveniently placed on the table. There was some kerfuffle and then Gudinski got up and said the same thing, so I hit him in the chest with another bread roll.

Dave Dawson

Dave's partner in crime was a young, eager reporter by the name of Steve Butcher. The dynamic duo bonded at a Billy Thorpe function in Prahran. Steve wanted Dave's advice: 'How do you think I can get upgraded from copy boy to cadet?' Dave replied, 'Why don't you fuck that sheila over there in the ticket box?' So he did. And the next issue of *The Truth* contained a story about 'a long-haired youth having public intercourse with a busty blonde at a Billy Thorpe function'. Steve was upgraded.

The legendary publicist Patti Mostyn and I called Dawson and Butcher 'Tweedledee and Tweedledum'. They made my life hell back then. They would turn up to functions and start a food fight. Of course, they were the only ones throwing food at each other, but when the story appeared in the paper, their names were not mentioned. The story would always be something like: 'Record company function degenerates into food fight farce. Guests in attendance included Ian "Molly" Meldrum . . .' I was always guilty just by being there. They were very wicked!

The Moir Sisters had their only national hit in 1974 with their debut single, 'Good Morning (How Are You?)'. Dave and Steve decided to liven up one of their functions by throwing hot dogs at me. The story appeared in *The Truth* under the headline 'The Hot Dog Sisters'.

I recall a King of Pop ceremony at Channel Ten in Nunawading. Gary Glitter was the special guest. Dave thought things were getting a little dull, so he said to Steve, 'Why don't you go and check if Gary Glitter's hair is real or not?'

Steve pulled out a cigarette lighter and set fire to Gary's hair, which turned out to be a wig.

I was a little disturbed by this behaviour. 'You can't set fire to his hair!' I shrieked.

'Bit late now,' Steve replied.

You could guarantee if there was a function with women and booze, there was going to be a story about the function rather than the artist. And the good thing was you could sort of live off the functions. There'd be two or three a week, and you'd always get plenty to eat and drink.

Dave Dawson

Dave's first trouble with the Press Council followed a Sherbet function when someone put LSD in the punch. The story appeared in *The Truth* as 'Four Drugged At Sherbet Party'. But when it was reprinted in *The Daily Mirror* it had become '40 Drugged At Sherbet Party'.

Dave had a knack for creating 'a good yarn'. After a Rolling Stones function, Keith Richards and a couple of other band members went to a party at writer Jenny Brown's house in North Balwyn. Dave and Steve decided it was going to be a nude pool party, so they jumped into the pool, naked. They had their headline: 'Rolling Stones At Nude Pool Party'.

Dave and Steve didn't restrict their activities to rock stars. At one function at Luna Park, they spotted Bob Hawke, then with the ACTU, on the merry-go-round, and they hit him in the head with a couple of bread rolls. The story was 'Hawke Pelted By Drunken Youths'.

Even innocent stories could become headlines. Sherbet guitarist Clive Shakespeare liked to make model aeroplanes while on the road. At one hotel, he left behind some glue. The story got out and the implication was that Sherbet were glue-sniffing pop stars.

Dave also got great mileage out of my house being burgled.

When I was at the ABC taping an episode of *Countdown* in September 1976, my house was broken into. Stolen was electrical equipment valued at $14,000, and 1500 LPs.

They found the guys and there were all these separate hearings. So every second week, one of the defendants who handled stolen goods would front the court, which gave us an excuse to run another story about Molly Meldrum's house being robbed.

Dave Dawson

It looked like my house was being broken into all the time. The insurance company I was with dropped my policy, so I had to find another one.

Having to attend court all the time was a nightmare. One of the court cases was particularly annoying because the defence barrister turned on me. 'Are you a homosexual?' he asked. 'With all respect to the court,' I replied, 'I'd like to go down and bop him on the nose, Your Honour.'

Basically, I was able to say no to that question—not that it had any relevance—because I'm bisexual. You have to get your terminology right.

Dave Dawson later became Melbourne's king of country, writing about country music, and programming Melbourne community radio station Nu Country. In 1981 he co-wrote the novelty hit, 'I'd Love To Have A Joint With Willie', based on Slim Dusty's 'Duncan'.

I think Dave misses living in the '70s. In 1988, he did a front-page story in *The Truth*, which was like one 'for old-time's sake'. Next to a picture of a topless blonde, ran the article 'Molly In Row Over Blonde. Disco Scuffle'.

In the '70s, there was always a fracas with Molly and women. He'd always be going in to defend some woman's virtue and get hit on the head. I'd always be like, 'Get your hands off the women, Molly, they're no good to you!'

Dave Dawson

The 1988 story started:

Popular TV star Molly Meldrum and a record company executive have been involved in a wild scuffle over a blonde in a trendy Melbourne disco.

The blonde—a WEA promo person, Jo Wilson—actually had nothing to do with the fight I had with her boss at the Underground, a popular Melbourne club.

Ms Wilson, from Camperdown in Victoria's western district, was drenched with beer from her own glass as she fell to the floor . . . Guests scattered as Meldrum reeled away and his hat flew through the air at the crowded King Street disco. Bouncers ran past shocked onlookers to separate the two angry rock celebrities.

'The funny thing was Molly was more worried about his hat than anything else,' an Underground staffer said.

Meldrum admitted there was a fracas, but denied punching Ms Wilson. 'I didn't whack her,' Molly said. 'I just pushed her away and said, "Please, stay out of this, for heaven's sake."'

Jo later told me her mum was so mortified by the story, she made her dad drive to the newsagents and buy every copy of *The Truth* in Camperdown.

Molly's longstanding deal at *TV Week* originally was negotiated by his then manager, Brian de Courcy, and obviously was not big on finer details. I first recall him 'writing' his weekly *Humdrum* piece by dictating it to the editor's secretary, a lissom brunette named Debbie, who probably was still in her teens, and upon whose desk Molly would lounge/sit/stretch out/put his feet. Next time you see Molly on TV or hear him on radio, try taking dictation from him and you will wind up with the same thing Debbie used to present to the *TV Week* sub-editors each week after Molly's departure—absolute drivel. Well, being educated, literary types, the subs actually referred to it as absolute shit, or worse. It soon reached a point where they threatened mutiny unless Molly was given a 'ghost'—someone who could weld together his infinite wisdom and uncanny observances of the pop music industry into tightly written copy.

I'm not sure what I did to deserve it, but I got the job.

This would have been some time in 1979, and somehow I continued as Molly's silent partner on the *Humdrum* team for the next seven years or so (I also did similar work with radio king John Laws for quite some time, which probably says something about my appetite for punishment).

In the beginning, Molly continued to come to *TV Week's* West Melbourne offices each week and we would work on the column at my desk. But as he became more and more unreliable—sometimes a couple of days late, which can be vital in the production schedule of a weekly magazine—it became obvious that a better alternative was for me to go to him. Pin him down, so to speak. And that, to my mind, was when the fun really started.

Rather than Molly dropping in and disrupting the entire *TV Week* office, I would drop out—portable typewriter and a ream of paper under my arm—and become part of his world for a couple of hours each week. Mornings were best because Molly was a late starter and you usually found him at home, sometimes still in bed.

We started that routine—if anything in Molly's life can be referred to as 'routine'—when he lived in Alfred Street, Prahran, in a tiny Victorian terrace about as big as the living room of his current Egyptian palace. The bathroom was right off the lounge, and, as I recall it, there was a noticeable gap between the bottom of the door and the floor. Occasionally, we did the column as Molly went about his morning ablutions, sitting on the loo, studying *Billboard* and, between grunts, shouting his opinions about various songs or artists for me to translate into readable English.

The sub-editors had been right. Absolute shit could be refined!

Lawrie Masterson, former *TV Week* editor

4: DEEP WATER

1977: It's my party and I'll cry if I want to—*Countdown* turns 100, and this was one party that was not my cup of tea—Too many Sherbets—JP . . . Why?—Hits and myths—Where can I get arrested?

*A journalist asked Michael [Shrimpton] if he could sum Molly up,
and Michael had a lovely description: 'A collection
of nouns searching for a verb.'*
Robbie Weekes

On April Fools' Day 1977, *Countdown* executive producer Michael Shrimpton met Melbourne *Herald* journalist Lawrie Masterson in the ABC canteen, and over a cup of coffee spoke about that week's episode. 'It will be the biggest rock show ever put together in this country,' Michael declared. 'It's astounding.'

On April 3, 1977, *Countdown* celebrated its 100th episode. Michael had convinced ABC management that because it was such a big occasion, the show should be two hours long and filmed completely live.

It proved to be a landmark show in more ways than one.

The 100th show was an exciting but daunting project, mainly because Michael and the ABC had deemed it would be a 'Television Event'. I'll never forget being at home with Caroline, who gushed, 'It'll be the best show in the world!' (God bless Caroline. After successfully undergoing the operation from man to woman, she thought *anything* was possible.)

I went to London to shoot segments for the 100th show, with Leo Sayer as my co-host. Back then, satellite facilities cost an arm and a leg, so we decided to cheat with the visuals. The idea was I would then return to Melbourne and broadcast the show live across Australia. And within the two-hour extravaganza, I would cross 'live' to Leo in a London studio, introducing major acts including Elton John, AC/DC and Suzi Quatro.

I was very excited when Bruce Gowers, one of London's top TV directors—who I'd met through Elton John's manager John Reid—agreed to direct the UK segments from the famous Shepperton Studios. Bruce was the genius who made Queen's 'Bohemian Rhapsody' video.

It was hard yakka over those ten days in the United Kingdom because I also had to get interview grabs from artists who could not come into the studio.

Everyone was on tenterhooks when it finally came to taping the London links.

Leo Sayer was the perfect choice as UK host. His classic song 'When I Need You' was one of the year's biggest hits and Leo was the consummate performer, greeting all the other artists and proudly showing them our brilliant Union Jack/Aussie flag on the *Countdown* set. It was a real hoot to see Leo with Elton John, Suzi and AC/DC, all getting along famously, though there was some trouble when Leo confronted the mischievous Bon Scott. I'm not exactly sure what happened; Leo says it wasn't a punch, but he did push Bon over. I've been in a few punch-ups over the years, but this was definitely one of the stranger bouts—Leo Sayer versus Bon Scott.

The odd thing was that AC/DC were the least known of all the acts in the English leg of the show. Though they were having great success in some parts of Europe, they were yet to break into the UK charts. I remember Suzi Quatro saying to me, 'Who is this amazing band?'

After finishing the taping, we all celebrated with a huge party. Then I had to dash to the United States to do more interviews for the show. After a couple of sleepless days in New York and Los Angeles, I flew back to Melbourne the night before the actual live show.

Caroline could see how stressed and tired I was. 'Look,' she said, helpfully, 'take these two tablets half an hour before you do the show, it will calm your nerves.' Little did I know she'd given me very strong Valium. For Caroline, it might as well have been Smarties.

Renée Geyer also tried to soothe my nerves by kindly offering me a drink just prior to the show. 'Here,' she said, 'have a vodka and orange, it will settle your stomach.'

Well, the combination of the vodka, Caroline's little helpers, and the stress of it all . . . this was not going to end well.

Molly just wasn't himself. He wouldn't speak to anyone and I just didn't know what was going on. He must be a ground-breaker when it comes to dealing with jet lag, but on this day he just didn't look too well at all.

John Paul Young

Sending Molly overseas and asking him to organise crews and studios is like asking Tony Lockett to lecture at a Rhodes Scholars' Convention. I think at one stage I was going to go overseas with him but I couldn't for some reason, so there was no actual producer with him. Molly is not good at negotiating with facilities companies and things like that, and neither should he have been asked to. So when he came back, he was a bit spaced out.

Robbie Weekes, *Countdown* **director**

John Paul Young and Daryl Braithwaite were the local hosts of the 100th show. I've relied on their recollections and tapes of the episode, because I can't remember a thing.

At one stage during the show, I invited the cameraman to follow me into the crowd. 'Now let's go down into the *Countdown* audience,' I said. 'This is the one I say "Shh, Shh, Shh" to. This is the one . . . Where are we?'

I was facing the wrong way, talking to a non-existent camera.

A make-up woman appeared on set to touch up my make-up. I thanked her and she said, 'You're welcome, Ian', to which I replied, 'I'm welcome Ian, I tell you what, I'm very welcome Ian because I mean, like, that's the one that makes it all together.'

The poor make-up lady left the set more confused than I was.

I was also looking dazed and confused when the floor manager instructed me to cross to the Elton John interview. It looked like I thought Elton was actually in the studio. John Paul Young tried to help out. 'Mate, it's the Elton John interview from London. Do you want to do that?'

'Ooh yes, let's do that,' I said deliriously.

It sort of fell apart about halfway through. Things got very slow. And a tilt became a lean, then a dive, both for Molly and the show. The other hosts came from everywhere to try to save it. They did a fair job, but there was no way to disguise it. It was a total disaster. I sat there with my life flashing before my eyes. There was nothing I could do about it. I could go to black or stay with the zoo. Robbie used to have a marvellous line: 'Stay wide and shoot for news.' So I called the control room and said, 'Just keep it wide, go with the crowd, everything's going to be fine.' I think Paul Drane was directing. He said, 'You are fucking joking!'

Michael Shrimpton, *Countdown* executive producer

Later in the show, I gave JPY—who I called 'Squeak'—an invitation he could not refuse. 'Now Squeak, because there have been many times when I've sent you up and criticised you, and also your mates Sherbet, why don't you just, on behalf of your fans, here it is [touching his nose] punch me on the nose. A left hook, come on.'

Even though Squeak was one of my best friends and he knew I was joking, he was not going to miss the chance to bop me. So he delivered a straight left, right on the hooter. I reeled back, slightly dazed, and looked at Renée Geyer. 'What about your fans?' I said.

Renée joined in the fun and gave me a slap across the face.

I was down for the count.

With about fifteen minutes to go, Daryl and JPY got word that I might not be able to finish the show.

John and I were both mates of Ian's, so we thought we could go and have a chat to him and sort things out. But we went in there and he was just so angry. He swore and swung a punch at me and I remember thinking, 'Fuck this.' We ended up doing the last ten minutes of the show on our own.

Daryl Braithwaite

Leo did his final London link, finishing with, 'Now it's back to you in the studio, Molly.' Only problem was I was nowhere to be seen. Daryl said, 'Thanks, Leo.'

Leo, who now calls Australia home, never got to see the show, 'but it must have been mad'.

At the end of the show, Daryl told the confused audience: 'What a night it's been. Listen, Ian Meldrum has been exhausted. Completely out of his . . . He's had enough and he's gone, but he said to say thanks to everyone for coming in tonight.'

As the hosts walked out of the studio after the show, JPY said simply: 'He's fucked.'

Renée Geyer lurched into the VIP Room, with a glass of champagne in her hand, exclaiming, 'Three cheers for Molly!'

But my performance was not over.

The show had organised a huge party at the Elsternwick Hotel.

Was Molly going to give up then? Oh, no. There must have been 200 people at the pub. Every record company had sent a tribe down. My main aim was to keep Meldrum away from the press because he was so out of it.

Michael Shrimpton

Ian had woken up and he was a raging bull. He was going to fight everybody and kill everyone in sight.

Brian de Courcy, Molly's manager

I think he'd given Daryl a bit of a slap. I was standing at the bar, getting a couple of beers when, all of a sudden, he was next to me. He had this look of cold death in his eyes. Just staring at me, not saying anything. I said, 'What, are you going to fucking slap me, too?' He looked and quivered a little and then turned away.

John Paul Young

I went over to see him, and he just lost it and threw one. It was a bloody good punch actually. Hit me right on the jaw. Because we had known each other for a long time, I thought it was totally appropriate to give him one back, so I gave him one. A few punches were thrown, but it didn't really develop. It was never mentioned again, until now.

Robbie Weekes

Apparently, as JPY and his manager, Wayne de Gruchy, stood at the hotel's bottle shop, buying some drinks for the drive home, the side door to the bar opened and Robbie walked out.

A few seconds later, the same door flew open and I leapt on Robbie's back.

Molly started laying into him, but unbeknownst to both of them, a police paddy wagon was sitting at the bottle shop. The cops get out, and I say to Wayne, 'Stay where you are.' I ran over and said, 'Take him away. He's nothing but a fucking nuisance. Lock him up!'

I was giggling, I thought it was the greatest thing.

John Paul Young

Obviously, I didn't think it was a bad idea, because apparently I told the police: 'Yes, take me away.' And then I got into the back of the divvy van.

Afterwards, JPY and Wayne went to Pellegrini's, a restaurant in the city, where they saw Brian de Courcy. As Brian tucked into a bowl of pasta, JPY informed him: 'You'll never guess where your star is—in jail!' Brian spat out his mozzarella and went off into the night, in search of his client.

Fortunately, the fast-talking Michael Shrimpton averted my arrest, convincing the police to let me go. He tried to bundle me into a taxi, but the driver refused to take me alone. Michael decided to take me back to his place.

He was all over me in the cab, saying things like, 'You're wonderful'.

All I said was, 'Sit up straight and don't say a word!'

Michael Shrimpton

When we arrived at Michael's house, in nearby Bentleigh, Michael told his wife, Jude, that I was going to stay the night. I don't think she was surprised because she had seen the show.

I woke up the next morning to be greeted by Michael's two daughters and their dog. We had a lot of fun in the kitchen. In fact, the girls taught me how to make a proper cup of tea. They explained that first you put a little bit of hot water in the pot and swirl it around to make the pot warm. Then you put the tea in, and then the boiling water, and then you turn the pot three times to your right, three to your left, three to your right, and that makes the perfect pot of tea. Every time I've made a pot of tea since, I've thought of this. It's always 'turn, turn, turn' . . .

We live and learn, but obviously Meldrum had learnt nothing from the night before, because he acted as if it had never happened. Here he was bouncing on the end of my bed with my two kids and the dog, having a great time.

Michael Shrimpton

I was really worried Molly was going to lose his job and that this would be the end of *Countdown*. The show had become so strong. Some critics were saying it had too much power over pop music. Certain people were gunning for *Countdown* and for Ian.

Brian de Courcy

With stories sweeping Melbourne that my career was dead (one crazy rumour was that I had actually died!), Brian called the ABC's head of light entertainment, Alan Bateman, whose response surprised him: 'I didn't see the show because I was away at the weekend, but the kids saw it and they loved it.'

Brian decided to get on the first flight to Sydney. By the time he arrived, Bateman had seen the show. Michael had told him that I'd just been suffering from jet lag after a stressful overseas trip. Brian got Bateman's assurance that *Countdown* would continue.

It's not easy being Meldrum. I think there are some ghosts in there. There are some demons that drive him. There is a self-destructive demon.

Michael Shrimpton

Michael told me to take two weeks off. I went to Lorne, a holiday town on the Victorian coast, with The Ferrets lead singer Billy Miller, whose advice was simple: 'Fuck 'em, don't worry about any of that shit—we should take over the St Kilda Football Club.'

I was the state manager of Festival Records and I was going to go on the 100th show and present Molly with a special gold record, in recognition of *Countdown's* support of Australian artists. But I was bumped when the show was running over time. Molly was really apologetic. I said, 'No worries, these things happen. The only thing I'm a bit sorry about is my son, Stuart, who's in grade six, had told all his mates to watch *Countdown* because his dad was going to be on the show.'

The next morning, I'm getting breakfast and my home phone rang. It was Ian Meldrum. 'Bill,' he said, 'I want to talk to your son.' I put Stuart on and Molly apologised.

When Stuart went to school on Monday, as his mates had a go at him for my no-show, he had an even better story to tell—Molly had called him!

Bill Duff, Festival Records

I have to admit I sat stunned as I tuned into the repeat of the 100th episode the following Saturday. Fortunately, the repeat was edited down to 90 minutes. It was a weird feeling; I felt like I'd had nothing to do with it.

I guess there were two things I learnt from the experience. One—how to make a proper cup of tea. And two—the show definitely must go on.

AC/DC's last big appearance before they went overseas was a huge gig in Adelaide. Ian was to compere the show, but that week his romantic involvement had broken up and he was a complete wreck. I arrived at his house to take him to the airport and he was sobbing, saying he wasn't going to go. I managed to get him into his Celica and he was driving, but on the Tullamarine Freeway, he decided he didn't want me in the car. We're doing 100 kilometres an hour and he opens my door and tries to kick me out.

Eventually we get on the plane, and the first people we see are a loving couple, holding hands. Ian falls apart. He said, 'I want to get off.' I remember Billy Thorpe was also on the plane. He said, 'Brian, can't you control your fucking client?'

It wasn't easy, but we made it. And it was an awesome gig. Bon Scott was brilliant.

Brian de Courcy, Molly's manager

5: IT AIN'T NECESSARILY SO

1975–1979: Backslappers, backstabbers and bribers—Yesterday's heroes—Mamma Mia, it's ABBA-mania—The plot to kill *Countdown*— How I nearly ended up at Seven with Norman Gunston— My Humdrum life—Getting Iggy with it—The golf war.

That Molly Meldrum is a shock to your aesthetic system, isn't he? Do you let your children watch that sort of thing? All Australia should complain. I've often said that the ABC should be closed down, and Countdown *is a classic reason for doing so.*
Bernard King on *King's Kitchen*

'Like a recording star who can't sing or a best-selling author who can't write, Molly Meldrum has no obvious talent,' Bryan Patterson wrote in *Listener In-TV* in February 1977. Thanks Bryan!

But with *Countdown* attracting about three million viewers a week, I was dubbed 'The Power Broker Of Pop'—a position I never wanted.

Countdown had become a monster. And not everyone was happy.

Record stores would ring the show, wanting advance lists of what was going to be played on the Sunday night—to make sure they had it in stock on the Monday. Before *Countdown*, the biggest-selling Australian album had been Daddy Cool's *Daddy Who? Daddy Cool* album, which had sold 50,000 copies.

A year after *Countdown* started, Skyhooks' *Living In The 70's*—released the week before *Countdown* went to air—had sold more than 200,000 copies.

Countdown had the power to create stars.

John Paul Young was one of the first *Countdown* creations. Producer Robbie Weekes believes that John walked into the *Countdown* studios 'a nobody and walked out a star'.

At the start of 1972, a 21-year-old sheet-metal worker called John Young (not to be confused with the *Young Talent Time* creator and 'The Real Thing' writer) appeared on the scene with his debut single, 'Pasadena', saying that one day he hoped to own an Aston Martin. He also played Annas in *Jesus Christ Superstar*, where the show's publicist, Patti Mostyn, dubbed him 'Squeak'.

> Because of my outrageous laugh, she called me 'Little Squeaker'. I didn't like it at first, but then a mate of mine told me that Johnny O'Keefe was known as 'Pip Squeak' when he was a kid because he was so small. All of a sudden, the name didn't seem so bad after all.
>
> **John Paul Young**

John's career had stalled by the time *Countdown* came along. In March 1975, when John's 'day gig' was welding security grills on windows, he came on the show to perform the Vanda & Young composition 'Yesterday's Hero'. I remember Robbie Weekes saying, 'This is a great song, but the wrong singer. They should have got Johnny O'Keefe to record it.'

But Robbie was determined to make it work. He shot footage of young girls shaking a cyclone fence. Robbie, liked a crazed movie director, was on the other side of the fence, screaming, '*Love him, love him!*' The kids were like, 'Who is he?' But Robbie told them: 'It doesn't matter who he is, just yell!'

It was a make-or-break gig for John, who became known as

John Paul Young soon after. He looked a million bucks, having gone to Paddy's Market before the show, spending $35 on a shirt that was made of old silk scarves.

John was not happy when the shirt was ripped from his back as he was dragged from the platform and into the *Countdown* crowd.

Everyone in the studio knew what was going to happen, except me. When the cord was ripped from the microphone, I looked at the floor manager. He just said, 'Don't worry, keep singing.' I was so concerned about everything being right, but nobody else was. I guess for them it *was* right—it was absolute mayhem. For me, that appearance was all about fear.

John Paul Young

The expression on Squeak's face—at first bewildered, then a little shy, then getting seriously pissed off . . . it was very funny—for me.

Jon English

In April 1975, I wrote in my *Listener In-TV* column about 'Yesterday's Hero': 'Now if this record is not a hit all over Australia then I'll burn my Beatles collection.' I didn't have to look for a lighter. 'Yesterday's Hero' hit number one in Australia and number 42 in the United States.

Robbie Weekes and Michael Shrimpton were masters at generating excitement. When *Countdown* started, the ABC's publicity department had no idea what to do with the show, so Michael said, 'Don't worry, we'll do our own publicity.'

When the Bay City Rollers appeared on the show, it was Rollermania.

The Bay City Rollers' appearance coincided with a total solar eclipse. We even put the eclipse into the rundown. This was a once-in-a-lifetime experience, but the kids missed it—they were pressed up against the window trying to get a glimpse of those tartan idiots.

Ted Emery, *Countdown* producer

Watched by the TV writer from *The Truth* newspaper, Robbie and Michael tried to repel the screaming, tartan-clad fans. One young girl hit Michael in the stomach with her handbag. He fell to his knees and staggered away. After the commotion, the TV writer asked Robbie where Michael was. Minutes later, Michael appeared and revealed a huge bruise covering his stomach. Robbie and the TV writer were shocked. The banner for the next edition of *The Truth* screamed: 'TV Man Bashed At Station'. What the writer didn't know was that after the incident, Michael had rushed to the make-up department and had the bruise painted on.

In 1975, a reel of clips arrived from Sweden. It contained songs from a band called ABBA, including 'Bang-A-Boomerang', 'Tropical Loveland', 'Mamma Mia' and 'I Do, I Do, I Do, I Do, I Do'. Tony Vuat, who was in charge of the incoming clips, took a liking to 'Mamma Mia'. He played it for me, then he played it for Robbie Weekes, and then for the rest of the *Countdown* crew.

Robbie remembers one of the crew reacting to the close-ups of Agnetha and Frida mouthing the words 'Mamma mia'. 'Look at those mouths,' the crew member said. 'Imagine them going down on you!'

Strangely, RCA, their record label, refused to release 'Mamma Mia' as a single. In fact, they told us, 'Don't bother playing that clip because we're not going to release it.' But we played it. And RCA still refused to release it. Then we played it again . . . We finally forced RCA to release it as a single. Then, after it went to number one in Australia, RCA in Europe decided to release it as a single. It topped the UK charts in

January 1976. And years later, it became the name of the ABBA musical.

At the end of 1975, ABBA had become the first group since The Beatles to have three singles in the Australian Top 40 at the same time. The Beatles did it in 1964 with 'She Loves Me', 'Love Me Do' and 'I Want To Hold Your Hand'. ABBA did it with 'I Do, I Do, I Do, I Do, I Do', 'Mamma Mia' and 'SOS'. And 'Fernando' spent a record-breaking fourteen weeks on top of the *Countdown* charts.

Mark Holden was another pop star *Countdown* helped to create. In 1975, Mark came on the show to perform 'Firefly', a little-known song from his debut album, *Dawn In Darkness*. Mark, then a folk singer, had long hair and was wearing leather.

With his record company promo guy, Michael Matthews, Mark decided he needed to make more of an impact next time he appeared on the show. And what they did would change Mark's life forever. On the way from the airport to the ABC studios, Mark was thinking, 'What can I do to suck up to the girls?' They stopped at a florist and bought red carnations.

> I gave them out to the girls in the audience before I sang, and as I was singing, they threw them back on stage. From that moment, I didn't have to do anything more. It had all started.
>
> **Mark Holden**

Mark Holden became 'The Carnation Kid' and ended up having five Top 40 hits, including 'Never Gonna Fall In Love Again' and 'I Want To Make You My Lady'.

In 1977, pioneering Aussie rocker Johnny O'Keefe told an Industries Assistance Commission inquiry: 'At present the pop business in Australia is almost in the grip of television clips on *Countdown*. This *Countdown* is the most influential factor in the pop business. If you don't have a clip, you are nowhere.'

JO'K cited the example of Peter Allen's 'I Go To Rio': 'It was out for nine months before it got any reaction, and somebody decided he [Peter Allen] should make a film clip. He got it placed on *Countdown* and immediately the thing was a hit.'

> What I love about the music industry is so many things are pure luck. All the record companies would make up VHS reels of clips for *Countdown*. I think Ted Emery was working one weekend when he decided to put on the Festival reel. He was just about to switch it off when he discovered a guy in a floral shirt playing the maracas. He rang Molly and said, 'You've gotta see this.' Now, Peter Allen's talent probably would have got him there, but sometimes you just need a lucky break, and his lucky break was Ted Emery seeing that clip.
>
> **Bill Duff, Festival Records**

But it's a myth that everything *Countdown* played became a hit. Some songs simply failed to connect with the public. For example, we gave an Adelaide singer named Andy Upton a big push in 1977. Andy—who was the writer and original singer of the *Here's Humphrey* theme—did a brilliant cover of The Supremes' 'Stop! In The Name Of Love'. It was a hit in South Australia, but failed to take off nationally, and the last I heard of Andy he was delivering bread, to supplement his music income.

Also in 1977, EMI, then the biggest record company in Australia, commissioned a survey that concluded that *Countdown* had an 'almost totally dominating effect' on the Australian record market. It found that 96 per cent of the singles that made the Top 10 in 1977 had been played on *Countdown*.

The National Times ran a story on December 30, 1978 headed: 'How Aunty Controls The Pop Game'. Three ABC commissioners—Richard Harding, Marius Webb and David Gunn—complained about the show's commercialism. The more *Countdown* rated, the more its internal critics said it was too commercial.

A mate of Michael Shrimpton's, an ABC executive named Frank Ward, would say to him, through clenched teeth as he took a drag on a menthol cigarette: 'The ABC can stand anything but success.'

And it's so true. And because our success came from a youthful area, it was even more dubious. There were two people in Sydney [at the ABC] who tried very hard to kill it, because it came from Melbourne, basically. But because it was hugely successful, it was too hard for them to touch. So they tried to starve it instead.

Michael Shrimpton

Michael once asked one of the *Countdown* staffers, Stephen Jones, to go back over the show's rundowns from the previous twelve months to work out each record company's percentage of play. The figures showed that we didn't play favourites.

Michael was a stickler for staffers doing the right thing by the ABC.

We weren't even allowed to take up lunch invitations. Record companies would ask us to lunches and we'd have to say no. I could never work out what Molly was getting out of it. Everyone thought he'd be a multi-millionaire, but he wasn't. I guess he just loved the whole scene.

Ted Emery

In the early days of *Countdown*, there was an understanding that the ABC would send me on one overseas trip a year to do interviews for the show. During 1979, Michael contacted his boss, Alan Bateman, to inform him that he wanted me to go to London, New York, San Francisco and Chicago in three weeks' time. A blazing row ensued.

Bateman: Sorry, travel budget's all dried up . . . you should have got your request in earlier.

Shrimpton: But this is standard, you knew it was happening.

Bateman: I don't have any memory of that.

Michael then did what you should never do at the ABC—he went above his boss's head, calling the controller of programs . . . who backed Bateman.

We were within a small step of going to Channel Nine *en masse*. It was the beginning of my disenchantment with ABC management.

Michael Shrimpton

I also almost ended up at Channel Seven. This is how my manager at the time, Brian de Courcy, remembers the story.

It's 1977 and Garry McDonald's alter ego, Norman Gunston, is one of the biggest stars in the land. In fact, he wins the Gold Logie for Most Popular Personality On Australian Television. I managed Garry and I also managed Molly.

I negotiated a new Gunston series with the ABC and also convinced him to make a record and go on the road. We got an amazing reaction right around the country. That's the one thing about the ABC—no matter where you go, you're known. True national acts are made by the ABC. It established Molly, too.

Garry and I realised there was more money to be made. I told Garry that if he wanted to make real money out of TV, he had to get out of the ABC. So we went and resigned. It was a real gamble because at this stage we hadn't spoken to Seven, Nine or Ten. The ABC stayed mum because they had the new series. The next day I rang the commercials. Ten and Seven said they'd love to have him. Nine didn't think he was funny. Two weeks later, I put him on *The Don Lane Show* doing his punk rock single. It got a huge reaction. Nine rang and said they wanted to talk.

Seven offered the best deal—four one-hour specials a year for two years, and Garry was able to bring his crew and writers.

As I was going to Sydney to do the deal with Seven's Ted Thomas, I remembered a conversation I'd recently had with Molly. 'I'm sick of *Countdown*, you're my manager, get me something else.' Was Molly just in one of his moods, or was he serious?

I went to see Molly. 'Do you really, genuinely this time want to leave *Countdown*?'

'Yes,' he replied.

I rang Ted Thomas. 'Would you like Meldrum, too?'

'Does he want to replace Donnie Sutherland?' Thomas asked.

Donnie Sutherland, the host of *Sounds*, was Molly's pop rival. The two shows were locked in a constant battle to premiere film clips. 'No,' I insisted, 'we don't want Saturday mornings. We want a prime-time show, but not up against *Countdown*. Maybe something on a Monday.'

Thomas liked the idea. The deal was on.

As Molly and I drove into Seven in Sydney, Donnie Sutherland walked out the front door and spotted us. He went pale. Molly did, too.

Thomas and I did the Gunston deal. Then Thomas said, 'Right, now let's talk about Ian.'

Molly appeared and said: 'I don't want to do it, I don't want to leave *Countdown*.' I will never forget the look Ted Thomas gave me. It was a 'What the fuck is going on?' look.

I leant over to Molly and whispered: 'What do you mean?'

'The ABC has been good to me . . .'

Ted Thomas stood up. 'I think I'll leave you two alone for a minute.'

'What the fuck are you doing?' I screamed after Thomas had left the room.

Molly ran from the room. 'I'm going to the toilet.' He was still in the toilet when Ted Thomas reappeared. 'What are you doing,

Brian? This was a package—Gunston and Meldrum.'

'Well, Ted,' I stammered, 'it was never a package. And I don't know why he's changed his mind.'

When Molly walked back into the room, Thomas was furious. 'You really owe me, Brian.'

'Don't worry, Ted,' I said, 'the first interview Norman Gunston will do for you is Mick Jagger.'

Molly glared at me.

As we left Thomas' office, Molly grabbed my arm: 'How the hell did you get Mick Jagger? We can't get Jagger!'

What Molly didn't know was the Jagger deal hadn't been done. In fact, it hadn't been thought of until that moment in Ted Thomas' office.

We *did* get him, but that's another story.

A few years later, *TV Week* ran a story stating that Kerry Packer had told Channel Nine executives to 'offer Molly whatever he wants' to switch from the ABC. These sorts of stories would pop up from time to time. In 1980, I outlined why I wouldn't leave *Countdown* in an interview with *The Age*. I loved the fact that it was a truly national show, we had the best crew in the country, and the program had great 'flow' because there were no ad breaks. 'Also,' I added, 'I couldn't bear—and this is no reflection on any channel that's offered me anything—but I couldn't bear sitting on an enormous pile of money in the bank with the possibility of the show, if it didn't work, going off the air and for the next eight months to two years sitting around doing nothing.'

In 1980, Jennifer Byrne wrote in *The Age* that I was 'the most unlikely power-broker since squat Vince Gair' [the DLP leader who Gough Whitlam appointed Australian Ambassador to Ireland]. She quoted former ABC commissioner Marius Webb:

There's absolutely no doubt that *Countdown* has been a continuing cause of concern. It has been brought up by a number of commissioners as being so dangerously close to a commercial channel as to fall outside the ABC's charter.

Webb criticised my trips overseas to interview artists—paid for by the record companies—as well as the superimposing of a band's tour dates over their latest clip. 'Anywhere else that'd be called advertising,' he claimed.

Meldrum became the man with the power. Molly would never discuss it as power. I'm not sure he would even see it as power, but it was a very powerful position to be in.

Stephen Jones, *Countdown* producer

I hated the thought of power. Some people might get off on it, I don't. The pressure the record companies put me under was horrendous. That's why I encouraged them to come to my house, so they could mix with each other and realise how competitive the business was. Songs went on *Countdown* because they were worthy. I had no qualms about our exclusive policy; we were spending a fortune on making a world-class music show. *Sounds* was essentially a video show. Why would we regurgitate on a Sunday night what they had played on Saturday morning?

Countdown's 'first-pick' policy meant we wouldn't show an artist's clip if it had been shown on another program. I was forced to defend the policy in 1980 after we ditched Jon English from the line-up because he had appeared on *The Don Lane Show*. 'There are the ratings, no one gets close to us,' I told the press. 'We have about three million potential record buyers who watch us every week. We can't produce a refreshingly new show every week if artists perform on a lesser-rating show earlier in the week. Surely, we have the right to get film clips first?'

In another interview, I said: 'We get offered 50 clips a week and if one has been shown before, why should we use it? I had 48 acts to consider last week and only 11 went on.'

The Australian newspaper quoted 'one aspiring musician' as saying, 'If Molly doesn't like you then you might as well give up.'

> We were never corrupt, and I can say that honestly. But we were ruthless in the sense that we wanted something first and we were going to have it.
>
> **Grant Rule, *Countdown* producer**

> If an artist was worthwhile, you'd get to go on. There was no graft or corruption.
>
> **Michael Matthews, EMI**

Only once was I seriously offered a bribe—and it was more laughable than serious. I was walking into the ABC canteen when a guy from an independent record label grabbed my arm. He thrust a wad of notes into my hand—he was trying to buy his act onto *Countdown*. I threw the cash in the air and walked out. It was raining money in the ABC canteen.

Being on *Countdown* pretty much destroyed my dream of being a record producer. For a start, I didn't have the time to do long stints in the studio, and I understood that there was an obvious conflict of interest. People would say, 'Well, they're only on *Countdown* because Molly produced their record.' But, if anything, an act that had an association with me was disadvantaged because their song had to be a hit before I would give it a run.

Conflict-of-interest accusations also hounded Michael Shrimpton because his brother, Stephen, was, at the height of *Countdown*'s success, the boss of EMI in Australia. When the issue came to a head, EMI had seven songs in the Top 10, but there was never any collusion between Michael and Stephen, and we never favoured EMI. Unfortunately, the issue had an impact on the brothers' relationship—and they barely spoke for years.

Critics also criticised me for not being more critical. I tried to explain my approach in a 1978 interview. 'For instance, I don't like the group Boney M., but I don't see any point in criticising them as a lot of people get enjoyment out of their records.'

About eighteen months into the show, to counter the critics who were saying *Countdown* was too commercial, Michael decided that I should do a 'rock report', to give the show some editorial clout. Michael wanted it to be a serious rock report, presented by 'Ian Meldrum'. He even wrote one of his famous memos, saying as much.

I was sensitive about the Molly thing because I thought it was a hangover from another era—you know, the kids' show with Molly The Monster, and that was not the age group we were going for. Also, I thought that the industry might have known him as Molly, but it's a camp name and camp was not the audience. I just felt it was a bit childish. Of course, I was probably a tad up myself as well. The attitude was if we're going to be the market leader, we had to get rid of all the crap and start afresh. Look how that worked!

Michael Shrimpton

The Rock Report's first week went according to Michael's plan. The second week's report was introduced by that week's host, John Paul Young. He was supposed to say: 'Here's Ian Meldrum with The Rock Report.' Michael even went to him before the show and ordered: 'Do not, *under any circumstances*, call him Molly.'

Of course, that was like a red rag to a bull with Squeak. His introduction was: 'Now here's boring old Molly with his boring old humdrum.'

Both names stuck—and Humdrum became an integral part of the show.

> I used to give it to Molly all the time. I didn't put him up on any pedestal. I came from a factory background—I had four years in a factory with people taking the piss out of me, so I knew how to do it. I would always say things to him like, 'What are you mumbling and grumbling about? Just speak, man!'
>
> **John Paul Young**

Squeak was a huge part of *Countdown*. He was a great pop star, though he was so laidback he drove me crazy.

> I think my lack of ambition frustrated Molly. He would regularly tell viewers, 'Squeak has gone fishing instead of touring overseas.' He couldn't fathom me at all. I used to say that I'd gone fishing to get him off my back. I remember sitting by the pool in Swan Hill and he tracked me down. 'What the fuck are you doing in Swan Hill? "Yesterday's Hero" is number 50 in America, why aren't you over there?'
>
> **John Paul Young**

One of *Countdown*'s classic catchphrases came after yet another screaming match with Michael Shrimpton. He was furious when I praised an album during the Humdrum segment, telling the viewers: 'Go out and buy it!'

Meldrum's inherent enthusiasm to promote something he liked caused problems for me with management in terms of advertising and commercialism. At the ABC, we weren't permitted to endorse a product. We had to tread a fine line.

Michael Shrimpton

So, my recommendation became 'Do yourself a favour'. It was my way of saying, 'You should buy this album.'

Working with Michael Shrimpton was always a delight. Even when he was yelling at me, he was entertaining. I would regularly receive a Shrimpton memo. **From**: Head TV Ent Vic. **To**: Ian Meldrum.

They [the memos] were glorious reading because Shrimpton is a brilliant, articulate man. Molly would be reading them and then he'd look up and ask you something like, 'What does this mean? *Incarcerated*?'

Ted Emery, *Countdown* producer

Michael and Robbie Weekes made a terrific team. As Michael said of Robbie, 'He was a truly great team leader. He could enthuse the dullest crew.'

Ted Emery was another brilliant member of the *Countdown* crew. He had a wonderful way of dealing with the bands.

One of my favourite bands was the Ted Mulry Gang. I remember eating baked beans and drinking scotch with them in the ABC canteen on a Saturday morning. Four young girls were banging on the window. They followed TMG everywhere. We were going out to make a clip at a church hall. We raced to the car and they chased us. They lifted up their dresses—they didn't have any underwear on—and pressed their bodies against the windows. This is 8 o'clock in the morning! The boys were yelling that I was Ted Mulry's brother. A little old guy in a blue Morris Minor drove past. All I can remember as we drove off is looking in the rear-vision mirror and seeing the Morris Minor crash into a brick fence. About half-an-hour later, the girls found us at the hall. We had a great day.

Ted Emery

One of Ted's roles was to look after *Countdown*'s guest hosts.

Having guest hosts was one of the beauties of the show. The presentation of the host was unimportant. That was such a simple and effective idea.

Ted Emery

Ray Burgess and Darryl Cotton were two of Ted's favourites. You could ring them up at the last minute and they would always do it, and do it well.

One day I shared the hosting duties with Alex Smith [Moving Pictures] and Mark Edwards [The Runners]. They told us not to worry about the script too much as they had cue cards. But I was too embarrassed to tell them I was as blind as a bat without my glasses, so I fumbled and mumbled my way through the whole show. I don't think I got one thing right . . . and no one seemed to care.

Wendy Stapleton, Wendy & The Rocketts

The late James Freud wrote about his first *Countdown* experience, singing the Teenage Radio Stars' debut, 'I Wanna Be Your Baby', in his book, *I Am The Voice Left From Drinking*, which I launched in 2002. In it, he says, 'I was finally going to be on the show I had sat and watched religiously as a teenager, while telling everyone, "One day I'll be up there."'.

The band was introduced by that week's guest host, Meat Loaf. Reclining on a large couch, after riding onto the set on a motorbike, Meat Loaf drawled, 'Ladies and gentlemen, Teenage Radio Stars!'

'It was a huge moment that lasted for about three minutes,' James recalled. 'Then it was suddenly over. We shlepped out to our bomb of a car and drove home as mere mortals, though, deep down inside, we knew we'd just been on *Countdown*.'

James later had a smash hit with 'Modern Girl', recorded an album with Gary Numan in London, and joined his old school friend Sean Kelly in the Models. James also hosted *Countdown* twice, realising, 'I didn't have a future as a television host. I battled through it, but I was no Brian Mannix, who was one of the best *Countdown* hosts.'

Countdown was a very generous show. One of the follow-up singles to 'I Hear Motion', from the Models' *The Pleasure Of Your Company* album, was a song called 'No Shoulders, No Head'. The week we performed the song on *Countdown*, we were the only band appearing live. The production crew allowed us to set up our equipment over two stages and assisted us in super-imposing song lyrics over the images, *Star Wars*-style. The song had a macabre subject matter—war, destitution . . . The end result was very satisfying—camouflage netting, incinerators, and we all played drums. *Countdown* gave us a tape, which we used as a self-produced film-clip. It was even played on other music shows.

Sean Kelly, Models

I was a huge fan of the Models. In Sean Kelly and Andrew Duffield and then James Freud, they had three wonderful songwriters. But they also liked to do things their own way.

With our first Models album, we came up with the unusual concept of not releasing a single. Molly spotted a couple of us in Chapel Street from his car and blocked traffic for several minutes to berate us, that we were doing no one any favours and that our song 'Happy Birthday IBM' could've been a hit!

Sean Kelly

In *Countdown*'s early days, the show went to air on a Sunday, was repeated on the following Saturday, and then it was gone, and we'd already moved onto the next show. There was no such thing as YouTube.

These days, you can re-live all of the show's 'magic moments'. One of the favourites is Iggy Pop's performance in 1979. I'd seen David Bowie play with Iggy in the United States, and I was a fan. So he came on the show to perform 'I'm Bored'. Now, Iggy appeared normal during the rehearsal. But something obviously happened between rehearsal and showtime. When Iggy reappeared for an interview during the Humdrum segment, he leapt onto the set—bare-chested with a cigarette in his hand. 'Hiya, Dogface,' he exclaimed.

With Iggy jumping up and down, saying 'G'day, G'day', it was one of the few times that I was forced to adopt the attitude of a serious interviewer. 'What's wrong, Iggy?' I asked. 'Don't you . . . You behave yourself.' But it didn't work. Iggy even did the old trick of pointing at my shirt and then slapping me in the face when I looked down.

Iggy then performed his song, forgetting every move he had worked out with the camera people earlier that day. Wielding the microphone stand like a maniac, Iggy also forgot the words to the song. He rolled on the ground, like a lizard, poking out his tongue. As he sang, he put the microphone down his pants.

My memory is fuzzy, but every time I talk to an Australian, they want to talk to me about that show. I vaguely remember I was miming my number and wielding the mike stand like an axe, very near the face of these really horrified eleven and twelve-year-old girls. They looked like they had seen a monster.

I remember thinking, 'Well, I don't think so much of you either, baby.' Gee, it was a strange booking. I didn't have any band with me. Actually, I've got no idea what happened that night, or during that trip to Australia, for that matter.

Iggy Pop

I remember being at home and watching that episode. It was great television when Iggy spat on the little girls at the front of the stage. You have to remember, the live audience was not totally reflective of the audience at home. It was usually young girls, who'd come to see the current pop star, like JPY. When a band like Mondo Rock played, the little girls would be like, 'Who are these guys?', and we'd be trying to get their attention. Iggy certainly got their attention.

Ross Wilson

Stephen Jones was *Countdown*'s first assistant director on the night of the Iggy incident. In his mind, he can still see a globule of Pop's spit swinging from one of the camera lenses.

It was the closest I ever came to walking in front of the camera and stopping the show. I was worried about what he was going to do, and we had a responsibility to the audience. A floor manager is a bit like a flight attendant—you have to ensure the safety of the audience. One member of the crowd, a girl about thirteen, was traumatised by the experience and needed first aid afterwards. It was very frightening. But I don't think Molly was frightened, he was just bemused.

Stephen Jones

Visually, what he [Iggy] did was, of its time, fairly remarkable. It brought the powers that be down on us like a ton of bricks. It went all the way to the [ABC] Commission. The ABC can be extraordinary about how it reacts to letters. One will catch a spark somewhere and this one did. It was the microphone down the pants in front of all these 'innocent' young ladies that caused the trouble. Nothing actually came of it, but it was a burden. I think one of the reasons I wanted to leave the show after year five was that I realised I was starting to self-censor, and self-censorship is a malicious thing. It creeps up on you, and you're not doing what you should be doing. This was a very serious time for me.

Michael Shrimpton

Michael found himself making cuts to David Bowie and Johnny Cougar film clips—but he let a Devo clip through unedited.

In this clip, they put a fork in a toaster. I looked at it as a surrealist work, and that's what they did, and I quite liked it. I let it go and we ran it twice. We didn't receive one complaint. Not a word. But I came to realise what a dreadful mistake it was. I beat myself up about that.

Michael Shrimpton

Watching the taping of another show in the VIP Room, Michael Shrimpton took a call from Alan Bateman, who declared: 'You will not be putting that to air.' He was referring to the Sex Pistols' 'God Save The Queen'.

Michael replied, 'Excuse me, I am the EP [executive producer] of this program, responsible for its content. Are you giving me an instruction that undermines my authority?'

Michael told me that Bateman's response was: 'I wouldn't go so far as to say that, but I'm taking this to the Commission.'

Michael and I had a chat and we decided to drop the clip. But we ran it the following week.

To appease the internal critics, we decided to film some shows in Sydney. It was not a good idea. The Sydney shows didn't have the same vibe as the Melbourne productions. And Michael had another major run-in with Bateman while taping a show in Sydney in September 1978. Michael says Bateman came into the control room uninvited.

> That is something in the ABC hierarchy that you never do—you never go into someone else's control room, especially if you're the superior and you haven't been invited or requested. It's because there would then be a second-guessing problem—everyone is watching what the department head is going to do. I never went into a control room without asking. Multi-camera TV is a benign dictatorship and, by definition, there can only be one dictator, and that's the person whose bum is in the chair. Not the fucking cheer squad.
>
> **Michael Shrimpton**

This was the night of what became known as 'The Rose Tattoo Chewing Gum Incident'. It was thought that singer Angry Anderson traded his chewing gum with the band's guitarist Mick Cocks mouth-to-mouth during a performance of 'Rock 'n' Roll Outlaw'.

Mick Cocks later revealed what actually happened to author Murray Engleheart: 'We got up there and we're goofing around, and one of the things I used to do was lay my head on his head. And he's just turned around and stuck his tongue in my mouth. Because he'd done it so many times before, I never thought of it as being anything.'

Bateman went off his head, demanding that the performance be cut from the show. Michael was furious. 'Jesus Christ, it's a rock 'n' roll show, baby. What is this confused middle-class niceties, this *Women's Weekly* kind of pap?'

It was an ugly period for everyone working on the show.

Looking back, I have a couple of regrets. I should have said, 'Fuck you, sack me if you will. But I will go down with thunderbolts and I'll take you with me.' But I didn't have the balls for that. And I was too protective of the show, thinking I had to tread carefully.

Michael Shrimpton

Rose Tattoo were banned from the show—a ban that lasted nearly three years. And Mick Cocks was forced to go to his little sister's school to explain their *Countdown* performance.

> I had to have a little yak and say, 'Look, we're just grown men and it's theatre and don't give my sister a hard time about this and I'm not a poofter.' I had politicians ringing my mother. I'm serious! It was a fucking huge thing.

The *Countdown* ban actually pleased Australian guitar great Lobby Loyde, who joined Rose Tattoo in 1979. Lobby was a great mate of one of my best friends, Michael Gudinski, and was someone I admired. But he was not a fan of the show. 'The death of music was *Countdown*,' Lobby claimed in Murray Engleheart's book *Blood, Sweat & Beers*.

> All they ever talked to you about was how it looked, what colour shirts you were going to wear, and was your make-up right . . . We just thought it was fucking definite Satan land. Everybody that I knew pathologically hated that show. Yet today they talk about it like it was the birth of rock 'n' roll. It was a shit show and everyone knows it. As sissy and camp as the day is long. It did awful stuff to music and it slowly replaced all the good rock 'n' roll with crap. It was the beginning of the fucking end.

I used to have a go at Molly for always pushing lightweight pop stuff. But one day he told me that acts such as Kylie are the catalyst that got young kids involved in music. For a long time, I didn't see it, but he's absolutely right. And now I realise how important that is. He is fostering the acts that will get people involved in music.

Jim Keays, The Masters Apprentices

Countdown was the ultimate squirm television. It was something you loved to watch to hate. Every week you would think, 'Oh my God, why doesn't this man get it together? Who is he, why is he on national TV and why is he so powerful?' He was the antithesis of a slick pop show host. He was inarticulate, clumsy, not very well groomed, and he was always in awe, which kind of gave him a very tenuous control over the interview. It was great to know you were watching something a whole nation was plugged into. There is something beautifully universal about that, knowing you could go to school the next day and say, 'Did you see what Agnetha was wearing?'

Deborah Conway

Yep, everyone's a critic. But, as they say, I guess it's better to be hated than ignored!

A show like *Countdown* should never have caused so much drama. In its heyday, it was just some frothy, silly, flashing-lights, bubbly, screaming kids . . . a harmless entertainment program, not trying to say or do anything, not aggressive, not anything. As was its talent coordinator, really.

Ted Emery

Band behaviour was not the only source of grief.

My brother Brian is a top golf writer, but when people say to me, 'Don't you like golf?', I say, 'No, I hate golf!' The first *Countdown* for 1979 was cut in half because there was a play-off in the Victorian Open golf championship. I protested to ABC management, saying, 'They should have started *Countdown* at 6 p.m. and interrupted it for the highlights of the golf. As it was, most of the golf was shots of people walking from green to green.'

I can respect the achievements of all of our great golfers, but I've never grown to like the game!

When the Bay City Rollers came to Australia in 1976, Ian was the compere of the tour. The day he was to go on the road, I went to get him. As I was walking up the stairs, I could hear this sobbing. I opened the front door and the house was in darkness. I found Ian on his knees on the floor, ironing a pair of trousers with a travel iron.

'What are you doing?' I asked.

'Ironing trousers,' he replied.

'Why don't you turn on the light?'

'Because my electricity's been cut off. My gas has been cut off, too. You, as my manager, should be looking after all these things.'

Then we had a big argument.

Brian de Courcy, Molly's manager

6: HOME ON MONDAY

1977: Fashion tips for Nicks—Raging at Regine's—Grant Rules OK—Getting Rod and Rotten—Meeting a new Idol—Get me home— I need to meet my Prince!

This business eats you up. It exhausts you.
John-Michael Howson

By 1977, *Countdown* had become a respected show, both locally and overseas. In fact, it seemed that every man and his dog wanted to be on *Countdown*. Yes, believe it or not, in that year a record was released with a barking dog.

At the end of the year, it was decided I would go overseas to gather interviews for the show. I was relieved to go because there was quite a power struggle going on at the ABC and within the *Countdown* camp.

So I headed overseas with producer Grant Rule, for 19 days, to the United States, Europe and the United Kingdom. During that period, I would do 54 interviews.

Grant got his start in TV the same way I did—as a mimer on *Kommotion* in the mid-'60s. He was one of the stars of the *Kommotion* cast. He did an interview with *Go-Set*'s Lily Brett, who wrote that he 'is considered by most people the best-looking *Kommotion* boy. He likes the colour black, greyhounds, girls with skinny legs, making movies and most important—sultanas.'

I would regularly see Grant at The Thumpin' Tum. Grant, Ronnie Burns, Denise Drysdale and Tony Healey ran a restaurant upstairs at the club called Top Of The Tum.

The 1977 trip was our only overseas adventure together.

I avoided them forever after that, but it's fair to say that I experienced one of the great ones.

Grant Rule, *Countdown* **producer**

Los Angeles was our first stop. We checked into the 'in' hotel at the time, the Sunset Marquis, and started to set up the interviews. Things were rolling along and all indications were that this trip was going to be a breeze. But then, to my horror, Grant took a phone call from the *Countdown* office, informing him that he would no longer be working on the show—after the trip, he would be assigned to another part of the ABC.

It totally knocked the wind out of Grant's sails, and I was furious. So much so that I rang them back and told them what they could do with themselves and Aunty ABC. I was very aware that in some quarters they were gunning for my position, but the Grant decision floored me. And I felt it was cowardly to do it over the phone.

I sat down with a devastated Grant. 'Come on,' I declared, 'we're going to have fun with this trip. Don't let those pricks spoil it.' And fun we had—though it was sprinkled with drama.

Without a doubt, one of the biggest things in America in 1977 was Fleetwood Mac. Their *Rumours* album was a monster. I had never met Fleetwood Mac, but it was arranged that towards the end of our trip we would get a big exclusive with one of the band's female singers, Stevie Nicks.

After doing a few general interviews in Los Angeles, Grant and I headed for New York to tackle some of the big ones, including Rod Stewart.

Of course, Rod and Elton were great friends/foes. But as much as I was a friend of Elton's, I hardly knew Rod, or his manager, Billy Gaff. But his publicist, Tony Toon, had become an acquaintance during Rod's Australian tour. Tony was great fun. Rod called him 'mincing, waspish, scurrilous, incorrigible'. At the end of every dinner, Tony would say to the waiter: 'Bring me a large amaretto and a big butch man.'

During Rod's Australian tour, they had a reception at the SCG, where everyone had to wear white. It was very much a who's who affair, what with the Bermuda jackets, tuxedos and bow ties. To be different, I decided to arrive in white cricket gear, pads and all, waving a cricket bat. Tony Toon thought it was hysterical, and I believe Rod and Billy were also amused.

> It was another way of Molly not only being noticed but remembered. In this particular instance, it helped to get us what we wanted in New York. You've got to remember that back then Molly didn't wear a cowboy hat, but the name Molly was enough.
>
> **Grant Rule**

In New York, we checked into the prestigious Waldorf Astoria. It was a very swish hotel and we felt very important.

Peter Ikin, the head of WEA's promotions department in Australia, was also in New York, as was WEA's international boss, Tom Ruffino. Peter's nickname was Iris, and *Countdown's* overseas trips were often referred to as 'The Molly and Iris Show'.

The night before the interview, Rod's record company threw a big party at Regine's, a restaurant, bar and discotheque. Grant and I scored an invitation, as did the members of Air Supply, who had impressed Billy Gaff when they supported Rod on his Australian tour, and he was determined to break them in the States.

We arrived at Regine's, showed our invitations and went in. Now, I don't know who was to blame, maybe it was me . . . We had a few drinks at the bar and couldn't see any stars. After about an hour, I turned to Grant and said, 'This could be the duddest party I've ever been to.'

We were just about to leave, when a friend of Tom Ruffino's spotted us. 'What are you doing, why aren't you down at the party?'

The party was actually *downstairs* at Regine's.

Well, I rushed down those stairs like a frenzied housewife trying to get those first bargains at a stocktake sale.

Now, *this* was a party. It was like a who's who of the music and movie business. Much to my delight, John and Yoko were there, and I spent about fifteen minutes talking to them about my days at Apple and that world exclusive. They laughed when I told them I didn't realise during the interview how important it was. Little did I know, but it would be the last time I would see and speak to John Lennon.

The party was a hoot. They had a dance floor, which was absolutely packed with celebrities. I was sitting next to this very pretty girl, so I asked if she'd like to dance. She obliged and we hit the floor.

After about fifteen minutes, I sat down. Tom Ruffino grabbed my arm. 'I didn't realise you knew Stevie Nicks.'

I didn't know what he was talking about. 'I don't. In fact, I've never met her.'

'But you've just been dancing with her!'

I was stunned. 'Oh really, where is she?'

But Stevie had disappeared into the night.

After the party, I went with some friends to a club. I ended up going back to the Waldorf with a guy I'd met at the party, who was a tennis player-cum-stroke coach.

The next morning we woke up and I ordered some breakfast.

I got out of bed to prepare for the press conference and possible interview with Rod Stewart, which was scheduled for 1 p.m. at Rod's hotel, The Pierre.

Grant rang my room and was happy to hear that I was up. 'Good,' he said, 'I'll come around.'

'No, not yet, don't, don't,' I stammered. Grant knew something was going on. 'Have you got a number in there?'

'No, of course not,' I lied.

My guest explained that he really should get back to his hotel because his friend from England would be wondering where he was. I nearly died when he told me that the hotel in question was The Pierre, and that he was the boyfriend of Rod's manager's best friend.

Imagine my horror when Tony Toon rang me and revealed that all hell had broken loose at The Pierre because Billy Gaff's best friend's boyfriend had gone missing. And back then, if there was a drama in the Stewart camp, or the Elton camp, everyone got involved—including the artiste. Rod was threatening to cancel the press conference and interview.

I quickly got dressed, my guest departed, and Grant arrived. He must have guessed something was up because he kept asking what was wrong.

We arrived at The Pierre and mixed with all the other film crews, international press and photographers. It was a *big* event. Along with Fleetwood Mac, Rod was the hottest act in the world. Tony Toon was in panic mode, flitting around. 'That's terrible what happened with that guy's boyfriend,' I said. 'I'd kill him if it was me.'

Word got out that Rod would not be coming down. 'This is ridiculous,' Grant said, shaking his head, 'all over some stupid queen.' Grant was getting worried—he didn't want to have to call the *Countdown* office and tell them we hadn't got our biggest interview.

I excused myself, saying I needed to go to the toilet. I actually ran down to the bar and downed two scotch and cokes. When I returned to the main room, Grant was in a panic—Tony Toon was trying to find me.

'Quick,' Tony said, 'get your crew into the next room and set up. I think the artiste will come down and do something with you.'

When Rod finally appeared, he barked, 'Who let that fucking crew in?'

'It's Molly,' Tony replied.

'That's okay then. Get your arse over here, Molly!'

We sat down and talked for 35 minutes. Billy Gaff then asked if I could include a question for European television. After that, Rod stood up and said, 'Thank you everyone.' He then walked out of the room.

This truly was a world scoop. With media from all over the world, no one got anything except Ian. I then spent the next two hours negotiating with the European media about the rights for our interview to be shown in their respective countries.

During my time with the show, a lot of producers would come to me and say, 'Anyone could program a music television show.' And there's an argument for that, because anyone with a reasonable ear can pick a hit song. But I always used to answer that by saying, 'If you can deliver me Paul McCartney, I'm happy for you to be whatever you want to be.'

I have this view that Molly was really a newsman. He had this great capacity to generate news on the spot. We [once] went to a movie premiere and there was a big party afterwards, but we didn't have an invitation, so Ian generated a distraction, a false fight, grabbed some passes, and in we went and filmed it all. He was a great news guy.

Grant Rule

When I finally introduced the Rod Stewart exclusive on *Countdown*, I said, 'We went back to Los Angeles for Rod Stewart. No, yes, no, it was in New York—I got so confused in America, it was ridiculous.'

When the interview started, Rod—unshaven and dishevelled—picked up my notes and called me 'an amateur'. He then said, 'I came from warm sheets to do this interview. I've had only four hours sleep.'

'You went to bed at 7 a.m. and it's now 5 p.m.,' I challenged him.

'Took me five hours to get ready.'

I then told Rod how much I enjoyed his concert. 'The band was great,' I said, 'really tight.'

'They *are* tight,' Rod agreed. 'They haven't bought me a drink in months.'

Of course, Rod has a reputation for being tight with his money. The story goes that he once made a 30-kilometre round trip back to a restaurant in Los Angeles because they had charged him $4 for a mineral water that he hadn't ordered. It wasn't true, but it was true that when Rod and Elton once exchanged Christmas gifts, Rod gave Elton a bar fridge worth £300, and Elton gave Rod a Rembrandt.

Rod and Elton have a wonderful love–hate relationship. Rod calls Elton 'Sharon'; Elton calls Rod 'Phyllis'. At one of his London shows, Rod had a huge 'Blondes Have More Fun' banner. Beneath it, Elton placed his own banner: 'But Brunettes Have More Money'. At another show, Rod had a giant soccer ball floating above the arena. Elton hired a marksman to shoot it down.

In 1979, I did interviews with both Rod and Elton. Rod couldn't resist having a jibe at Elton: 'He phoned up and said, "I've made a disco album." I said, "You're a bit late, aren't you, dear?"'

Elton shot back: 'He made a very big disco record, which he stole the tune of from Brazil.' I'll always remember the look of delight on Elton's face when he related the story of going to the Rio Carnival with Rod and Freddie Mercury (who they called 'Melina'); Rod heard a record called 'Taj Mahal' by a Brazilian singer named Jorge Ben Jor, and subconsciously ripped off the melody for 'Da Ya Think I'm Sexy?'—subsequently losing all the royalties to one of his biggest hits.

I've had some great times and classic interviews with Rod. I once asked if he liked blondes better than brunettes. He replied: 'That's the most silly question I've ever heard.'

Another time, I gave him a big introduction and then said: 'What did you think of that?'

'Useless.'

In July 1983, I announced on *Countdown* that Rod would be touring Australia in February 1984 with Elton John. 'That should be a concert and a half and a real circus and, I'd imagine, a lot of drama.' Unfortunately, the tour never happened, and in November 1983, I had this to say on the show:

Now I know I made a bit of a fool of myself because I said Rod and Elton were gonna come out to this country next February, but, ah, Rod's thrown in the dummy, thrown another mood again and decided not to come out. But then I can understand because *Too Low For Zero* is still Top 5 in this country, and you could say that Rod's album stiffed. The publicist of the tour said last week when Rod decided to cancel the tour, 'Don't worry about that, because he was only the support act anyhow.'

Ooh, I can be a bitch sometimes!

Rod has been a regular visitor to Australia, and we've had a lot of fun on the road. On one Australian tour, I pestered Rod's people about doing an interview. They kept putting it off. By the day of the gig at Rod Laver Arena, I was seriously frustrated. I got a friend to go home and get my video camera. When the concert started, I ran to the front, pointed the camera straight at Rod and said, 'Talk, you bastard!'

I got the interview.

When Rod did a song, 'All For Love', with Bryan Adams and Sting, for the movie *The Three Musketeers*, I had great fun interviewing all three of them separately, making up stories. When I caught up with Rod, I took great delight in saying, 'They both said you were a real prick. Now, we know you are, but . . .'

'What?!'

Even though I've had plenty of bitchy fights with Rod, he's always been very supportive. In 1979, a journalist in *The Australian* wrote: 'What is wrong with humdrum Meldrum? There's so much he wants to say but however much he opens and shuts his mouth, moves his tongue around and things like that, it remains inside him.' On Adelaide radio, Rod sprung to my defence. 'Look,' he said, 'we have a lot of fun doing all that, which is probably what some critics don't realise. Anyway, I'll talk to Molly, but I won't talk to most of those people who've been slating him.'

Thanks, Rod. And you know what? I kind of owe my life to Rod and his then manager, Billy Gaff. I was booked on an Air India flight, but Rod and Billy—after much argument from me—convinced me to stay with them for one more dinner party. Good move: a bomb went off on the plane and it crashed into the Atlantic, killing all 329 passengers.

Some guys have all the luck, indeed.

Anyway, back to New York in 1977 . . . After we left The Pierre, we went for a drink with Peter Ikin and Tom Ruffino at The

Plaza hotel. I finally plucked up the courage to reveal that I was kind of responsible for all the drama. They swore me to secrecy. 'You must never tell Billy Gaff, Rod or Tony Toon!' Tom instructed.

It was only years later, when Billy became a great mate of mine, that I confessed. We laughed for about an hour.

Obviously the incident had improved my status as a television interviewer, but I can tell you it did nothing for my tennis.

Sadly, Rod would later split with both Billy Gaff and Tony Toon. Tony got his revenge by planting a story—which was reported as news in America—that Rod had been rushed to hospital in San Diego after servicing a gang of sailors at a gay bar. The story went that he had his stomach pumped and they found eight pints of semen. 'This story has stayed with me ever since,' Rod admitted in his autobiography. 'Say what you like about Tony Toon—and God rest his soul—but he was good at his job.'

For the rest of the New York trip, I tried to keep out of trouble. I was certainly on my best behaviour when I spent a night with Olivia Newton-John and John Travolta at Studio 54, the world's hippest disco. I thought of the song 'The In Crowd' when Olivia and I walked straight in, bypassing the enormous queue. Studio 54 was mind-blowing. I was in awe of the dance floor, the music, the speakers and the sound. It was like being in another world. (Two decades later, I was sitting in a Melbourne cinema watching the *Studio 54* movie. In the opening scenes, someone says, 'We've got to get down there because Olivia Newton-John's there!' 'My God,' I thought, having a flashback to those times, 'I was there, too.')

When Grant and I returned to Los Angeles, we did the interview with Stevie Nicks at her house in the Hollywood Hills, which once belonged to the silent-movie star Vilma Bánky.

Stevie was very spiritual, almost psychedelic. She kept us waiting for about an hour and then she drifted down the stairs, carrying her little white dog, Jennifer.

'Don't I know you from somewhere?' she asked.

'No, I don't think so,' I replied, still embarrassed about not knowing who she was when we'd been dancing in New York.

It was a fun interview.

'Excuse me for saying it,' I said, 'but you've become an immense sex symbol to many rock followers throughout the world. Are you aware of that?'

Stevie: I'm aware of it because people tell me that. I'm not aware of it in the way I look at it. That's not something I set out to do. I consider myself an entertainer, maybe an old-school entertainer. I probably would have been in vaudeville or on Broadway or something thereabouts.

Molly: You became a household name almost overnight with Australian audiences. The guys were going nuts over you. And then this sort of Stevie Nicks hairstyle started to come.

Stevie: I'm going to open a beauty salon, due to the fact I cut it. I decided I'm gonna have to really cash in on this hairstyle.

This was the first of many interviews I would do with Stevie.

Steve Millard from Sony Records did many overseas trips with me. Twenty-one years after that first encounter with Stevie, an Afro-American guy bumped into me at the Mondrian Hotel in Los Angeles. 'Hey Molly, remember me?' he said, slapping my hand, 'I met you in Australia with Stevie.'

'Of course,' I replied, 'but she's a bit crazy these days, isn't she? Although I do hear she may be getting back with the group, which is great.'

I then wondered why the guy looked a little confused. He made his excuses and walked away. Steve Millard had to explain to me that the guy we met was part of the security team for Stevie Wonder. Talk about the blind leading the blind!

Another major interview in Los Angeles during the 1977 trip was on the set of the *Sgt. Pepper's Lonely Hearts Club Band* movie. Even though this was based on The Beatles' classic album, the film didn't feature any of the Fab Four. Instead, the stars were the Bee Gees and Peter Frampton.

Produced by Robert Stigwood, the Bee Gees manager and mentor, the film was a far cry from Stigwood's productions of *Saturday Night Fever*, *Grease* and *Jesus Christ Superstar*. To this day, I'm still not sure what the movie is all about. But for Grant and me it was an exciting adventure because we hired, for the very first time, a limo—a big white limo. Grant wasn't sure whether the ABC could afford it, but I said, 'Bugger it, we'll have one on Aunty.' Even the commissionaire at the studio gates was impressed by its size.

It was the first time I'd been on a major Hollywood set and I was totally awestruck. It was like a fantasy land. The Bee Gees, dressed in their Sgt. Pepper's gear, took time out to give us an interview, though I think they were a little annoyed that I kept referring to *Saturday Night Fever*. After all, they'd been there, done that and wanted to move on.

Peter Frampton had been a star in England over the previous decade, but had exploded worldwide with his multi-platinum *Frampton Comes Alive!* He seemed a little disoriented on the film set, or maybe he was still trying to work out the plot. In fact, we talked more about his current album, *I'm In You*, than the movie.

Sgt. Pepper's pretty much killed Frampton's career. *Rolling Stone's* Paul Nelson declared he had 'absolutely no future in

Hollywood'. And the movie copped a caning. The *Newsweek* critic called it 'a film with a dangerous resemblance to wallpaper'.

As Grant and I left the film lot, we were still not sure what *Sgt. Pepper's* was all about, but it had been a thrilling trip. From Los Angeles, we headed to London, where we would average nine interviews a day.

Ian was becoming a bit testy by this time, and occasionally would throw the odd tantrum and start throwing things. I remember Ian not liking the hotel we were staying at. He threw an ashtray, missed me and hit the mirror. We had to change hotels.

Grant Rule

My mood brightened when I got to interview Paul and Linda McCartney.

The interview went off without a hitch. I just couldn't believe how warm they were to Molly, and to everyone, including myself. It was fantastic.

Grant Rule

Paul and Linda were in great spirits. We did the interview at Studio One at Abbey Road. They were finishing the final mixes for their single 'Mull of Kintyre', which was to be released for Christmas 1977. At the end of the interview, Paul said, 'Look, we'll give you an exclusive of "Mull Of Kintyre" to take back to Australia for *Countdown*.'

Two days later, a videotape master of the song arrived at my hotel.

'Mull of Kintyre' ended up spending eleven weeks on top of the Australian charts—only ABBA's 'Fernando' spent more time at number one in the '70s.

Being handed an exclusive by one of my heroes had my mind racing back to when I was thrown out of Festival Hall at

The Beatles' concert. To this day, I haven't told Paul that one of the reasons I was ejected was because I was screaming, '*I love you, Paul!*'

Apart from a couple of studio visits, most of the London interviews were done at the ABC's headquarters in Portland Place—much to the horror of the rest of the staff, who were used to, shall we say, a more reserved atmosphere. Suddenly the office was transformed into a joint that resembled the 'green room' at *Top Of The Pops*.

It was a fascinating time to be in London because music was going through a giant transition. Punk was the buzz, and the Sex Pistols and their manager, Malcolm McLaren, were at the forefront.

Foolishly, the ABC's London head gave us permission to use his rather grand office—a move he would regret. I'll never forget this leather-clad figure swaggering into the boss's office, plonking himself down in the boss's chair, putting his feet up on the desk and declaring, 'Come on, let's get this over and done with, I haven't got much time.'

It was Billy Idol, then the lead singer of Generation X. He had spiky blond hair, a lip curled like Elvis, and almost no regard for anything. But he had a charisma that shone like a beacon.

Grant was horrified when Billy started butting his cigarette on the table, then the floor. I think Grant spent more time running around with an ashtray trying to catch his ash than directing the interview. But I have to admit I wasn't much better because I was totally spellbound by this guy's presence.

After the interview, Grant reprimanded me. 'These people have to have more respect for ABC property!' he ordered.

I didn't know what to say, except, 'Grant, the guy's going to be a star.'

If Billy Idol was too much for Grant, it was just a warm-up for the Sex Pistols. This band had exploded onto the UK scene with a bunch of expletives. Bill Grundy caused a sensation when he interviewed them on the TV show *Today*. Guitarist Steve Jones called Grundy 'a dirty bastard', 'a dirty fucker' and 'a fucking rotter'.

I couldn't wait to meet the band. But I was disappointed when only two members—Steve Jones and drummer Paul Cook—arrived at the ABC offices. I'd been promised all four (and being a bit of a royalist, I was looking forward to having a go at them for their single 'God Save The Queen').

After doing the interview with Steve and Paul, I decided to track down their manager, Malcolm McLaren. I finally found him at a post-production studio, where he was working on some Sex Pistols' videos. Malcolm was very gracious, apologising, and promising that Johnny Rotten and Sid Vicious would be available the following evening.

It was great news, though I had a problem—we were due to fly back to Australia that afternoon, so we'd be home two days before my interview with Prince Charles.

What to do?

Without consulting Grant, I cancelled our flight and told Qantas I'd ring back to re-book. But when I did, two and a half hours later, all the seats on the following day's flight had gone. In fact, all the flights for the next ten days were fully booked.

'Oh, well,' I thought, 'there goes my chance to chat with Johnny Rotten and Sid Vicious.' I told the booking agent to put us back on the flight that I'd cancelled.

'I'm sorry, sir, we can't do that because we've already given those tickets away.'

I burst into tears. Between sobs, I explained my dilemma to the sympathetic Qantas representative—I had to go home because I was interviewing Prince Charles. He managed to find a TWA flight that would allow us to connect to the only available Qantas flight in San Francisco. I gladly accepted it.

I then rang Malcolm McLaren, who told me to meet him at the film studios at 5 p.m. He would then take us to an English pub where the boys were meeting with a Russian writer. I was happy again, even more so because the delay meant I could also do an interview with Freddie Mercury from Queen.

Grant, well, he was not so happy. In fact, he called me 'totally irresponsible'. 'But, Grant,' I protested, 'when am I going to get another chance to interview the Sex Pistols, Freddie Mercury and Prince Charles all in the same week?'

I can't be absolutely certain, but I'm sure Grant muttered under his breath, 'You stupid old queen.' He obviously didn't like the group.

And so the stage was set for our final day. Grant was praying it would go smoothly, but there were ominous signs . . .

London was in the midst of a power strike, which led to regular blackouts. This meant we had to carry a high-powered sun gun, in case we needed extra lighting.

Queen shared management with Elton, and the interview with Freddie Mercury was held in John Reid's office in South Audley Street—very plush and very posh. The centrepiece of the room was a Rolls-Royce coffee table, a birthday present to John Reid from Ringo Starr. It featured two Rolls-Royce radiator grilles, with the emblems and glass in the middle.

Freddie was in top form, as Queen's tour was selling out everywhere. Their brilliant album *A Day At The Races* had topped the charts, and they had just released the follow-up, *News Of The World*. The only testing time came when Freddie talked about Australia—he was still angry about the band's bad reception at the Sunbury Festival back in 1974.

Halfway through the interview, the room suddenly blacked out. We decided to do the rest of the interview on the balcony, in the sunlight. As we were packing up, we discovered that the lighting man had scratched the Rolls-Royce table. Fortunately, John Reid was away; I quickly looked around the office and found a statue to place on top of the scratch.

One down, one to go . . .

We caught up with Malcolm McLaren, who took us to the pub, where we found Johnny Rotten and Sid Vicious huddled in a corner with a group of people. It was there that Malcolm confessed that he hadn't actually told Johnny and Sid about our interview.

'What are we going to do now?' Grant whispered in my ear.

'We're going to do the interview,' I insisted.

Suddenly the main lights went out.

Here we were in the depths of a pub in Soho, almost totally in darkness, with these two punks who don't know that we're about to interview them. I asked permission for us to film in the pub and the publican said to me very sternly, 'I don't want any trouble.' I assured him there wouldn't be, but, I must admit, I wasn't confident.

Grant Rule

As the crew set up by candlelight, I repeatedly told Grant, 'Whatever happens, we keep filming.'

He had no idea what I had planned.

Malcolm McLaren put his hand on my shoulder: 'Go for it,' he ordered, 'do it now!'

Grant was holding the sun gun, a light so bright it's like an atomic explosion when it's turned on in a dark room. I gave Grant the nod, and he flicked the switch. For a moment there was stunned silence, then I walked up to Johnny Rotten and shoved a microphone in his face. 'We spoke to Steve and Paul,' I declared, 'and now we'd like to talk to you and Sid.'

Johnny Rotten looked up and scowled. 'Get fucked,' he spat. I persisted with my approach and Rotten decided to flick a cigarette at the camera. It hit the cameraman's eye.

There is a bit of confusion about what happened next.

Grant Rule

A brawl erupted. I unloaded with an almighty right hook, connecting with Rotten. Sid Vicious leapt to his feet and applauded. 'Hit him again!'

Grant was hit in the back of the head, the camera was knocked to the ground, while I unleashed a barrage of blows on Rotten. I gave him a right for me and my cameraman, and another right for the Queen of England.

Grant was in a state of panic as a headline flashed through his mind: '*Countdown* Crew Runs Amok In Soho Pub'. He turned off the sun gun.

I don't think Ian's ever forgiven me. In retrospect, it would have been good to get another five minutes of worldwide headlines, but I made a snap decision.

Grant Rule

I was furious. We packed up and returned to our hotel in silence.

The next day, it was time to head home to interview Prince Charles.

I think Molly was actually feeling a bit guilty about the night before, because he was up early and ready to go, and not making excuses that he had one more bag to pack.

Grant Rule

When we arrived at Heathrow Airport, with 90 minutes to spare, I told Grant that because we'd been working so hard, I hadn't had time to do any shopping, so I would now buy some gifts to take home. 'Don't worry,' I said, 'I'll see you back at this restaurant in twenty minutes and then we'll go through immigration.'

Thirty minutes later, Grant started to worry. An hour went by, and worry had switched to panic. What can I say? I've got a lot of friends, so I had a lot of gifts to buy. When I finally reappeared, I said, 'Come on Grant, we've really got to go!'

We looked up at the departures board but could not see our TWA flight. I raced to the TWA counter, only to be told that the flight had closed. I could see that Grant wanted to curl up in the corner. If he didn't deliver me in time for the Prince Charles interview, his career was as good as over. I had to take charge. 'Follow me,' I ordered.

We ran to the gate, where the TWA attendant was packing up his documents. The door was open, but there was a rope across it. I grabbed Grant: 'When I count to three, run and jump the rope.'

I counted to three, we hurdled the rope, and took off down the stairs—with the TWA guy in hot pursuit.

We found ourselves on the tarmac. I spotted a TWA plane in the distance. 'That has to be it!' An empty bus was idling near the doorway. 'Jump in!' I yelled.

I threw twenty quid at the driver, pointed at the plane and screamed, 'We've got to get on that TWA plane.'

As we tore across the tarmac, I could see the attendants removing the steps from the plane's door. Jumping out of the bus, I demanded, 'Put the steps back!'

Sirens were blaring and security people were coming from everywhere, brandishing guns. Grant was shaking.

I'm not sure how Molly explained it to them, but he pulled out all these official papers plus the script from Buckingham Palace, screaming, 'I've got to get home to interview the future King of England!'

Grant Rule

The steps are put back, the doors open, and we're on our way home.

After one American trip, we were at the airport in Los Angeles. We checked our bags at the Pan Am desk and they gave us our boarding passes. Molly then went to do some shopping and he lost his briefcase, containing his passport and his boarding pass. Molly simply had to be on that flight—he was going home for the Logies or the football or something terribly important. But the Pan Am people weren't going to let him on.

'How do we know you're Mr Meldrum?' they said.

'But everyone knows me,' Molly replied.

'Excuse me,' the Pan Am woman said to the people in the queue, 'do any of you know this gentleman?'

Yes, several people said, it's Molly.

And they let him on the plane.

Peter Ikin, former record company executive

7: MY MISTAKE

1977: Prince Charles in South Melbourne—'M' for 'muffed it'—A boy
and his mum—A dreadful blunder—Royal liaisons.

To err is human, to umm is unforgivable.
Greedy Smith, Mental As Anything

There was a knock on the door at my Alfred Street house. It
was *Countdown* producer Grant Rule. I opened the door and
burst into tears. Both Grant and I were wearing identical blue
shirts that we'd bought in London.

'Don't worry, Ian,' Grant said, placing a reassuring hand on
my shoulder. 'I'll borrow one of your shirts, it'll be fine.' Of
course, it wasn't just the shirt—I was nervous about doing the
biggest interview of my life. It's not every day that you meet
your Prince.

Grant walked inside to see that I was surrounded by a group
of friends. My mood immediately brightened. 'Watch this,
lovey,' I said to Grant. 'Watch this!'

I delivered the Prince Charles script *word perfect*.

I went weak at the knees. I knew he'd never do it twice.
Grant Rule, *Countdown* producer

I'd been up till 2.30 a.m., rehearsing, with neighbour Fay (Brian
Flaherty) playing the role of Prince Charles.

So, how did a man named Molly come to interview the future King of England? Well, the Prince Charles saga started when showbiz entrepreneur Harry M. Miller—who was the Chairman of the Queen's Silver Jubilee Commemorative Organisation—was planning the functions and duties that Prince Charles would be required to do on his official trip to Australia.

Harry suggested to me that perhaps there could be an album of Australian tracks to coincide with his visit, with the proceeds going to the Silver Jubilee Organisation.

'That's a great idea,' I said.

In the weeks after that first meeting, I negotiated with record companies, managers and artists and came up with the concept of an album of previously unreleased tracks and B-sides.

Harry then organised a meeting with *Countdown* executive producer Michael Shrimpton, the record company bosses and myself. Halfway through the meeting, he dropped a bombshell: 'So when the Prince comes to Australia, he's going to be on *Countdown*, talking to Molly . . .'

'What?' I shrieked. 'You've got to be joking!'

Michael Shrimpton was even more blunt: 'Over my dead body. It can't happen. It's a recipe for disaster.'

But the interview was locked in—Prince Charles was going to appear on *Countdown*.

I learned the script on the plane on the way home from London. The other passengers must have thought I'd lost my mind. Over and over, I'd say, 'And now I'd like to introduce His Royal Highness, The Prince of Wales, Prince Charles.'

This was new territory for me, but Michael and Harry insisted I had to stick to the script.

We had to submit scripts to Buckingham Palace. We were saying quietly to ourselves, 'Do they think for one minute he's going to say any of these words?

Or even understand them?' Consecutive sentences made it rather difficult.

Michael Shrimpton

When I got home, I was devastated to learn that Glenys Long, my assistant during the *Go-Set* years, had died. Glenys had been a big part of my life.

> The paper attracted all of these weird people and it needed a glue to hold it all together. Glenys was that glue. She and Ian were quite a team. One time, she threw a typewriter at him. Another time, he locked her in a filing cabinet. She was obviously in love with Ian and wanted more.
>
> **Ed Nimmervoll, *Go-Set* and *Juke* magazines**

Glenys—who always carried a flask of whisky wherever she went—worked for Sherbet when she left *Go-Set*, falling in love with guitarist Clive Shakespeare. But again her love was not reciprocated. Glenys was a fiery red-head. I loved her, calling her Glenisabelle. She typed my *Go-Set* column and, boy, did we have some fights. When The Rolling Stones were here in 1973, I was going to have lunch with Mick Jagger. I was so excited, I bought a new suit. On the way to meet Mick, I popped into the *Go-Set* offices in Collingwood, had a fight with Glenys and she threw a cup of coffee on me. I was devastated!

Sadly, Glenys overdosed on cough syrup. Her death also rocked Ed Nimmervoll, who wrote a poem, which Little River Band's Beeb Birtles turned into a song.

The song, 'Red-Headed Wild Flower', appeared on LRB's *Sleeper Catcher* album.

Unfortunately, Glenys' funeral was scheduled for 11 a.m. on the Tuesday—clashing with the Prince Charles interview, so I couldn't go.

A friend of mine, Dale Harper, officially known as Lady Tryon, asked me to a party she was having for Prince Charles on the eve of the interview. Now, it wasn't like me to knock back a party invitation, but I said, 'No, no, no, I can't go, I'm still learning the script.'

Dale Harper, a Melbourne girl, met Prince Charles at a Buckingham Palace reception in 1973. She married one of Charles's best friends, The Honourable Anthony Tryon, who became Lord Tryon after his father died. During the '70s, Dale became good friends with the Royal Family, especially Prince Charles, who nicknamed her 'Kanga'. In fact, Dale accompanied Prince Charles and her husband on annual fishing trips to the Arctic. Prince Charles famously described Dale as 'the only woman who ever understood me'. For Dale, it was a far cry from her days in Melbourne when her boyfriend—much to the horror of her socialite Toorak mother—was pop singer Buddy England. Another one of Dale's close friends was Rosie Ham, who married Max Ross, The Groop's bass player.

The Prince Charles interview was being taped at the AAV studios in South Melbourne, which was close to Government House, where Prince Charles was officially staying. As Prince Charles was required to fly to Adelaide straight after the interview, it was felt that the ABC studios in Elsternwick were too far away.

Prince Charles arrived at AAV at 10.11 a.m. He left thirteen minutes later, but for me it was a very long thirteen minutes.

I told the press afterwards: 'It was like a dream, but it developed into a nightmare. I became panic stricken. I had never felt this feeling of such panic before.'

I remember turning into Bank Street, South Melbourne, where the studios were situated, and seeing rows of Commonwealth and Victorian Police. It then hit me—I was about to interview the future King of England. It was a momentous occasion, because the Royal Family, certainly at that stage, didn't do television interviews.

God, why did it have to be *me*?

Also unsettling was the fact they had turned the small studio into a little theatre. The set was a *Countdown* backdrop with two chairs for Prince Charles and myself, and rows of chairs for the audience.

Well, it wasn't exactly an *audience*, it was the press, travelling on the Royal Tour. Suddenly I knew exactly what a fish felt like in a fish bowl. Just before Prince Charles arrived, I had an uncontrollable urge to go to the toilet. I found myself standing next to a good mate, Sydney journalist James Oram, who could be outrageous at the best of times.

So there I was, having a pee, trying to remember my script, and Jim confronted me: 'Come on, Molly, give us the goss. You're a mate of Dale Harper's, is she rooting Charlie or not? Because I know he's been staying at her place, not Government House.'

I got such a shock that I mumbled something like, 'Don't be so silly, Jim', and I accidentally put my little fella back into my pants. Consequently, I had wet pants and a wet leg.

Luckily, the ABC make-up artist had a hair dryer. I guess it's one of the rare times I've ever had to use one.

All zipped up and ready to go, the *Countdown* crew lined up to meet Prince Charles. Everyone was dressed immaculately, except floor manager Ted Emery, who was wearing pink flared cords, sandals and a Fleetwood Mac T-shirt.

As Prince Charles shook Ted's hand, he pointed to the T-shirt. 'Oh, an Australian band?'

'Um, yeah,' replied a perplexed Ted, not wanting to contradict the future King.

The press was all seated in front of the set. The cameramen were ready. Grant Rule was in the control room. Michael Shrimpton was at the back of the room. And Jim Oram was in the front row, winking at me.

Sitting very upright in a navy suit with a sky-blue shirt and white collar, and grey, navy and pink tie, I adopted a voice even toffier than Prince Charles and began the most horrific interview of my life.

I remember sitting with Prince Charles and thinking, 'I wish all of this would go away', just as Ted Emery yelled: 'Molly, 10 seconds to go . . . 5, 4, 3, 2, 1, *action!*'

I proceeded with an incredibly long introduction. Everything was going fine until '. . . and now we come to the most important part of tonight's program. In fact, the most important part of the program's history. Some months ago, the Chairman of the Queen's Silver Jubilee Commemorative Organisation, Mr Harry um, MMM, um, MMM Miller . . . oh no.'

Why couldn't his name be just plain Harry Miller? The M was really posing a problem. It was like I had a whole bag of M&Ms in my mouth.

Ted Emery looked at me a little bemused and barked, 'Take two!'

And so I restart the intro. I get to Harry's name and stumble on the Ms again.

I look at Prince Charles, he looks at me with a rather astonished look, and Ted says, 'Just relax, we're going to re-set the cameras.'

It was at this stage that Prince Charles, obviously trying to break the ice, kindly remarked, 'I believe you've just got back from London.'

'Yes, yes,' I replied enthusiastically. 'As a matter of fact, I saw your mum driving along in an open carriage in London the other day. She was on her way to open Parliament.'

Prince Charles corrected me: 'You mean Her Majesty The Queen.'

'Yes, yes, The Queen, The Queen, Oh my God!'

Ted Emery: 'Take three.'

I cleared my throat, rambled on and got to the point of:

'And now we come to the most important part of the . . . sorry. Could I just have one glass of water please?'

Looking at Prince Charles, I said, 'I'm terribly sorry about this.'

Prince Charles: 'Don't worry, it happens all the time.'

Me: 'Does it?'

It was around this stage of my life that I took to calling just about everyone 'Lovey'. When Ted handed me the glass of water, I turned to Prince Charles, put my arm around his shoulder and said, 'It's all right, Lovey, I'll get this together in a moment.'

An awkward giggle reverberated through the press contingent. All I can remember is Michael Shrimpton at the back of the room, pacing up and down with his hands over his eyes. One of the ABC cameramen claims Michael was saying: 'The man's a fool.'

Grant Rule was sitting outside in the broadcast van. 'Just keep rolling,' he instructed the crew, 'we're living history.'

Back on the set, Prince Charles helpfully asked me: 'Do you have one of those [rolling his hands] teleprompters?'

'Um, no.'

It was then decided that I would record the intro after Prince Charles had left the studio.

This is how the interview ran on *Countdown* on 13 November, 1977 (after my studio introduction, admitting 'I did muff it').

Molly: Would you now make welcome to *Countdown*, His Royal Highness, Prince Charles. Your Royal Highness, it is a pleasure to have you here to help us support the Queen's Silver Jubilee Appeal for young Australians.

Prince Charles: I am delighted to be here, obviously as the patron. And I am particularly grateful that this program should have produced this marvellous album, the *Countdown* album, which I know has taken a lot of effort and problems to produce.

Molly: Yes, a lot of effort. But I'm sure you'll be delighted to know that all the artists and composers represented on this LP have waived their royalties as a donation to the appeal, and the recording companies involved have given their very generous support.

Prince Charles: It's extremely generous of them. I don't know how they did it.

Molly: Oh, it was a lot of difficulty. Could you perhaps tell us what benefits the young Australians will receive from the money raised from this appeal?

Prince Charles: Basically, the idea has been to try and raise at least a target of $5 million, and the Australian Government has been very generous and has given a certain amount. And we've raised jolly nearly five million already, which is very encouraging. So by the time the appeal ends next May, with a bit of luck, we'll raise even more, but if so, you get a complete $5 million, if you invest that, you should get back $500,000 a year. [*I whistle to show how impressed I am.*]

Prince Charles: And that I'm hoping will be used to make money available for projects for young Australians to get involved in various community activities and things like that to help in the community generally. To various youth organisations, like the Scouts, the Guides and all these things, but also—which I'm particularly keen about—to try and get at the sort of person who doesn't normally get involved in these kind of activities. I often believe that if these people actually had a chance and the opportunity to get involved in adventurous activities or useful things with the old, the handicapped and the sick and this sort of thing, they'd find it's a marvellous way of discovering themselves to a certain extent, and finding that they can do something useful. So that's one part. The other thing is we hope that it will also contribute towards enabling particularly talented young Australians to achieve their ambitions in their chosen vocations. In other words, if the best training is somewhere abroad, then they can be helped to go and get that training and then come back here and make an even bigger contribution to Australia. That's, you know, the main idea.

Molly: Well, that's fantastic. And it's great to know then that the sales of this LP will help many other activities in that field then.

Prince Charles: That's if anyone buys it, I don't know. I hope it's been recorded correctly.

Molly: Very correctly, I assure you of that. In fact, we're very proud of it because it's the Top 20 artists we're very proud of in this country. Your Royal Highness, on behalf of the Australian recording industry, we are very grateful for you coming onto *Countdown*, sparing your time, to launch this project. We really are. And, ah, without any ado, I'd just like to thank you also for helping us promote this album, the *Countdown Silver Jubilee Australian Top 20 Album*, which is in the record stores now for $5.99. And, if we now may sit back, Your Royal Highness, and for the first time on Australian television, here is a countdown of the *Countdown* Australian Top 20.

The line-up for the album was then revealed—Sherbet, Skyhooks, Little River Band, Dragon, Air Supply, Ariel, Supernaut, Hush, The Ferrets, Flash and the Pan, Ol' 55, AC/DC, John Paul Young, Mark Holden, Marty Rhone, Richard Clapton, Marcia Hines, Renée Geyer, Jon English and the Ted Mulry Gang.

At the end of the interview, Prince Charles said to me: 'I think that was all right. Probably talked nonsense actually, but still, thanks very much.'

'Yes, that was fine,' I replied, as we stood and shook hands.

I was there for the Prince Charles interview. I think it shows why Molly has such empathy with kids and why I think they identify with him—he stuffs up all the time.

Tim Swallow, *Countdown* crew

It was a landmark edition of *Countdown*. As well as the Prince Charles interview, the episode featured the world premiere of the video for what would become Paul McCartney's biggest solo single, 'Mull of Kintyre', the premiere of David Bowie's 'Heroes', a live performance by Stars (the Adelaide band Michael Gudinski signed instead of Cold Chisel), a cross to Peter Frampton on the set of the ill-fated *Sgt. Pepper's Lonely Hearts Club Band* movie, news that LRB's 'Help Is On Its Way' had reached number fourteen in the States, and a live performance by Dragon of their track on the *Silver Jubilee* album, 'The Dreaded Moroczy Bind', a song about a chess move. Mark Holden was the show's host.

After the Prince Charles episode went to air, Grant Rule stamped the interview out-takes in big letters: 'NEVER TO BE USED'.

> I thought it didn't do Ian any good. It was a bit tragic. But slowly, bits of it have filtered out over the years, and we can all laugh about it now.
>
> **Grant Rule**

I recently watched a clip of the interview on YouTube. With the editing tricks, it looks like I said 'fuck, fuck, fuck' in front of Prince Charles. I swear this never happened!

I guess I can laugh about it now, but back then it was a nightmare. I'll always remember the Melbourne afternoon *Herald* related the whole episode on the front page with the headline, 'Molly Mumbles . . . "Saw your mum" he tells Prince Charles'.

I guess the only way you can sum it up is to give a different spin to Gough Whitlam's historic speech on the steps of Parliament House after he'd been dismissed by the Governor-General. 'Well may we say God save the Queen, because nothing will save the Governor-General.'

In my case, it was Michael Shrimpton saying: 'Well may we say God save Prince Charles, because nothing can save Meldrum!'

Years after I'd been on *Countdown*, I was sitting in my house in the Hollywood Hills, watching TV. There was a knock on the door, which is always a bit disconcerting in America. You don't just turn up, even to a friend's house. I opened the door and it was Molly. 'Hey Mark, how's it going?' It was like we'd seen each other only yesterday. I don't even know how he got my address. It was similar to when Norman Gunston came to my house and did an interview. Because he looked so bizarre, my neighbours and friends thought he was truly bizarre. But they thought Molly was more bizarre.

Mark Holden

8: SOUNDS OF THEN

1974–1987: It's a long way to the top—A Wilde question—
Am I ever gonna see your face again?—Cougar town—
Tattoo you—Marching in the Kiss Army—The Police arrive—
Having a Leo Sayer—Who Dares wins—Gimme Ted—Duran Duran take
a trip to the Nile—Tales of rock 'n' roll adventures.

Molly: I gotta say, what a spunk! She's great!
Grace Jones: What's a spank? What does that mean?
Molly: No, spunk. It means you're pretty good in Australian terms.
Grace Jones: Pretty good? That's all?
Countdown, 2 May, 1982

I've seen them burn bright and burn out. I've seen them take off and soar. And I've seen them bomb and fade away.

I've been fortunate to meet and interview just about all of the major music acts of the past six decades. Some acts—such as John Farnham, the Stones and AC/DC—are still going strong. But many have disappeared. For all its glitz and glamour, show business is a tough business.

During the *Countdown* years, our budget was so tight, sometimes we'd pretend to do interviews to preserve the person's ego. Because we couldn't afford to waste the tape, we would do the interview without any tape in the camera, or the camera operator would not press the record button.

Sad, but true.

The problem with this business is when you're hot, there's a long queue of people who will bend over backwards to talk to you. But when you're not, it can be very lonely.

Though Jennifer Byrne said of me in 1980, 'He is a truly awful interviewer', I take great pride in the interviews I have done. Talking to people about their work is a responsibility I take very seriously. Research is paramount. You need to treat the interviewee with the respect they deserve. Of course, sometimes even all the research doesn't count for much when you're nervous. My interview with Kim Wilde is a celebrated example.

Molly: When you look back at sort of the three hits that you've had, do you and your brother purposefully go out to find, you know, like, I mean, in other words, do you knock back tracks that you may write, or what? Is it a calculated thing? I mean, I'm . . . it's a strange question, you know. I mean, like . . . Let me start again.
Kim Wilde: I don't understand the question at all.
Molly: I got a bit mixed up myself.

I tried to explain to Sydney's *Sun Herald* in 1981 what was going through my head when I was doing interviews:

When I'm interviewing, I'm conscious of time, so I start clipping my sentences, then the *ums* and *ers* start. That's me on television. I can't stop the *ums* and *ers* for the sake of them. But I don't want people to remember me for that.

Later, I told *The Australian*: 'I do *um* and *er*. Whenever I was being slagged off, I could laugh at it because I knew I was a bigger communicator to the public than they'll ever be.'

What I mean is it has been a great privilege to make a connection with people—both the subject and the audience.

Molly's strength is he's impervious to criticism. He can be whoever he is, because he's genuinely enthusiastic about what he does. He loves music and he loves being friends with the stars. He might stumble over his words during an interview, but they still get to say what they want to say, and he doesn't pretend to be a bigger star than them. Some interviewers get lost and think, 'I'm just as big a star as you are', but Molly never takes that stand. That's why he has endured.

Ross Wilson

I was fortunate to make many connections during the *Countdown* years—many of which continue to this day.

My first hit record was in Australia. Molly was the first guy to play that record. Molly made 'I Need A Lover' a hit. No question. He made it a hit.

John Mellencamp

When John Mellencamp, then known as Johnny Cougar, arrived in Australia, he was greeted by screaming fans. 'Who are these people here for?' he asked, wondering which other artist was arriving that day. 'You!' his record company rep replied.

John appeared on *Countdown* on 6 August, 1978. The following day he did an interview with *Juke* magazine and bagged the show. I was furious, as was his manager, Billy Gaff. Billy made John write me a letter of apology: 'Dear Mr Meldrum, I am sorry that I criticised your show . . .'

We've been great mates ever since.

John told the tale to *Billboard* when he received The Century Award, *Billboard*'s highest honour for distinguished creative achievement, in 2001. 'I was so burnt out that when some journalist asked me about being on Australian TV, I sighed and said it was stupid. What I meant was, "I'm tired and I wanna go home."'

In response, I wrote a piece in *TV Week*: 'Johnny Cougar Bares His Immature Claws'. 'He was right,' John later acknowledged. 'I apologised and he forgave me. We're still friends.'

In a John Mellencamp biography, I was amused to see that I was referred to as 'well-known music journalist Molly Melbourne'. It's actually a great name, reflecting how much I love my home town.

John can be arrogant at times and rather petulant—the name he gave himself 'Little Bastard' is very apt—but I love him. He's also an accomplished artist. John did a painting of me and called it 'The Ghost Cowboy'. He sent me the painting and it hangs in my home.

Speaking of art, I was actually with John Mellencamp when I got my first tattoo. I was out to dinner with John and Sean Penn in Los Angeles. They both had tattoos and I said I'd always wanted to get one. 'Well, let's do it,' John said. I opted for a traditional heart with a scroll, on my left arm, with Molly inscribed in the scroll. 'Oh, your wife or girlfriend is going to love that,' the tattooist remarked as we all laughed.

The next morning, I woke up at The Park Hotel, saw myself in the mirror and thought, 'Oh my God, what's that?' When I got home, *Countdown* producer Grant Rule saw it and told me to 'go to the make-up department and wash it off'. Tattoos weren't fashionable back then. (A few years later, I returned to the tattooist and had the St Kilda emblem inked above the Molly tattoo. It's also rumoured that I have a tattoo on my bum, of me lying naked on my back. It's been called 'The Naked Cowboy'. But I've never seen my butt, so I'm not sure if this story is true.)

Countdown gave many great international artists their first hits.

We met Ian in 1977 when we were supporting Iggy Pop in the States. He asked us if we had any videos. We gave him videos for 'X-Offender' and 'In The Flesh'. On *Countdown* they were meant to play 'X-Offender', but they played 'In The Flesh' instead. So our success in Australia was one big mistake! By the end of 1977, 'In The Flesh' had hit number two in Australia. It was Blondie's first hit anywhere in the world. Thanks, Molly.

Debbie Harry

During the *Countdown* years, a wonderful lady by the name of Carolyn James ran what we called the *Countdown* Council. Every Monday night, Carolyn would do a report, getting reaction to the songs we played on the previous night's show from designated *Countdown* watchers across the country. In the days before office computers and email, this was quite a laborious task, but the feedback was invaluable. Of course, with music, more often than not, you have to rely on your gut feeling; if you rely on research, you'll end up sounding like commercial radio, which is often bland and unimaginative.

One of the biggest fights I had with Carolyn was in 1978 over a strange Belgian singer by the name of Plastic Bertrand. The viewers said they thought it was awful and they never wanted to hear it again. I thought if it was getting such an extreme reaction, we might be onto something. I demanded that we play it again. And 'Ça Plane Pour Moi' hit number one.

Countdown initiated my popularity in Australia, and I will never forget the encouraging smile of Molly.

Plastic Bertrand

The *Countdown* Council was a great way of keeping in touch with the audience. I also loved hearing directly from the fans. Everywhere I went during the *Countdown* years, people would chat to me about their favourite artists and tell me what I should be playing.

For a long time, I thought that Kiss were a poor Alice Cooper rip-off. But one night I was shopping at Coles in Prahran when I was confronted by a group of kids. 'Why aren't you playing Kiss?' they demanded. 'Me and my mates love 'em, you've got to put 'em on.' On the Monday, I went into the office and said, 'Let's have another look at Kiss.' Of course, their 1980 tour ended up being one of the biggest this country has ever seen—even Norman Gunston was marching in the Kiss Army.

> I remember when the Kiss tour was happening and their fans were lining up to get tickets. A bunch of skinheads came along and threw bottles at them, so Molly gave them a lecture: 'Gene Simmons is disappointed, I'm disappointed . . . If you kids wanna behave like that, do it in your own lounge room or, better still, just get out of the country!' Here was a bloke, reviewing music, and telling people to get out of the country. Only Molly could do that.
>
> **Brian Mannix, Uncanny X-Men**

The first interview I did with Kiss was on top of Tower One of the World Trade Center. The guys had to stand right on the edge because the building's communication equipment was affecting our radio microphones. I was worried they were going to fall off. I thought of this interview when I saw the Twin Towers collapse on September 11, 2001.

In 1980, I did an overseas trip with *Countdown* producer Robbie Weekes. In New York, The Police were doing a secret gig at the Roxy and I was to interview the band in their dressing room. Their hit at the time was called 'De Do Do Do, De Da Da Da'. Try saying that after a few drinks!

Robbie: Rolling, action!

Molly: Welcome to Australia, welcome to *Countdown*. Congratulations on the success of 'De Do Do Ba Da De Da Do' . . .

Robbie: Cut! What's wrong with you?!

Molly: I'm trying to pronounce the name of the song.

Robbie: What is it, Camptown Races Doo-dah Doo-dah, is it?

[Keen to avoid another Prince Charles debacle, I decided to take a different approach.]

Robbie: Rolling, action!

Molly: Welcome to the show. Congratulations on the number one, you must be very happy.

Sting: Yes, but what's the name of it, Molly?

I could have killed him.

On that same trip, we had another big interview. I was in another room when the band arrived. Robbie Weekes came to see me. 'Meldrum!' he shrieked, 'There are these strange people in there and they're wearing flower pots on their heads.'

'Oh, that's Devo,' I replied.

'With flower pots on their heads? I thought we were doing a *rock* group, not the Flower Pot Men!'

We also interviewed Debbie Harry. Now, before the trip, my son had said, 'Dad, if you get to meet Debbie Harry, could you get me a pair of her knickers?' So I asked Debbie, and she said, 'Please thank your son, that's a lovely request. But I'm not wearing any.'

Robbie Weekes

The *Countdown* crew were wonderfully creative people. I remember when Robert Palmer appeared on the show, Ted Emery came up with a great visual idea—he would get a group of models and they would groove away behind him, playing guitars.

Molly said, 'He'll love that.' But when Robert Palmer arrived and saw the girls, he said, 'No way.' There was unbelievable tension. It was an awful day. But I was more furious when I saw his 'Addicted To Love' film clip. What was in the background? Beautiful women, pretending to be musicians. I wanted to kill him.

Ted Emery

Of course, rock groups like to do things their own way. I was with Led Zeppelin in Adelaide when the band decided to glue everything in one of their hotel rooms to the ceiling—and I mean everything. Then they ordered room service and the poor guy walked in and thought the whole room had turned upside down.

I was also there when Queen came to town—and stormed out of town. They came to Australia for the first time in January 1974 to do two shows at the Sunbury Festival. And they were given some of the roughest treatment I have ever seen dished out to an international act. The cheeky music promoter Michael Chugg—who was angry that an overseas band was one of the headline acts—incited the crowd, and there was a constant drone of 'Pommy go home' and 'Go back to Pommyland, ya poofters!' I tried to take charge. 'Excuse me,' I told the fiery fans, 'this band will be *big* and this man [*pointing to Chugg*] is an idiot.' Of course, Chuggi would become one of my best friends. I often remind him—don't ever put down a Queen!

The call was, 'As soon as these Pommy bastards are off stage, we'll have Madder Lake!' The place went crazy. For the bulk of the crowd, Queen was an unknown quantity, and they really blew it. They came on late in the afternoon and they were stalling, so the sun would go down and they would get the benefit of the big light show. They kept mucking around and the good old Aussie audience just spat the dummy. It set the most beautiful stage for us—we literally could have got up there and played nursery rhymes and bared our arses and we would have been a hit.

Brenden Mason, Madder Lake

The next night, Queen got their only cheer when it was announced they would not appear because Freddie Mercury was ill. Members of the band were terribly upset about the response and before they flew out, they phoned me and vowed they would only return when they were one of the biggest groups in the world. In 1975, they broke through with the single 'Killer Queen'.

Queen returned to Australia in April 1976. I met them in Perth. The concert was great, but I asked them why they didn't do a full version of 'Bohemian Rhapsody'. Guitarist Brian May told me it was too hard to re-create live. That night, we went to a club and as we walked in, I thought they were playing a Queen record. 'How embarrassing,' I thought. We walked in and it was actually a cover band doing an absolutely brilliant version of 'Bohemian Rhapsody'. I turned to Brian and remarked, 'I thought you said you couldn't do this live?' He was furious.

Freddie was a real gentleman and party man. I remember I lectured him in Melbourne about condoms at a time when I was getting paranoid about AIDS. Unfortunately, Freddie seemed to dismiss the idea that AIDS could happen to him. He told me not to be so silly.

Sadly, Freddie died at the end of 1991.

Another English star was a big part of *Countdown* in the '70s. I first saw Leo Sayer—the curly-headed, five-foot-four-inch cross between a singing Charlie Chaplin and Marcel Marceau—live in 1975. I wrote: 'I sat there completely stunned by this little chap's talent.'

Of course, Leo co-hosted the ill-fated 100th show. Leo's 'You Make Me Feel Like Dancing' was as much a part of *Countdown* as John Paul Young's 'Yesterday's Hero'. Any time we went overseas, we always did an interview with Leo. And he was always a joy to work with.

It's great that Leo now calls Australia home. He wrote a lovely note for the tour program when we did the *Countdown* Spectacular together:

> Well, lots of people have stories of their adventures with Molly from the past, but I've got a new one, or a recent one. I hadn't seen Molly for ages, but I found out that we were due to perform together at a big charity ball at Palm Beach in Sydney. Molly was in great form, working up the crowd as I walked in. We greeted each other like the old mates we are and I told him about this new remix of one of my old hits that was about to be released in the UK. I'd brought a CD of it, just to listen to it in the car on the way down, but Molly insisted that I perform it on stage, there and then. He gave me the biggest intro I've ever had in my life, raving about the track (which he hadn't heard yet!). It was the first performance of 'Thunder In My Heart Again' anywhere in the world and, thanks to Molly's introduction, it brought the house down. Since then, it's been number one in the UK, number one on the dance charts here, and Top 10 all over Europe. I came offstage and Molly was ecstatic, saying, 'It could have been crap, but knowing you, I guessed it'd be good!' That's classic Molly. He took a chance on me that night, one that most people in his shoes would never have done. His kind of support and enthusiasm is what keeps us artists going. Cheers, mate. You ARE *Countdown*. So here's to a new generation discovering the Molly Meldrum magic!

I have forged close friendships with many stars. But we don't always instantly bond. Billy Joel's first *Countdown* appearance was a disaster. He didn't want to be there. And I guess my first question didn't help:

> I, um, over the last couple of weeks, um, we've had many, many international tours coming through—we've had Boz Scaggs, Bob Dylan, The Beach Boys. Some have been good, some have been bad, right. But I have never, like, last week I went on the, ah, *Countdown* Council to Perth and to Adelaide and you're leaving a day earlier and you've just done a concert that night and then Adelaide, you've just done a concert the night before et cetera. And I have never read reviews, rave reviews, for any artist that I've read for you.

All Billy said in reply was: 'All right.'

We cut to a clip and Billy then started talking. I screamed at Ted Emery, the floor manager: 'He's talking, for God's sake, come back to us!'

Fortunately, my interviews with Billy got better over the years. In fact, when I talked to him about his 1993 album, *River Of Dreams*, he said to me: 'Molly, you've unlocked me. You've unlocked me.'

The '80s are often criticised, but it was actually a great time for music, with Michael Jackson, Madonna, Bruce Springsteen and Prince leading the way. Prince never appeared on *Countdown*, though we played a lot of his videos and I was a massive fan. In fact, I spent a lot of time in the '80s bagging radio for refusing to play his music.

I've caught up with him a few times, but I have interviewed Prince (or The Artist Formerly Known As Prince, aka 'Love Symbol') only once—in Tokyo in 1996 as he prepared to release his three-CD set *Emancipation*. He had flown in journalists from around the world.

When I woke up on the day of my interview, I discovered there had been some drama the day before. The Artist had walked out of two interviews, one with Channel [V], the other with Sydney's Keith Williams from 2Day FM. Keith got to ask only two questions before The Artist decided he didn't like the sound of his own voice. He walked out and his minder seized Keith's tape. The Artist then banned all electronic media because he didn't want his voice or image to be recorded.

I assumed that my interview would be cancelled because I had a crew with me to shoot the interview. But then I got a message: 'The Artist wants to talk to you—but just you, no crew.'

I was ushered into his room, where it was just me, The Artist and a Japanese interpreter. We were both surprised by the presence of the interpreter. 'But, Molly, you speak English, don't you?' The Artist said.

'Um, that's debatable,' I laughed.

As we spoke, the interpreter took notes. The only hiccup in the interview came when I called him 'Lovey'. He didn't know that I called just about everyone Lovey.

As he glared at me, I asked what you were meant to call him. He told me his name had no sound, but people called him 'The Artist' and his friends called him 'friend'. Later, when his manager asked why I had called him 'Lovey', I explained that it was an Aussie thing—it was our way of abbreviating 'Love Symbol'.

Two of my favourite local acts in the '80s had major success internationally. I don't think many Australians truly understand just how big Men At Work were overseas. Their debut album, *Business As Usual*, spent fifteen weeks at number one in the States. At the start of 1983, they became the only non-US/UK act to have a number one single *and* album in the US *and* UK *at the same time*. Only six other acts have achieved this feat— The Beatles, The Monkees, Simon & Garfunkel, Rod Stewart, Michael Jackson and Beyoncé. I remember Men At Work's first appearance on *Countdown*. The director came down from the control booth and said: 'Could you ask the lead singer to at least look at the camera?' I had to tell him that Colin Hay had a lazy eye and that he *was* looking at the camera.

The Divinyls are one of my all-time favourite bands. Chrissy Amphlett was a magnificent performer. I remember the first time I saw the band, at the Prince of Wales Hotel in St Kilda. Chrissy was squatting on stage and spitting at me down the front. We had a strange relationship at the start. It wasn't until I became friends with her mum, who barracked for Colling-wood, that we became mates.

I always thought it was a little strange that two of the major Australian acts to break in America both featured someone wearing a school uniform—Angus in AC/DC and Chrissy in the Divinyls.

We like to claim the great New Zealand acts as our own, and plenty of Kiwi stars were a big part of *Countdown*, including Split Enz, Dragon, Mi-Sex and Sharon O'Neill. And a young guy named Richard Wilde even appeared on the show; he later reverted to his real name and became a great mate of mine, Richard Wilkins.

One of Split Enz's many classic songs is 'My Mistake'. It's an apt title when I think about one of my biggest blunders. In the late '70s, Michael Gudinski was making some cuts at his Mushroom Records label. 'Maybe you'll have to let Split Enz go,' I suggested. Fortunately, Michael believed in the band so much, he ignored my advice. Of course, a couple of years later, Split Enz had the landmark *True Colours* album, containing the classic 'I Got You'. I don't like to say this too often, but Michael, you were right.

There were plenty of other blunders during the *Countdown* years.

My friend Andre and I were DJ-ing at the Underground in Melbourne in 1986 when I suggested we should play a new song from a band called Bon Jovi. 'No way!' Andre replied.

We had to do a Saturday afternoon under-18s gig, so I said, 'Let's give it a try.' Well, the place went off. And that song, 'Livin' On A Prayer', is still a part of my playlist when I DJ today.

I met Jon Bon Jovi when the band released its self-titled debut album in 1984. Interviewing him in New York, I was struck by an extraordinary-looking guy with long hair and piercing, blue eyes. In 1987, we ran a Bon Jovi competition just before the end of *Countdown*. The winner was to be the show's guest reporter at one of their concerts overseas. One of the questions was the band's state of origin. When I was handed the envelope, I made the terrible mistake of reading out the winner's name—a girl from Ballarat. Then I scanned over the list of answers. Instead of New Jersey, she'd written New York. She was just a tunnel away, but we had to draw another envelope. There was a huge outcry and we were forced to find a substitute prize for the girl from Ballarat. It taught me a valuable lesson—always read the answers before announcing the name.

In 1979, I interviewed a new English band called The Human League, who had just released their debut album, *Reproduction*.

Because ABC budgets were always so tight, producer Ted Emery made a snap decision that the band wouldn't amount to much and he did the old trick of pointing the camera but not pressing the record button. When we got home, I asked, 'Where's that interview with Human League?'

'Um, the tape didn't work,' Ted said.

Later, he confessed what he'd done.

Of course, The Human League went on to release the *Dare* album, which was huge and contained the classic single, 'Don't You Want Me'. This was one of my favourite albums of the '80s. On the 21 March, 1982 edition of *Countdown*, I had this to say:

> Dare I say—I have no qualms in saying this—I now put this album against all The Beatles albums, the Elton John *Goodbye Yellow Brick Road* album, the *Ziggy Stardust* David Bowie album, *The Dark Side of the Moon* Pink Floyd album, the *Holland* album by The Beach Boys, and it goes on and on. They're my favourite albums; this one is a great album. Believe me, this group are going to get bigger and bigger and this is one of the perfect albums. If you have not heard this album, I suggest you go out and have a listen to it because you cannot help but be impressed . . . this album is an absolute classic.

This statement caused an absolute uproar, culminating in some ugly scenes when The Human League played at the Palais Theatre in St Kilda in May 1982. Australian audiences at the time were not used to programmed music and they were stunned when just Philip Oakey, the two female singers and a programmer appeared on stage. Where was the drummer? Where was the band? I was accosted in the foyer by a group of angry people, almost demanding that I give them their money back. 'You told us these guys were good!' they bellowed.

You know what, I maintain that *Dare* is one of the great albums.

That trip with Ted Emery was an unforgettable experience. We went to Europe and the United States for six weeks to film a 90-minute end-of-the-decade special, featuring interviews with Paul McCartney, David Bowie, Elton John, ABBA, Fleetwood Mac, Alice Cooper, Suzi Quatro, the Bee Gees, Bette Midler, Meat Loaf, Supertramp and Earth, Wind & Fire. Along for the ride was the photographer David Parker (who later became a wonderful film-maker with his wife Nadia Tass), and we met the crew in the States—cameraman David Etherton, who we called Ethel, and the sound recordist, who we called Muppet.

> Molly thrives on chaos—if he doesn't have chaos, he'll create it.
>
> **David Etherton, cameraman**

Not all of the interviews went according to plan. In Florida, we weren't allowed to go to the floor of the hotel where the Bee Gees were staying. So I snuck Ted and the crew into the hotel's kitchen and we crammed into the dumbwaiter. We got the interview.

Here's how Ted Emery remembers the trip:

> I arrived at the airport in Melbourne and boarded the plane. There was an empty seat beside me. I started to sweat. I had $25,000 worth of traveller's cheques in my pocket and no talent coordinator. And I had no contacts, or interest in the subject. I was slowly dying.
>
> Fortunately, Molly boarded the plane in Sydney.

To get approval for the trip, Molly had written an itinerary. All the times and dates were listed. The only people who didn't know anything about it were the artists and their management. The moment we arrive, I can hear Molly in his hotel room making phone calls.

I'm panicking.

Also, none of the hotels in America would take our traveller's cheques—they wanted a credit card. Fortunately, David Parker had a credit card and he paid for everything.

Molly would always be off, smoking or drinking or having a meeting—and I could never tell which one, until he got back and I'd have a sniff and work it out.

We had a fight at LaGuardia Airport in New York. Molly was still angry that Michael Shrimpton had docked his pay when he'd been working with Cheetah. He left to make a phone call. Then he lost his wallet. I'd had enough, so I boarded the plane. Minutes later, Molly appeared. He always carried two briefcases, but he had only one. So I went looking for the other briefcase. I found it near the phones. The case was open, with a crowd of people looking at it. 'Excuse me,' I said, 'that's mine.' The case contained some interesting male magazines, the sort you could only get in America in 1979. Things like *Golden Schlong* and *Thunder Buns*. I quietly picked up the case and walked away.

It's now all very laughable. But that whole trip was nerve-racking.

I remember when Ted got home, I asked if he'd had the chance to go to Disneyland.

'Disneyland?' he replied. 'I was travelling with fantasy land.'

Stephen Jones, *Countdown producer*

During that trip, we were running late for a Paul McCartney press conference at The Dorchester. We snuck in the back door, but Paul spotted us. 'It's fucking Molly,' he smiled. He then invited Molly up on stage. 'I'd like to introduce you to one hundred of my closest friends,' he said, pointing to the assembled press. I then realised the magic of Molly—he *did* know these superstars.

David Etherton, cameraman

We also got to do a one-on-one interview with McCartney.

This is what I remember most about that interview with Paul McCartney for the end-of-the-decade special in 1979. 'Are we rolling?' Molly said. Then he asked Paul, 'How did you see music in the '70s?' McCartney turned away from Molly, looked straight at the camera and said, 'Just like that.' Molly had no idea what was going on. He just gave Paul his 'What, Lovey?' look.

Ted Emery

The '80s were a great time for English music. Sure, there were a stack of one-hit wonders, including A Flock of Seagulls, The Vapors and Ultravox, but, as I've said many times, there's no shame in being a one-hit wonder—it's better than being a *no*-hit wonder. Skyhooks' Shirley Strachan once told Joe Dolce he felt sorry for him because his only hit was a novelty song. 'It wasn't a hit,' Joe replied, 'it was a *phenomenon*. Better to have one phenomenon than ten piddly hits.'

Of course, many '80s stars went on to have phenomenal careers. When 'Wake Me Up Before You Go-Go' was huge, I went to London to interview Wham! When I got to the studio, I was told that only Andrew Ridgeley would do the interview because George Michael had a boil or something. I was furious. I went on *Countdown* and said that George couldn't go on camera because he had a case of herpes. This comment got back to London, and George and I were distant for a long time.

George later came to Australia for a solo tour, and Sony had a huge reception for him on Sydney Harbour, with a mammoth sign: 'George Michael—Welcome To Australia'. The only problem was someone had stuffed up and misspelled Michael. He was not happy.

Since then, I've got to know George better, and we have become friends. He's always been very polite, and I respect him for that. And I think his work is fantastic.

Twelve inches. That's what we all wanted in the '80s.

I remember I went to see INXS at The Club in Collingwood. They were great, as usual. Afterwards, I talked to them about one of their new songs. 'You've got to do a twelve-inch version,' I said.

'A what?'

'An extended mix.'

'What are you talking about?'

Of course, INXS went on to do some fantastic extended mixes of their songs. One night, I was having a barbecue at my place for Duran Duran, and INXS's 'Original Sin' was on the stereo. 'What's *this*?' keyboards player Nick Rhodes demanded. 'Who did it?'

Nick was so excited he rang the producer, Nile Rodgers, from my phone. As I worried about my phone bill, Nick said, 'We've got this song called "The Reflex", we'd like you to do a twelve-inch mix of it.'

The Nile Rodgers remix hit number one in the States and United Kingdom. It was Duran Duran's first US chart-topper. Simon Le Bon later told the tale on stage when he did a gig with Chic at Budokan in Japan in 1996:

Me and Duran Duran were at a party in Australia and a friend of mine called Molly Meldrum put this song on—it was a song by INXS, 'Original Sin'. He didn't play it once or twice or three times, he ended up playing it twelve times in a row. By the end of listening to it, there was only one man in the world that Duran Duran wanted to be produced by and that was Nile Rodgers.

At the start of 1981, my friend Russell Mulcahy did the video for Duran Duran's debut single, 'Planet Earth'. And I did an interview with bass player John Taylor. I remember having dinner with Russell and saying, 'I've just done an interview with this guy from Duran Duran. Wait till you see him.' Russell replied, 'I've just done a video with them—wait till you see the *rest* of them!'

> Molly was a real champion of the band. We had our first Top 10 hit in Australia with 'Planet Earth', thanks to *Countdown*. We came here and everyone went completely nuts.
>
> **Nick Rhodes, Duran Duran**

We all became great friends, and Duran Duran were a major part of *Countdown* in the '80s. An interview with Simon Le Bon and Nick Rhodes ran on *Countdown* in March 1982.

> **Simon:** It's a nice surprise when you wake up and there's a letter on your doorstep that says, 'Hey, you've got a number one on the Melbourne charts with "Planet Earth".'
> **Nick:** We never dreamed we'd have a string of hits in Australia.

I remember during a trip to the United Kingdom I had to interview both Duran Duran and Boy George on one Sunday. As Nick Rhodes was getting his make-up done, someone said, 'After this, Molly has to go back and talk to Boy George.' Even though he was straight, Nick could be a bit of a bitch at times, so he took more than an hour getting his make-up done—just so I would be late for Boy George. When I finally arrived, George said, 'What kept you?' When a member of the crew told him 'Duran Duran', he started to slag the band. Because I grew up in the days of Elton and Rod, I was like, 'I've been there done that, kids, get over it!'

In his autobiography *Wild Boy: My Life In Duran Duran*, guitarist Andy Taylor wrote about going to a party at my place, where he got drunk on Jack Daniel's with Dennis Lillee, and met Greg Chappell and the team, 'people you only normally got to see on the BBC'. Andy called me a 'lovable old bloke'—a bit of a backhander!—who was 'famous for wearing a big cowboy hat and his catchphrase was "Molly Meldrum loves you lots".'

I have to point out, I have never used that expression in my life!

Not all of the *Countdown* discoveries became superstars like Duran Duran, but many of them went on to have lasting careers.

In 1979, I became great friends with Martha Davis from The Motels—by accident. Ted Emery and I had gone to Germany to interview Bette Midler, who was on *Musikladen*, the German equivalent of *Countdown*. The Motels were also on the show, so we decided to do an interview with Martha and the two of us clicked. She became a real *Countdown* favourite. I remember at the end of one show, she was on with Annie Lennox, then of The Tourists, and Martha came out with two sayings which became favourites of mine: 'Lost the plot' and 'You're talking to two girls who have been around the block and back again.'

I can certainly say, I've lost the plot many times, and I've definitely been around the block and back again.

In 1978, Ian and I went to the launch of Dragon's *O Zambezi* album at Bombay Rock. I always avoided driving with Ian, but on this occasion he had convinced me to go with him, and I left my car at his house in Alfred Street.

Not long after we got there, I looked up to see that Ian was crying. 'Let's go,' I said, and he agreed. I thought, 'My wife is going to think this is great—I'm going to be home early.' I knew that Ian wasn't drunk. I thought he was okay, just upset.

We got into his Celica and he threw a U-turn that would have defied a racing car driver. I tried to calm him down. Then I looked up to see we're on the freeway. 'Ian, we're going to Doncaster!' I yelled.

'What are you talking about? Don't be stupid.' But then he spotted the Doncaster sign and, suddenly, we flew across the median strip to go back the other way. We are doing unbelievable speeds. I'm terrified. I know I'm going to die.

He overtook a tram and went through a red light. I am begging to save my own life and the father of my kids.

Two hundred metres from his house, I start to feel better. One hundred metres . . . we're going to make it. I'm going to live.

We turn into Alfred Street and I can see my car.

Crash! Ian slams into the back of my car, a Volkswagen, sending the motor onto the back seat.

Ian is out cold. A neighbour, Brian, comes running out. I drag Ian out of the car and say to Brian, 'Get this prick out of my life.'

I have never been in a car with him since.

Grant Rule, *Countdown* executive producer

Whatever happened? I was such a little angel! (Molly's collection)

My first true love, Sandy Breen, at a ball for our other true love—the St Kilda Football Club, in the mid-'60s. I asked Sandy to marry me around this time; fortunately, she said no, and we're still best friends nearly 50 years later. (Molly's collection)

At the *Go-Set* offices when I was still known as Ian Meldrum. I was trying to look very serious in those days—I still had aspirations to be a lawyer. Thankfully, for the justice system, I pursued a pop career instead. (Molly's collection)

Don't shoot me, I'm only the fan—next to the musician and the magician. With Elton John and Ian Buckland on the set of *Do It* at Channel Seven in 1974. (Molly's collection)

'I feel like a permanent fixture,' Elton said when he hosted *Countdown* at the end of 1980. No international star appeared more regularly. And Elton was always entertaining. During that 1980 show, I reviewed Steely Dan's *Gaucho* album.

Elton: It's a real bore and it cost a million dollars to make.

Me: I think this album's great!

Elton: It's the worst album they've ever made.

Me: I quite like this album, so do yourself a favour and have a listen to it.

Elton: And drop dead. (Molly's collection)

'Do you have one of those teleprompters?' my Prince asked. No, and I also seem to have misplaced my brain. I called his mum a queen. Actually, I called the Queen a mum. (Molly's collection)

Mamma Mia, I went to Stockholm in 1976 to do a special with Benny, Bjorn, Agnetha and Frida. Australia fell in love with ABBA. All we could say was 'I Do, I Do, I Do, I Do, I Do'. (© Newspix)

John Paul Young was an integral part of *Countdown*. He even helped save the 100th show when things went a little, er, awry. (© Newspix)

The Tartan Terror. Rod Stewart once said, 'We all need a good hobby, good sport and good sex.' Words to live by. We've had a lot of fun over the years. On one Rod tour, everyone got an official tour T-shirt, like you were part of a soccer team. Mine said, 'Water Girl'. (Molly's collection)

I love Livvy. And when she came on *Countdown* to host the final of the *Xanadu* Dance Competition, I couldn't stop kissing her! (© Newspix)

The Divine Miss M! When I saw *The Rose*, I remarked on *Countdown*: 'To see such an amazing performance from a woman who's been so closely associated with *Countdown* ... I'm speechless.' (Molly's collection)

The legendary Robbie Weekes, who created *Countdown* with Michael Shrimpton and myself. We got away with so much in the '70s—even smoking on TV! (Photograph by gregnoakes.com)

I can't sing. I can't dance. But I've been lucky enough to have a lifetime in the music industry. (Photograph by gregnoakes.com)

The Village People hosted *Countdown* in 1980 when *Can't Stop The Music* premiered in Australia. If they didn't already have a cowboy, I could have joined the group. (Photograph by gregnoakes.com)

I'm just an excitable boy. And anything could happen on the Humdrum set. Look out for cream pies, egg on your face, sudden rain storms and exploding sauce bottles! (Photograph by gregnoakes.com)

I love having a 'Leo Sayer' (an all-day drinking session)—almost as much as I love the man himself. Leo was a massive part of *Countdown*, and I'm proud that he now calls Australia home. (Photograph by gregnoakes.com)

Queens means Hines! Marcia was Queen of Pop three times in the '70s, and nearly 40 years later, she still looks great—she's got the secret to eternal youth. I also have to thank Marcia for being Peter Andre's vocal coach. She helped Peter become a star. (Photograph by gregnoakes.com)

The Boy from Oz, Peter Allen, with the boy from Quambatook. (© David Parker)

Do yourself a favour . . . Air Supply's *The Whole Thing's Started* album in 1977. I wear my sunglasses at night! (Photograph by gregnoakes.com)

I walked the plank on *Countdown* in 1982 when American actor Christopher Atkins appeared to promote *The Pirate Movie* (which was Rated *ARRRH!*). A very intelligent, friendly, humble guy. (Photograph by gregnoakes.com)

'And I'm still a bachelor,' I declared on *Countdown*, before turning to Martha Davis from The Motels and asking: 'Do you want to marry me?' (Photograph by gregnoakes.com)

With one of 'The Countdown Sisters', Linda Freedman, who's still a massive Duran Duran fan more than 30 years later. (© The Countdown Sisters)

Duran Duran were a big part of *Countdown* in the '80s, with my good friend Russell Mulcahy making many classic videos for the band. This photo shows Simon Le Bon and Nick Rhodes at the Countdown Awards in April 1982. (Photograph by gregnoakes.com)

Cheeky Elton once called David Bowie 'a pseudo-intellectual', adding, 'And I can't bear pseudo-intellectuals'. But David is always a delight to spend time with—even though he insists on unusual locations for our interviews, including an elephant safari in Africa, a strange Japanese restaurant in New York, and a tennis court. We had to get permission from the navy to do this interview at Garden Island in Sydney in 1983, just before Bowie released the blockbuster *Let's Dance*. I love Bowie so much, all of my dogs have been named Ziggy, after Ziggy Stardust. (Molly's collection)

After my first Ziggy was sadly hit by a car and killed, I visited The Lost Dogs' Home in Melbourne to do a photo shoot for *TV Week*. When I was told that this little black dog was going to be put down the next day if no one claimed him, I had to take him home. He then appeared alongside me when I said 'Goodnight, Australia' on *Countdown*. When the repeat went to air the following Saturday, a woman called the ABC and claimed, 'You've got my dog!' I had to pay her $500 to keep Ziggy 2. (Molly's collection)

Hats off, step lively! Receiving my Order of Australia from the Victorian Governor, Dr Davis McCaughey, in 1986. (© Newspix)

Of course, John Farnham is The Voice, but Gavin Wood was the Voice of *Countdown*. Gavin is also very heterosexual, which is why I knighted him a queen when I was King of Moomba. (Molly's collection)

Driving up to Mount Buller, I found an injured kookaburra by the side of the road. I took him home to Melbourne, nursed him back to health, and then returned him to where I found him. I called him Cougar—after Johnny Cougar. (© Newspix)

I interviewed Bob Hawke for *Go-Set* when he was president of the ACTU. Then, when he was Prime Minister, Bob was a guest on *Countdown*. A great bloke. Here we are at the Priority One Concert in Sydney in 1985. (© Newspix)

Molly meets Charlene. We've been friends since I appeared in *Neighbours* in 1986. I admire Kylie so much. (© Newspix)

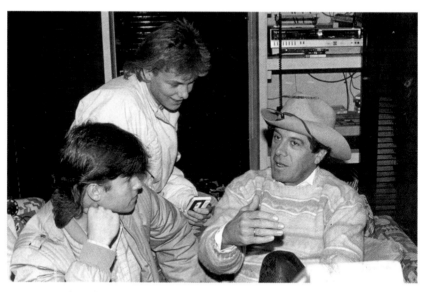

I'm not sure if I've been the best neighbour over the years (I do like to have the occasional party), but I was on *Neighbours* in 1986, offering some musical advice to Mike (Guy Pearce) and Scott (Jason Donovan). Two lovely and talented guys. Jason ended up having four number one singles and a number one album in the UK, while Guy finally released his debut album in 2014, *Broken Bones*. (Molly's collection)

9: EGO IS NOT A DIRTY WORD

1969–2014: Years and tears and great times—
Friends and feuds—Don't shoot me, I'm only the TV host—
Jail in New Zealand—A wedding—A split—A fairy godmother—
Life is what happens while you are busy making other plans.

Molly: *When it comes to the second and then the third album . . .*
Elton: *She's gone mad. I've made 28, dear. It's unbelievable.*
Molly: *Well, you have been around for a long time.*
Elton: *So has herpes, but we don't have to talk about it.*
Molly interviewing Elton John in 1985

In the mid-'80s, I interviewed Elton John for *The Meldrum Tapes*. Looking back at that interview, I can see why I love Elton so much. And we also have many similarities, though I have none of Elton's musical genius.

We both had humble beginnings, came to terms with our sexuality and led remarkable lives, which surprised even ourselves. And, yes, we can both be drama queens at times, but we've managed to survive in an industry that's not noted for longevity.

I asked Elton if he'd always wanted to be part of the rock world.

Well, I didn't really know what I wanted to be, because I wasn't exactly a rock 'n' roll-looking person. I was sort of like Billy Bunter goes frantic.

Then I was living my teenage years in my 20s. I didn't have much fun in my teenage years. [My 20s] were the first time I had the chance to express myself and, boy, did I! For the first time in my life I was able to wear high-heel shoes and dresses and stand on top of the piano.

I have had a personal life as well, God knows how, but I have. My career, I find it a game. I love it, it's a constant game and a battle and I love it. The personal thing is much harder to cope with. Without the people around me, I'd be the biggest monster of all time. Elvis, for example, must have known he was being an idiot, but, unfortunately, nobody from the word go said, 'You're being unbearable', and he just got away with it.

I've never said this in public before, but I played Prince Andrew's 21st at Windsor Castle. Incredible things have happened to me, and I danced with the Queen to 'Rock Around The Clock'. The odds against that when I was born!

In life, if anybody's got a bit of talent, if they go for it, they can succeed.

At the end of 1989, I had a barbecue for Elton at my house. It was a fun day. Elton's mum, Sheila, pushed one of my friends into the pool, and Elton wrote on the wall in my TV room:

Dear Molly,
So many years,
So many tears,
But so many great times.
Your friend Elton.
Love you.

And it's true. We have had plenty of tears, but we've also had so many great times.

I actually first got to know Elton's manager, John Reid. People always ask me, 'How do you get access to all these people?' Well, it's through knowing great people like John Reid. He was working for a publishing company in London, which had the rights to 'The Real Thing', so he was trying to push that song. At the end of 1969, John, myself and a couple of other people went to a Christmas party at Apple and we decided we would steal one of The Beatles' gold records. I had a big coat on, so I grabbed the American gold record of *Abbey Road* and put it under my coat. We were walking down Regent Street when I panicked. 'We can't do this,' I said, but they replied, 'Well, we've done it.' But I decided we had to take it back. So we returned to the party and I quietly put it back. John and his friends thought I was mad.

John's boss, a great guy called Phil Greenup, then came to Australia to work for WEA. He said, 'Have a listen to this album, Reidy is managing him.' It was Elton John and already I absolutely loved 'Your Song'.

When I returned to London in 1971, John organised a dinner with Elton. But I got stuck at *Top Of The Pops*, talking to Slade. I remember I glanced at my watch and it said five past nine. I was meant to be at Elton's place at 7 p.m. I finally got there to see a note on the door, telling me they couldn't wait and I could meet them at a restaurant down the road. Elton was not happy.

After dinner, we returned to Elton's apartment for drinks. Thirty minutes later, there was a knock on the door and a spiky-haired guy bowled into the room. 'Ian, this is Rod Stewart.' Twenty minutes later, the phone started ringing. 'Sure, sure,' I heard Elton saying. 'Come over.' Soon after, Neil Young walked through the door.

After my first meeting with Elton, I wrote in *Go-Set*: 'It's great that this little guy, who dresses in anything from Mickey Mouse suits to hot pants, has made such an impression on the world pop scene. In my opinion, you can never get enough of Elton John.'

Hearing that Elton would soon be touring Australia, I wrote: 'Guess who'll be Australia's number one band moll?'

On 18 September, 1971, *Go-Set* announced: 'Ian Meldrum is a very good friend of Elton's personal manager John Reid, and on his recent visit to London had the chance to meet Elton in person. Ian found him a very quiet and sensitive person, which is in direct contrast to the zany rock wild image that he lashed out with on stage. Meldrum will be touring with Elton throughout his Australian concerts.'

Elton arrived for his first Australian tour on 20 October, 1971. He was approached at the airport by two policemen, who said that the four badges he was wearing would be 'damaging to our society'. One said 'Bitch, Bitch, Bitch'. Another was a zodiac sign with a sexual intercourse position. Elton stuck a few band-aids over the badges and was then asked by customs officials if he smoked marijuana. As I said earlier, Australia was starting to swing in the '70s, but it was still a conservative time.

I must admit it's funny looking back on the things that I wrote in *Go-Set*:

Well, we're OFF! The Elton John tour has begun. So I guess it's WHOOPEE! I had a frantic call before I left for Perth from Lynne Randell in Los Angeles because she had promised when the tour arrived in Australia that she'd line some birds up for [drummer] Nigel Olsson, Elton and the rest of the gang . . . Elton John is mind-blowing. What a knockout Perth was. Everything I'd ever read or heard about Elton John became a visual and sound reality . . . What a concert. I doubt if the Randwick Racecourse will ever be the same again. My dears, I'm here to tell you that the whole thing was absolutely MIND BLOWING.

Was I really that camp back in those days?

It was on this tour that Elton fell in love with Daddy Cool. He loved 'Eagle Rock', and when he got back to London, he convinced Long John Baldry to record Daddy Cool's 'Come Back Again' on an album that Elton co-produced. Long John called Elton 'my podgy little piano player'. I have no doubt that 'Eagle Rock' inspired Elton to write his hit 'Crocodile Rock' a year later.

I was amazed by how much Elton loved music. Though he could get albums for free from his record company, everywhere he went he bought records. In fact, I have never seen anyone buy so many records.

I introduced Russell Morris to Elton in Brisbane. They talked for hours. And that night, Elton dedicated 'Take Me To The Pilot' to Russell because he had mentioned it was his favourite song. Russell was blown away.

In Melbourne, Elton was staying at the Southern Cross and was very excited when I revealed that The Beatles also stayed there. While he was here, Elton wanted to hear a test copy of his new album, *Madman Across The Water*. Bill Duff from Festival Records brought a copy to the hotel. Elton shrieked when he saw it. Instead of 'Madman Across The Water', the label read 'Madam Across The Water'. Bill went white, but Elton was in complete hysterics. It summed up the whole tour: Madam Across The Water. Elton signed the record and gave it to me. It became one of my most prized possessions.

Elton literally shrieked when he saw the record: 'Ahhhhh, they even know about me here in Australia—look at this!' And I remember he signed it, 'To my darling Molly, with love Elsie Johns xxx.'

Bill Duff, Festival Records

After the tour, I wrote in *Go-Set*:

To the public, I suppose he comes across as a complete extrovert with his high-heeled boots, bizarre clothes and outrageous sunglasses. But believe me, it's a bit of a shock when you see him first thing in the morning, lying in bed sporting a very straight night gown, pair of socks, horn-rimmed optical glasses, and poring over the daily papers and sipping a cup of tea.

A year after that tour, Elton savaged Australia in an English music paper, saying:

Everything [in Australia] is controversial, even *Coronation Street*. They have a sign flashing on the screen during the show: 'Not suitable for children'. They are so archaic and they hate the English, or at least the press hate us. We're still 'Limeys' to them. Since I found that out, I have willed every Australian team to lose. My cousin lives there and he had to accept the principles of a beer-drinking idiot to survive. It was a nightmare being there, but we'll go back. Why not?

New Zealand is nice, though. It's like England, years ago. It's lovely and green and the people are great. But Australia . . . the band had five days off in Adelaide and they went mad with boredom.

Elton added: 'Don't worry, they already know what I think about them.'

But I was shocked when I read the comments. I loved Elton, but I love Australia even more, so I hit back in *Go-Set*, writing Elton an open letter:

So Australia was a nightmare, was it? And we're terribly archaic and supposedly hate the English? Oh, Elton, don't you think you're exaggerating just a bit? Heavens forbid, we now have our own local telly series entitled *Number 96*, which makes the gang from *Coronation Street* look like a church choir.

I told Elton that he had caused problems for Australian promoters 'by kicking your Steinway piano occasionally.

They are having trouble hiring Steinway pianos for Rolling Stones concerts because of your treatment of them.

And what's this about the fact that we still consider you as Limeys and since you found out, you have willed every Australian team to lose? Good grief, is that why we lost the last Test series in England, and why poor old Evonne lost her [Wimbledon] crown to Billie Jean? Wow, what will power.

I reminded Elton he had made a lot of friends during his Australian tour.

And remember that friends are hard to get and when they read things like this they can be hurt.

To finish off, all I can say is that I was once a friend of yours and I hope I still am. I can still remember some really good times we had during your Australian tour. But I felt I had to write this letter because, after all, I am Australian and proud to be one, and I did think you were being more than unfair with your statements. You can rest assured that I will be one of the first to welcome you back to perform in this country.

All was forgiven a couple of weeks later when I heard Elton's *Don't Shoot Me I'm Only The Piano Player*: 'Believe me,' I gushed in *Go-Set*, 'it is the best LP he's EVER released. MAGNIFICENT is the word.'

Of course, Elton returned to Australia. His second Australian tour started in Perth on 17 February, 1974. He walked into Sydney airport with a walking cane with a gold handle.

I helped organise a party for Elton at Silvers nightclub in Melbourne. I thought we'd do it in grand style, so we picked Elton up from the Old Melbourne Hotel in a Rolls-Royce. Unfortunately, the drive to Toorak Road took forever, as the car went 'putt, putt, putt'. It was my first face-to-face altercation with Elton. 'Oh, this is ridiculous,' he hissed. 'Whose idea was this?'

I whispered to Bill Duff: 'Don't tell him it was my idea, say it was someone from Sydney.'

When we finally arrived, the reception was great. Guests were given plastic bags of crushed yellow bricks (to mark Elton's *Goodbye Yellow Brick Road* album), and a huge African-American guy got on stage, dressed only in a glittering G-string, and danced to Elton's 'Jamaica Jerk-Off'.

At the time, I was doing a children's show on Channel Seven, *Do It*, with magician Ian Buckland. I said to Elton, 'Why don't you come across and do it with us?' And he did. He played the piano and was fantastic. John Reid woke up at the Old Melbourne Hotel and wondered, 'Where's Elton?' He turned on the TV and saw him doing a kids' show.

He freaked out.

After the Australian tour, Elton went to New Zealand, and he and John invited me to join them for a holiday. That's when all the trouble started.

I arrived at the White Heron Hotel in Auckland, expecting to get dressed for a party. But I was greeted by Elton, who shrieked, 'Oh Molly, have you missed out on a drama tonight!'

'Bullshit,' I thought, 'what's a drama without me present?'

Earlier in the day, Festival Records had had a big party to celebrate Elton's arrival. But they ran out of whisky—John

Reid's favourite drink. Offered a glass of champagne instead, John threw the drink on the party's organiser, Kevin Williams. Later, one of Kevin's friends, model Judy Baragwanath, had a go at John Reid, allegedly saying: 'How could you do that to anyone, you rotten little bastard . . . You're just a couple of poofs, anyhow.' John knocked her to the floor.

That evening, Elton John and John Reid went to see David Cassidy play at the Auckland Town Hall, and then went to the concert party at a local club. A journalist, David Wheeler, reportedly said that Elton and his entourage were 'all marked men' because of what had happened earlier in the day.

Elton grabbed Wheeler by the shirt; John Reid got involved, and there was a bit of a scuffle.

As one of Elton's biographers, Philip Norman, said: To hit one person in the course of a day may be considered unfortunate. To hit two—especially in a foreign country, under a foreign legal system—exceeds even Lady Bracknell's definition of carelessness.

The next morning, detectives arrived at the hotel to question the touring party and to tell us to provide six people for a line-up. John, myself and four others went to Auckland Central Police Station. We were told to look straight ahead and not speak to each other. Judy Baragwanath appeared with sunglasses covering a black eye. I thought, 'Shit, what if she picks me out?' I started to shake. Then David Wheeler appeared, also with a black eye.

Both of them pointed at John Reid, and he was taken into custody and denied bail.

Elton had a big gig that night—for 34,000 people at Western Springs Stadium—and we knew if he found out what had happened to John, he could be too upset to perform. So we spent most of the day lying about John's whereabouts. As Elton was getting ready in his hotel room, he turned on the TV.

I leaned across, pretending I was getting something, and knocked the television off the table. But Elton merely rang room service and got another one. He turned it on and heard the news. He was distraught, and would not contemplate going on stage with John behind bars. He demanded a special hearing of the New Zealand Supreme Court—held at the judge's house—to appeal the magistrate's refusal to grant bail.

With just 90 minutes until showtime, John Reid was granted bail. And Elton put on one of the best shows I have ever seen.

But the next day was the court case. Elton had also been charged with assault because he had grabbed Wheeler's shirt. With a character reference from Princess Margaret, he was ordered to pay $50 costs and discharged without conviction. But John was sentenced to one month's jail in Mount Eden Prison. He appealed and lost. I remember he said to me: 'Well, I've been meaning to have a holiday for a couple of years now, so I guess this is it.'

On the Qantas flight home, I wore a Festival Records' Elton John promo T-shirt, which had a drawing of Elton and the words 'We've given Elton John 28 Days', meaning the month of February was 'Elton month'. I changed it to 'Auckland has given John Reid 28 days'.

Elton and John Reid actually asked me to return to Los Angeles to work as a publicist for Elton's label, Rocket Records. But I said no. There was always talk about working for Elton, and he and John would say, 'Come overseas and work with us.' But I just wasn't interested. I never wanted to leave Australia. I loved New York and I loved London, but I used to suffer from homesickness, so living overseas never interested me.

We featured Elton in *Countdown*'s end-of-the-decade special in 1979. He was touring Australia at the time, so we planned to have him compere an episode. But Elton happened to catch the Saturday repeat of the previous week's show, where I mentioned that the Hall & Oates concert was the best I had seen on my recent visit to America, and David Bowie had been the single biggest influence on rock in the 1970s.

John Reid rang me. 'The Artiste,' as he called Elton, 'was utterly insulted by your comments and he won't be hosting your show.' After the fight continued with Elton's publicist Patti Mostyn, I went to bed, awoken only by a phone call about 3 a.m. The voice on the end of the line sounded like Dame Edna's sister.

'It's Sharon.'

'Sharon who?'

'SHARON!'

'Sharon bloody WHO?'

'It's Elton, you silly bugger.'

'Well, why didn't you say so? I'm half asleep and you ring up trying . . .'

'Now, now, don't get upset, dear. None of this drama is my fault. It's just management trying to stir you up and give you a hard time. Of course I'll do your show next week. But you really should come to Sydney and talk about exactly what we're going to do.'

I flew to Sydney on the Tuesday, caught another concert, and then went backstage.

'I heard you were in the audience,' Elton said. 'Did you like the show?'

'Yes, it was very good . . . excellent.'

'That's not what I want to hear,' he moaned. 'Was it better than Hall & Oates?'

We both cracked up laughing.

Elton came to Melbourne and he did compere *Countdown*, though there was more drama when he called himself a 'horny little bastard' and said he had to sleep with producers' husbands to get to the top. The comments were deemed a little too risqué for our 6 p.m. timeslot, so a couple of little edits were made to the final show. Elton was not happy, and he and John had a fight in the car on the way back to the Hilton. Elton told John he was too upset to do that night's Festival Hall show. 'I'm going to bed,' he declared.

John thought it was a good idea for Elton to have some sleep. Just before 8 p.m., he knocked on Elton's door. When there was no answer, he let himself in. Elton was nowhere to be seen. By 8.15, John was freaking out. He looked under the bed, in the shower, in the wardrobe, thinking that Elton was playing a practical joke. At the very last minute, he phoned Festival Hall with the bad news. But the man on the other end of the line had no idea what John was talking about.

'What do you mean?' he said. 'Elton's just walked out on stage.'

In December 1979, *TV Scene* ran an article headed 'Elton–Molly Feud?' It started: 'Did Ian "Molly" Meldrum and Elton John fall out over the taping of Elton's Australian appearance on the ABC's *Countdown*?' It quoted me:

> Elton had a variety of hats and the last one he wore was complete with horns. I asked him what the horns were for and Elton replied: 'Because I'm a horny little bastard.' So we edited that out of the show. Elton wasn't too happy and he put on a little turn, but it was only a small one.

I don't think any international star appeared on *Countdown* more often than Elton.

Molly: Well, this seems like an annual occurrence, having you on *Countdown*.

Elton: It's like the Queen's speech.

You could always rely on Elton for a cheeky line. 'I want to go back to really simple things,' he remarked during one *Countdown* interview. 'That's why I'm talking to you.'

> It was the early-'80s and I was in London, directing videos like 'Vienna' and 'Video Killed The Radio Star'. Molly turned up to do a *Countdown* special with Elton. He asked me to direct it, but I said no, because I had never directed TV before.
>
> He chose someone else and it was all disaster from there . . . Arriving on the day, we walked into the studio just as a light came crashing down, nearly killing Molly and I. The recording started and Molly hated just about everything the director was doing. Eventually, the manic quality of the day took over as Elton sang his final song. As the cameras rolled, Molly pushed me around in a shopping trolley behind Elton. I was holding a mop, waving it behind his head, giving the impression of a rather bad hairdo. Why we weren't executed, I will never know. The footage went to air. Most people thought it was an unusual and brave approach.
>
> **Russell Mulcahy, video director**

During one visit to Australia, Elton had a harbour cruise in Sydney. Of course, I was running late, and when I arrived at the dock, my ship had sailed. The water police could see my distress. 'No worries, Molly,' they said, helpfully, 'we'll take you to the boat.'

We hurtled out to Elton's party, sirens blazing, but when I boarded, no one seemed pleased to see me. I later found out that all the party-goers thought they were being raided and as the water police drew close to the boat, all sorts of illicit substances were being thrown overboard.

The next major Elton Drama Down Under was The Wedding.

I remember I took a sleeping pill to get some sleep. I had the flu, but I wanted a good night's sleep because I was going to a one-day cricket match at the MCG the next day. The phone rang about 1.30 a.m. It was Patti Mostyn, publicist to the stars. Patti, John Reid and myself all had the terrible habit of ringing each other at absurd hours, usually about nothing at all. This time around, Patti said, 'Elton's just gotten engaged, he's getting married on Tuesday.'

'Patti,' I replied, 'I'm too tired for all this shit.' I hung up.

Apparently, she rang me again. Then Elton's boyfriend Gary Clarke was on the phone, crying.

'Enough of this joke!' I said, and went back to sleep.

The next morning, just before eleven, there was a knock on my door. I opened it to find two guys who looked like Mormons. 'We're from *The Age*,' they said, 'and we would like you to comment on the fact that Elton got engaged in Sydney last night. Will you be going to the wedding on Tuesday?'

My mouth was wide open. '*Pardon?*'

'This is the photographer, could we also get a shot?'

I excused myself and went to the bathroom. Splashing some water on my face, vague memories of the previous night's phone calls came back. But who was Elton going to marry? I said to the guys, 'Look, I have been invited to the wedding apparently, but I don't know much more about it and you can't have a photograph because that's a bit silly.'

Then I went to the cricket.

During the lunch break, Lorraine Willison from Channel Nine publicity came to see me. 'Molly,' she said, 'we've got a bit of a problem. All of these reporters are outside the Channel

Nine box and they want a comment from you about Elton's wedding.'

Fortunately, by this stage, I'd been able to track Patti down, so I at least knew a few details. 'Yes, gentlemen,' I told the press pack, 'Elton is getting married to Renate, she's a lovely girl, and they've known each other for a while.'

My old mate David Dawson from *The Truth* was there, smiling. 'So Molly, now that your mate's getting married, when are *you* getting married?' I could have killed him. 'David, I don't think that's appropriate right now, but I can assure you I *won't* be getting married.'

I didn't even have a partner at the time, so I asked Lorraine if she would accompany me to the wedding. She was very excited. Later in the day, Lorraine brought me the afternoon paper, *The Herald*. Renate was on the front page, walking down the steps of the Sebel. And next to her was Gary Clarke. To this day, I'm amused by that shot. The picture the English paparazzi really wanted was of Elton's boyfriend, and they had it on day one, but they had no idea.

Elton's bride-to-be was Renate Blauel, a German tape operator who worked on Elton's 1983 album, *Too Low For Zero*, which contained the prophetic song, 'Kiss The Bride'. The album's liner notes included 'Special thanks to Renate Blauel'.

As I mentioned, Elton's publicist in Australia is Patti Mostyn. She's a feisty, dramatic woman, who could easily have been the inspiration for the lead characters in *Absolutely Fabulous*. (Another Sydney publicist tells a story that she once asked whether Patti had flown overseas in economy class. She replied, 'Darling, I have never got on a plane and turned right.')

Patti's name is synonymous with most of the big stars from the '70s and '80s—Elton, Rod Stewart (whom she affectionately calls Rod 'Stupid'), Boz Scaggs, Billy Joel, Fleetwood Mac and

Barry Manilow. I regularly sniped at Patti in my *Go-Set* column. 'Patti Mostyn sadly lacked a hairstyle,' I wrote after the *Hair* premiere. 'Patti Mostyn looked stunning in red, but, really, does she always have to be the last one to leave the party?' I said after a *Jesus Christ Superstar* performance in Sydney.

> I do adore Molly. He's a nightmare, an absolute nightmare, but there aren't enough characters in our industry, and he is a character. Molly's not sane. He's just not. And that's what's so fabulous.
>
> **Patti Mostyn, publicist**

Patti put Sydney's Sebel Townhouse on the map, setting up her office in the hotel's cafe. Comedian Billy Connolly famously described the Sebel as the place where no one ever said, 'You can't do that here, Sir.'

> I convinced the promoters that it wasn't necessary for me to go everywhere on the tour. I could spend most of my time at the Sebel, so the hotel became part of the music industry. Everyone would party in the hotel's bar. Funnily enough, that continued until the hotel closed [in 2000], but I wasn't there in the later days. We used to stay up all night drinking. It was great, but I can't do it now. I have the odd late night now and I'm sick for 24 hours. Everything changes. I don't know how Molly does it.
>
> **Patti Mostyn**

It was Patti's job to organise Elton's wedding—in four days. Of course, she had a decent budget. The Champagne that Elton wanted—Louis Roederer Cristal—was flown in from overseas because there wasn't enough of it in Sydney. And the flowers were also flown in because they were out of season in Australia.

> Molly, of course, did the wrong thing. He was issued a single invitation, but he turned up with someone, which is supremely embarrassing at a seated

function. It was one of the few slightly tasteless things that he's done because you just don't do that.

Patti Mostyn

I dispute this. I always had a double invitation, it was just that Patti was fighting with Lorraine at the time and she didn't want me to bring her, so my double invitation became a single.

The wedding was on 14 February, 1984—St Valentine's Day. It was a traditional white wedding at St Mark's Anglican Church in Darling Point. Guests included Olivia Newton-John, Michael Parkinson and Barry Humphries.

What do you give the man who has everything? Well, I gave Elton and his bride some all-Australian gifts—flying kangaroos (instead of flying ducks) to put on the wall, gold placemats featuring kangaroos and emus, and a colonial cookbook.

It was a fantastic wedding, but kind of weird, too. As the priest was reading the wedding vows, it was as if the windows of the church opened and we could hear one of the ghetto blasters outside the church playing 'Crystal'. This was the song that Elton had written for Gary Clarke, the man who was back at the Sebel, booked in under the name 'Mr A.N Other'. I started laughing. I couldn't help it—it was all too much.

Then we got to the reception at the Sebel and, below portraits of the Queen and Prince Philip, the letters 'ER' were carved from two giant ice blocks. I thought, 'This is over-the-top', but then it was pointed out that the ice blocks weren't for 'Elizabeth Regina' but for Elton and Renate. We sat down and John Reid, who was best man, raised a toast to the Queen. Elton sat there and said, 'Thank you, thank you.'

'This marriage isn't going to last long,' I thought to myself.

Many people have asked me: why did Elton get married? All I can say is that, in his own way, he really loved Renate. And she was a lovely lady. Speaking personally, I know how hard it is to come to terms with your own sexuality. Sometimes you scream for normality. I have had many relationships with women—hell, I've been engaged five times!—and I think that just about every man thinks about having children. In fact, Elton's mum, Sheila, gave Elton and Renate a pram as their wedding gift.

It was a wonderful reception. Elton, with his wicked sense of humour, had a go at everyone in his speech, including Michael Jackson. He said that Michael had to set his hair on fire to get in the papers and not just do something simple like getting married. Of course, Michael would shock the world a little later with his own Sydney wedding. But that's another story.

After the reception, I went to Gary Clarke's room to make sure he was all right. I passed out on his bed and woke up the next morning with my arm around Gary. I sat bolt upright and thought, 'What is going on here?' I got up to open the curtains and knocked over what I thought was a bunch of flowers. I picked them up and realised it was the wedding bouquet. 'What's this?' I said to Gary. 'Oh, Renate brought that up for me.'

This was too much.

A decade later, Gary wrote a kiss-and-tell book about his time with Elton. There are people over the years who have ripped me off or done the wrong thing by me, but in nearly all of the cases I can understand why they've done it, and, in many ways, I have allowed for it to happen. I can't hold a grudge. And I can't hate people. I just feel sorry for Gary Clarke, that he had to sell his soul in a book. Some things should always remain private. Kiss-and-tell is wrong. I haven't spoken to Gary since.

Elton and Renate announced they were separating on 18 November, 1988. Elton said simply: 'I gave it my best shot.'

Elton and I have a lot of things in common, not the least being our love of cricket. And Elton has a wonderfully wicked sense of humour.

He once took a look at my pool and said: 'I love your spa. Where's your pool?'

I remember him co-hosting *Countdown* and the next song was Ian Dury and the Blockheads' 'I Want To Be Straight'. Elton turned to me and said: 'I don't think either of us is equipped to introduce this one.'

I have to admit I had many run-ins with Patti Mostyn in the '70s and '80s. But our fights didn't last forever. Many of our fights involved Elton.

We both lived through that heady period of Elton's, with the drugs and alcohol. There was many a fight. We were always fighting with Molly. But we always ended up doing that *Countdown* show. We'd be stuck in that dressing room and there'd always be a bottle of scotch for Elton.

Some of Elton's *Countdown* appearances were a nightmare. Some of the things he would say on there! Poor old Molly would try to cover, which was a change because people would usually be trying to cover for him.

Are Molly and Elton similar people? Well, they're both male and both gay, that's about it. Um, they're both in the entertainment industry. They wore hats, Molly still does [*Patti sighs*]. They're probably both volatile. I suppose you could say they're similar.

Sometimes people think their 'friendships' with stars are a lot more intense than they actually are. Sometimes people think they're a lot closer to the stars than the stars perceive it. I used to think I was best friends with everyone I worked with. Well, of course, you're not. You're their best friend while they're here because you happen to be good at your job and they feel comfortable with you.

But Molly and Elton's relationship has endured for years. And he will still always do an interview with Molly. There's still that loyalty factor.

Patti Mostyn

Do Elton and I fight a lot?

Well, I think we both like drama. John Reid, Elton, Patti and myself, we thrived on drama at one stage. Elton's humour can be cutting, as wicked as Dame Edna. In fact, sometimes I think they are the same person. I remember I bought a beautiful yellow jumper in Los Angeles, and Elton said, 'That's a nice yellow jumper you've got. Yes, it matches your teeth.'

Probably the biggest fight we had was at the Sebel in Sydney. I can't even recall what it was over, but it was a real punch-up, and I gave him a good bop on the nose. He stormed up to his room and tried to get me thrown out of the hotel.

It has been traumatic, but, most of all, it's been great fun with Elton. Even some of our little dramas have been funny. In 1996, I saw him at the VH1 Fashion Awards in New York, where he was receiving an award. He greeted me, 'Ah, Molly, I see you're still wearing that hat.'

I replied: 'Well, the people giving these awards have obviously gotten over those shirts you wear. They look more like silk scarves that I could buy in Bangkok for nothing!'

Elton then motioned to the man next to him. 'Molly, have you met Gianni Versace?' Of course, Versace was the designer of Elton's shirts.

Elton said to him: 'Don't worry, he's always putting his foot in it.'

Through the years and the tears, Elton has always been very

generous to me. I love him dearly and I admire him immensely. To be touched by Elton's genius is special. He had at least one Top 40 hit on the US charts every year between 1970 and 1995. No one else did that. And so many of the songs he has written with Bernie Taupin will live forever. For a songwriter, there's nothing bigger or better than that.

I've also had some horrendous fights with John Reid, but he has also been very good to me, always making sure that I got the exclusive. I was very sad when Elton and John split in 1998 (with Elton suing John for $25 million), because they had been a great team. I love them both and I will always love them. I will be very disappointed if either of them gets angry with me for keeping in contact with both of them.

Hopefully, Elton and John will work things out—just like Elton did with Billy Joel. When they toured Australia together in 1998, I took great delight in showing Elton one of my *TV Week* columns from 26 July, 1980. It was headed 'Bitter Duel At Piano Stool'. The story ran:

> Arch enemies Billy Joel and Elton John are enjoying a battle royal on the charts at the moment. Both megastars have expressed their dislike for one another on more than one occasion . . . An even more interesting battle between Billy and Elton could develop if it's true that both are going to tour the Land of Oz later this year. Wouldn't it be delicious if they hit in the same week? After all, there is a limited number of Steinway pianos available for hire in this country.

When Elton and Billy toured Australia, we had this exchange:

> **Molly:** I tell you what, Billy, you may not follow cricket, but you have one thing in common with cricket that Elton and I have never really experienced.

Elton: Balls.

Molly: No, you've bowled a maiden over.

I'll always remember the night Elton was playing Amadeus on *Countdown*. Five minutes before showtime, Elton said, 'That's it, I'm leaving', and got into his limo. I heard all of this unfold in my headphones. We were going live across Australia, it wasn't a pre-recorded show. And I think Elton didn't like the colour of his dressing room or something trivial like that, so he went to his limo and said, 'Driver, take me back to the hotel.'

Molly chased after him and grabbed on to the car door. He's being dragged along as he's pleading with Elton to come back. The drama is being relayed to me in the headphones: 'The limo's stopped . . . Elton's got out . . . He's walking back with Molly . . .'

It was so tight, everyone's heart was racing. I think it is a game to all these blokes. Fair dinkum, they get bored. I firmly believe that's why Elton got married to Renate in Sydney—because Michael Jackson got worldwide press for having his hair burnt in the Pepsi commercial. So Elton says, 'I'll fix that.'

Gavin Wood, *Countdown* announcer

I've had so many great times with Elton. I was lucky enough to be invited to his 50th birthday party. It was fancy dress; I went as a musical fairy.

Molly looked like an unmade bed. Elton came over to me and said: 'What does she look like?!'

Patti Mostyn

I gave the birthday boy one of the original wigs from *The Adventures Of Priscilla, Queen Of The Desert*. I took my dear friend Heloise Pratt, who looked beautiful. Elton's mum came dressed as the Queen. And Howard, Gary and Jason from Take That were Batman, Robin and The Riddler. A highlight for me was getting to talk with one of my heroes, The Beatles' producer Sir George Martin. It was a great party. I remember standing there and thinking about all the years I'd known Elton. And, yes, all the tears. And how we had both survived.

And I thought of our idol, John Lennon.

In September 1980, John and Yoko signed a new recording deal, with Geffen Records, and they released *Double Fantasy* on 17 November. On 8 December, John was in the studio with Yoko, working on one of her tracks, 'Walking On Thin Ice'. They returned to their New York apartment, where John was shot five times by Mark David Chapman, a 25-year-old drifter to whom John had given an autograph just a few hours earlier.

My manager Brian de Courcy was in a taxi on Toorak Road in South Yarra when he heard the news.

> The driver said, 'Bad about that Lennon guy.' I was only half-listening.
> 'What?' I asked.
> 'That Lennon guy being killed.'
> I thought he was trying to give me a history lesson.
> 'Yeah, but that was in Russia a long time ago.'
> 'No, the Beatle Lennon . . .'
> My mind was reeling. 'Let me out!' I yelled, and I ran to Molly's house in Alfred Street.
>
> **Brian de Courcy**

It was a hot day, and I was sitting on the house's sun deck when Brian appeared. 'I need to talk to you,' he said. 'Come down.'

Brian poured me a scotch & coke. Then he came out with it: 'John Lennon has been shot dead.'

I refused to believe the news. 'This is wrong, Brian. It can't be true.'

It was not until Elton's manager, John Reid, rang from the Hilton that it truly hit me. Elton, who was in town, was similarly devastated. He is Sean Lennon's godfather.

Soon after, there was a knock on my door. It was a reporter from *TV Week*.

I was in the office in West Melbourne when the Lennon news came through. After a few minutes of dazed silence, one of the editors said, 'We should do something.' Lawrie Masterson was Molly's 'ghost' at the time, but for some reason he was unavailable. The editor then turned to me. It was the old short-straw syndrome. I was the youngest cadet and this was the job that no one else wanted.

I had never met Molly, but the next thing I know I'm in a cab heading for his house. The cab driver knew we were going to Molly's place as soon as I gave him the address. In the cab, I was really starting to worry about what sort of shape he'd be in. I'd heard Lawrie talk about how emotional the guy was and though the stories seemed funny at the time, they didn't seem that funny as I was about to knock on his door.

A woman answered. I half-expected and half-hoped to be told to piss off. But she said it might be a good idea if Molly talked to someone, that it could help him. So I got shown in, with my stupid little notebook and my sixty-words-a-minute shorthand, and Molly's sitting on the couch, looking like a total wreck. He'd obviously been crying, but he was really polite and he offered me a drink, which I was happy to accept.

I didn't really know how to start, so I just sort of asked him if he was okay. He started to cry. Then he pulled himself together and went into a sort of automatic pilot interview mode, which kind of freaked me a bit. He talked about Lennon and how he worked with him and how that was a dream come true. It went okay for 10–15 minutes, but then he lost it. He was obviously deeply upset. The woman reappeared and said she'd called me a cab, which was waiting outside.

Back in the office, the page had already been laid out and I was told to fill the space, writing it in the first person as Molly. For some strange reason, it was a really easy story to write.

Garry Williams, journalist

I'd been organising a dinner party at my house to celebrate Christmas with Elton. I had a turkey, a tree and fake snow. I still had the dinner party, except it had turned into a wake. I also organised a memorial service at St Francis' Church in the city, and a tribute at the City Square.

Whenever I think of John, I look up at the copy of *The White Album* on my wall. It's inscribed: 'To Ian, love and peace, John Lennon.' Yoko Ono also signed it, writing 'Yoko Ono Lennon'. And John did a drawing of himself and Yoko. Paul McCartney and his wife Linda later added their signatures: 'Paul McCartney was here . . . and his old lady Linda McCartney.'

It's probably the only autographed piece in the world that's got those four signatures. Years later, I also got John's sons to sign the album:

Happiness, love, Julian Lennon.
To Molly with love, Sean Lennon.

I talked with Elton about John's passing, and he told me it was the first time he really had to confront death. I felt very empty for a long time afterwards. It was like a part of my life was gone. The Beatles could never be again. It was over.

John returned to the top of the charts after his death. In the United Kingdom, 'Imagine' hit number one for the first time, replaced by 'Woman'. John's reign was ended by Joe Dolce's 'Shaddap You Face'—with a film clip featuring my younger brother, Robert.

I had known Molly's brother, Rob Meldrum, from the alternative theatre scene in Melbourne, of which I was a part. When I had a chance to make the film clip for 'Shaddap You Face', I asked Rob if he would mime the accordion part for the video. I knew that he was Molly's brother and I hoped that when Molly saw his brother in the clip, it might mean he would show it on the air. To this day, I don't know if it made a difference. Probably not, because when the song went to number one in Australia, instead of showing the clip with his brother in it, I was invited to perform the song live on air—and Molly asked if he could mime the accordion part, which he did wonderfully in a black and white muscle shirt and French beret, in the same way that his brother did in the original film clip. (Hmmm, now that I think of it, why was he wearing that French beret, when the song had an Italian flavour?)

Secret dream: I have always hoped one day to have both brothers miming duelling accordions for a performance of the song.

Joe Dolce

John Lennon's last concert appearance was with Elton at Madison Square Garden in 1974. Elton played on John's song 'Whatever Gets You Thru The Night' and was convinced it would top the charts. John was not so sure, so he and Elton had a bet: if the song reached number one, John would do the song with Elton live.

Elton has touched so many lives, including my own.

He was one of the first interviews I did after I recovered from my fall. I'll always remember his kind words:

You're a legend and you're a friend, and you've stuck by me through the good times and the bad times and now the good times again, because you are an institution—a mental institution, but you're an institution.

I was walking out of the Sebel Townhouse in Sydney when I spotted Molly having an argument with the woman at the reception desk. 'I can't get into my fucking room,' Molly was yelling. 'There's something wrong with my key!'

The woman was trying to be helpful: 'Mr Meldrum . . .'

But Molly was going on and on. 'You'll have to get me another key, I can't get into my room.'

The woman finally got a chance to speak. 'Mr Meldrum, you're actually staying at the Ritz-Carlton.'

Ralph Carr, music/entertainment manager

10: SEEMED LIKE A GOOD IDEA

1976–1978: Don't fall in love—Saints and sinners—Oh Errol—
I feel like a call girl who's never been had—On a slide going down—A
hit I didn't want—Meet Willie Everfinish.

> *Following my heart and it takes me far away*
> *Through rivers strong, through yesterday*
> *Towards something I'm not too sure*
> **'Dreams Of A Love', The Ferrets**

At the start of 1976, I had a call from Frank Howson. He told me his mate Billy Miller—with whom he'd appeared in *Jesus Christ Superstar*—had a band, The Ferrets, who I should hear. Then I bumped into my friend Tony Cohen, who happened to be working with the band. Looking back, I think Alice Cooper came up with a title to explain all of this:

Welcome To My Nightmare!

It's a funny story, The Ferrets. And I always figure that it was my fault that Molly took over that band.

Tony Cohen, recording engineer

It's April 1976 and The Ferrets—who have recently relocated from Sydney to Melbourne—are doing a midnight-to-dawn recording session at Armstrong Studios in South Melbourne. Drummer Rick Brewer (ex-Zoot)—the replacement for the band's previous drummer, Ian Davis, who had been thrown in jail—asks recording engineer Tony Cohen if he can bring his bong into the studio.

The band puts down twelve or thirteen songs and Tony finishes mixing them by morning. The next afternoon he is making cassette copies at the studio. The music is pumping as I walk down the corridor. A song called 'Just Like The Stars' lures me in. By the time I leave, I'm apparently declaring that I have found 'the new Beatles'.

> That was the beginning of the end for The Ferrets. It was also the beginning of the start for them.
>
> **Tony Cohen**

I called my mate Michael Gudinski and convinced him to sign the band to Mushroom Records. Ferrets singer Billy Miller wanted me to produce an album for the band. He knew I was a huge fan of his favourite band, The Beatles; I'd produced one of his favourite recordings, 'The Real Thing'; and, just as importantly, I barracked for St Kilda. Billy is as fanatical about the Saints as I am. During one performance of *Superstar*, Billy listened to the broadcast of a game on a tiny radio.

> My main role was as an apostle, and the apostles doubled as lepers in the leper scene. It was a Saturday matinee—hence the footy on the tranny, which I had next to my ear. As Marcia Hines ploughed through the dead lepers, singing 'I Don't Know How To Love Him', the Saints hit the front against Collingwood and I came to life, yelling, 'Go Saints!'
>
> **Billy Miller, The Ferrets**

The Ferrets were a revelation. They were just so talented. Billy was a great singer and they were excellent songwriters. And I thought it was a great combination of different musical influences, everything from The Beatles to the Eagles and Steely Dan. I thought we could combine all of that, and do everything from really simplistic songs to rock opera-type pieces. I also suggested bringing Billy's two sisters—Pam and Jane—into the band, which caused a bit of friction. Blondie was breaking at the time, and I just thought the climate was right; women were being accepted in rock 'n' roll bands.

> I suppose I wanted it to be really big, with the orchestra and everything. I had come out of the theatre—four years with *Jesus Christ Superstar*—so I thought it was possible to combine all of that with rock 'n' roll.
>
> **Billy Miller**

I wrote in my *TV Week* column: 'The Ferrets consist of seven members, all of whom are suspected of madness . . . Billy Miller [is] under the impression that he's a poor man's Errol Flynn.'

> I don't know about the 'poor man's' bit. We had this big thing about Errol Flynn, that's why we ended up drinking vodka. We had all read his book, *My Wicked, Wicked Ways,* and I just identified with him. He was from Tasmania, where half of my family came from. I used to dress like him and in one photo I was standing there with a log of wood and an axe in my hand and I drew on a little Errol Flynn moustache.
>
> **Billy Miller**

The Ferrets' first single was even named after one of Errol's biggest movies, *Robin Hood*. It stiffed.

My manager at the time, Brian de Courcy, lived through The Ferrets' madness.

Oh my God, The Ferrets! A remarkable time. I remember one night in the studio, Ian fired the orchestra string section because they were reading the paper. But they were reading the paper because they were waiting for something to do!

Brian de Courcy

Making an album with The Ferrets was one of life's great adventures. Billy and I connected on a musical level and we felt we were making a landmark Australian album. But things did get out of control, with Michael Gudinski screaming, 'What the hell is going on in there?'

I was producing the album as well as managing the band. And, at the same time, *Countdown* was huge and I was going overseas to do interviews. At times, it all got a bit much and I felt close to a breakdown.

When we were making The Ferrets' album, Molly was screaming about 'separation' . . . 'We need more separation!'

I was at my wit's end, I didn't know what to do. So I called Roger Savage, the head engineer, and got him to come in. He winked at me and said, 'Okay, I'll plug it into the separator.'

Totally deadpan, he fiddled with a few leads and then we had a listen. Molly said, 'Ah, that's much better.'

Tony Cohen

I've always liked to create a party vibe in the studio, but with The Ferrets it was ridiculous. Billy's three-legged dog, Django, would be running around, and his mum would be sitting there, knitting, nodding her head and tapping her foot and occasionally saying, 'Mmm, yes, that sounds very good.'

It was a circus.

One day, we decided we wanted Django to bark on the record. We sat him on a stool in front of a microphone, but, alas, he wouldn't sit still.

Because I was living with Caroline, the transsexual, and her brothel was just around the corner from the studio, Billy and I would often drop around to visit the girls. One night they dressed us up as showgirls, covered in feathers. We ended up in the front room, pretending we were working girls. For some strange reason, we weren't getting picked, but then this panel van pulled up and in came a young guy with long, blond hair. He started talking to us, but as I reached for my drink, my wig fell off, and he nearly died. 'Fuck, you're Molly!' he shrieked. He bolted for the door and my days as a call girl were over.

The Ferrets ended up being in the studio for eighteen months.

During the making of the album, we would have 'production meetings' at Molly's house. When we'd arrive, he'd usually still be in bed. He'd get up, wrap a towel around himself and pour a scotch and coke. As the scotch kicked in, the meetings would get more and more outrageous.

One day he was telling us how to produce records and he wanted to play us 'The Real Thing', but he couldn't find a copy. So he took the gold one off the wall, smashed the glass and played us the gold record.

Tony Cohen

While The Ferrets continued to work in the studio, I had to go to London for a *Countdown* trip. Michael Gudinski tracked me down. He was ranting and raving, like he usually does, but he told me that he was getting bills for master tapes. 'Hold on a second,' I thought to myself, 'The Ferrets aren't at that stage yet, there shouldn't be bills for master tapes . . .'

When I got home, I went to the studio and confronted Tony Cohen. 'It had nothing to do with me,' he said.

It turned out that Billy's girlfriend, Lucy, was in London at the time and Billy was sending her audio postcards. I found all of these recordings marked 'Tape For Lucy'. Billy would sing a song and then suddenly someone would say, 'Hello Lucy, this is your cousin here, we're missing you.' There were a heap of these tapes. Billy's brother's band, The Wombats, had also been in the studio recording. It was madness. I had to do everything I could to make sure that Michael didn't find out.

While we were making the album, Nicky Hopkins—who I got to know during The Rolling Stones' Australian tour in 1973—was in town with Joe Cocker, and I asked him to play on the record. Nicky, unfortunately, had a serious alcohol problem and his hands wouldn't stop shaking. His friend/minder had to keep picking him up and sitting him back on the piano stool. But when he played the piano, he was a maestro. At the end of the recording, for some reason he yelled, 'Albatross, albatross!' It sounded so strange, we kept it on the record. It can be heard at the end of track three, 'Bye Bye Baby'.

The band and I had a lot of fights in the studio. After one incident, I fell asleep under the control desk. The band—who were still in the studio—thought I had gone home and they started calling me every name under the sun. All I had to do was keep my finger on the talk-back button to hear every word. After about half an hour, I took great delight in strolling in and saying, 'I heard all that.'

I guess I was very naive, but often I would ask, 'Where's so-and-so?', and the reply would be, 'Oh, he's sick.' I'd be like, 'Not again. Boy, we're having such bad luck.' It wasn't until later that I found out the extent of the drug problem within the band.

Billy Miller later told me his biggest regret was telling Pat

Bowring, *The Sun*'s rock writer, that members of the band had tried heroin. A two-page spread appeared the following day, headed: 'Ferrets Into Drugs'. Billy's mum—who wrote the newspaper's kids' page Corinella—was horrified.

One member of The Ferrets' entourage was so out of it on Mandrax that when she saw Billy's dog, she said, 'Do you wanna Mandy, love?', having no idea it was a dog.

All of these experiences just added to my hatred of drugs. As Nirvana singer Kurt Cobain would later say, 'Drugs are a waste of time. They destroy your memory and your self-respect and everything that goes along with your self-esteem.'

The Ferrets and Tony Cohen helped me make an ABC documentary looking at heroin, called *On A Slide Going Down*.

> Here we were making this anti-drug thing, and we were all totally fucked up.
> **Tony Cohen**

On A Slide Going Down went to air a week after my old *Tommy* buddy Keith Moon died of a drug overdose in London. At the time, I described the heroin documentary as 'the most important project of my life', and I stand by that statement today. I have lost too many friends to drugs. There is nothing cool about heroin use. A young person hooked on hard drugs is one of the most heartbreaking things you'll ever see. Drug use is not restricted to rock stars. It's an everyday problem for many Australians. Of course, a rock star dying from an overdose gets the big headlines, but below the headlines are many stories of real human suffering.

When I was living with Caroline, she was hooked on heroin. I devoted so much time to trying to get her off it. I literally cried myself to sleep because it hurt so much to see her become just like an animal. She simply couldn't help herself. (I once ran into one of her dealers. I told him that if I ever saw him dealing to her again, I would kill him. I meant it, too.)

For the documentary, I interviewed nine people—seven addicts, one ex-addict, and a mother of an addict. All of them had tragic tales to tell. One addict, Peter, told me he robbed a shop, but he and his mates had no getaway car, so they called a taxi. 'We all jumped in the back with our shotgun and masks and stuff,' he said. It was so pathetic, it was almost funny.

While we were shooting the doco, I was at home in Alfred Street, about 11 p.m., playing records with a mate of mine from EMI Records, Russell Thomas, when two guys appeared in the lounge room. I didn't know them, but that didn't worry me because there were often people in the house I had never seen before. One of them asked if I was looking for a girl named Caroline (not my old housemate), a heroin addict. I said I was. He told me to stop looking for her and give up the idea of making the doco. I told him it was going to be made and then they jumped us.

> We were playing Bob Seger's 'Hollywood Nights' when the two guys walked in and started hassling us. I asked them to leave and one of them head-butted me and I punched him. And Ian was punched in the nose. I had the other guy in a headlock and tried to get out the back door whilst being hit by the first guy. Realising the back door was locked, I tried to drag the guy in the headlock to the front door. As this happened, they rammed my head into the fireplace. I managed to get them both out the front and they took off.
>
> **Russell Thomas, EMI Records**

When I was hit in the nose, the pain was so intense that I thought, 'This is the end . . .' I had a broken nose and we rushed Russell to the nearby Alfred Hospital for stitches to his head.

I kept the incident quiet at the time because I didn't want to jeopardise the making of the doco.

My neighbour, John Hoffman, arrived to see the end of the fight.

> Russell saved him [Molly] from a pretty bad hiding. The guys were screaming, 'Why are you doing this doco?'
>
> **John Hoffman**

Billy Miller believes one of our attackers was an underworld figure called Gary The Boxer.

> I was going to work one Saturday morning about 6.30 a.m., when this guy jumped into my Falcon station wagon and said, 'Can you give us a lift? I've just woken up in The Alfred, I OD'd last night. I need to get to St Kilda.' A year later, I met him again as the guy who co-wrote 'Don't Fall In Love'.
>
> **John Hoffman**

In eighteen months of recording, 'Don't Fall In Love' was almost an afterthought. It was recorded and mixed in about eight hours with the intention of being a B-side for 'Lies', but I realised that the song was too good to be a B-side. It was released in June 1977 and hit number one in Melbourne and number three nationally.

But Ian Davis's share of the royalties go to Mushroom Publishing boss Michael Gudinski. Ian despised authority and disliked the music industry so much that he sold the rights to his songs to Gudinski for $500. A couple of years later, Ian died in his bedroom. With his fists still clenched and a glare on his face, it looked like he was having a go at the two policemen who carried his body out of the house. He died as he lived—defying authority.

With 'Don't Fall In Love' topping the charts, Mushroom Records was screaming for the album to capitalise on the success. Ironically, the album, *Dreams Of A Love*, was 'rush-released', in October 1977, in a plain white sleeve with just the band's name and the title stencilled on it, because the real artwork had not been finished. Buyers were told to return the cover for the proper cover a few weeks later.

> The paper bag cover was Molly's idea. It turned out to be brilliant decision. Nobody else has ever done it.
>
> **Billy Miller**

I was credited on the album as 'Willie Everfinish', and a photo showed me wearing a Sherbet T-shirt with my face covered in gaffer tape. Stencilled in the groove on the record was the message: 'Well, Williever Finish Finally Finished Hope You Liked It. Luv Molly X.'

> In the end, I think the album came out pretty shithouse. That's everyone's fault—you can't blame any one person, certainly not Molly. We were all pretty out of control. But the more it got out of hand, the more it got out of hand—the more money Molly wanted to fix what he'd half done. Molly would say, 'Live for the song!' and he'd get in orchestras and choirs. The band would then worry that they'd never be able to play the album live.
>
> **Tony Cohen**

The Ferrets tried to recreate the album at one glorious gig at the Palais Theatre in St Kilda. Only problem was there was only one conductor for the choir and the orchestra, so every time the conductor signalled for the orchestra to start playing, the choir would start singing as well.

A highlight of The Ferrets' shows was Billy re-enacting the commentary of the last 90 seconds of St Kilda's 1966 Grand Final victory.

Due to my *Countdown* commitments, I relinquished my role as manager of The Ferrets. It was suggested that my manager, Brian de Courcy, take over.

> Brian said to us, 'Right, I want everybody to go to the clothes shop tomorrow and we want silver costumes with a big flash on them, like Flash Gordon, and we're going to change the name to The Flashes.'

> We just looked at him. I can't remember what we said, but it was something like, 'Get fucked, Brian.'

> **Billy Miller**

The Ferrets made a second album with Tony Cohen, *Fame At Any Price*. I remember visiting the band in the studio with Michael Gudinski.

> One song was called 'Tate's Run', about the drug runner Donald Tate; another was called 'We Want It Legalised'. As they heard the lyrics 'The man in the moon is coming here soon/Show us how to grow our own', their faces just completely dropped. I guess that was it.

> **Billy Miller**

The Ferrets broke up at the start of 1979. But I remained great friends with Billy. In fact, I asked him to put a band together for *Countdown*'s *Xanadu* Dance Competition in August 1980, which I was hosting with Olivia Newton-John.

My wife was overseas, and I had this great idea that I was going to meet Olivia Newton-John and we would get together that night. I had it all worked out. I think I got to say hello to her at sound-check and that was that. At the end of the night, I was having a piss beside my car and the cops pulled up. So instead of spending the night with Olivia, I spent it in the Prahran lock-up.

Billy Miller

Billy and bass player Ken 'K.D' Firth formed a new band, The Great Blokes. In 1983, Billy teamed with Mick Pealing (ex-Stars) to form The Spaniards. They got me to produce their debut single, 'God Is A Shield'. I also worked with Billy on the Gillian Armstrong movie *Starstruck*, with Billy writing one of the soundtrack's songs, 'I Want To Live In A House'.

K.D ended up working for Telstra. Guitarist Dave Springfield (aka Dave Schofield) drove taxis in Sydney and does blues shows on community radio. He also released an acclaimed album in 2011, *Two Days*, as JD Love, co-produced by his daughter, Georgia Fields, who's also a recording artist. Georgia's mum is Jane Miller—Billy's sister, the subject of The Ferrets' 'Janie May'. And drummer Rick Brewer relocated to Byron Bay.

Tony Cohen became one of the major record producers in Australia, working with Nick Cave, Models, The Cruel Sea, Horsehead, Powderfinger, and his wife, Astrid Munday.

I learned a lot from Molly. It was one of the best educations you could get, and I'm not just talking about recording. I found out about some things I didn't even know were possible. I loved Molly's unforced imagination. I think that school of producers is pretty much gone. He's like a Phil Spector, where over-the-topness and the atmosphere are just so important. The only problem is Molly hasn't got an off-switch, which is probably his only downfall when it comes to working in the studio. There are times when you have to stand back and get a little serious.

Tony Cohen

Billy Miller continues to record. And his son, Eduardo Miller, formed his own band called Dr Mexico.

> I would like to do something with Molly again one day. Get him to produce something.
>
> **Billy Miller**

> I wish Ian had produced more records. He could have been the Phil Spector of Australia. I mention Phil Spector because if Phil Spector produced the record, it didn't matter who the singer was, they're Phil Spector records. With Ian, it would have been the same. It wouldn't have mattered who recorded them, they would have been Ian Meldrum records. But all we really got was a litter of singles, which is a pity.
>
> **Ed Nimmervoll, *Go-Set* and *Juke* magazines**

Billy has also dabbled in production, having done a three-year course at RMIT university and an Advanced Certificate in Sound Production. He still plays around Melbourne, having worked a lot with Mick Pealing, as well as being a member of Dave Graney and Stephen Cummings' bands.

He also had a Wiggles tribute band, The Waggles!

Many years ago, Molly owed me $100. He couldn't find his cheque book and he didn't have the cash. He went into his kitchen and returned with an egg. On it, he wrote: 'Please pay Jeff Joseph the sum of $100, signed Ian Meldrum.'

I looked at him as if he was a lunatic, but he said, 'Take that to the bank, lovey, buy a duty stamp, lick the stamp and put it on the egg, and they'll cash it.'

So when it came to doing that week's banking, I said to the teller, 'Please don't think I've lost my mind, but I've got this egg I want to cash. It's an egg from Ian Meldrum and he says you will honour it.'

And they did. They cashed the egg.

Jeff Joseph, manager

11: LIVING IN A CHILD'S DREAM

1969–2009: My brush with Michael Jackson—A meeting at Studio 54—A Thriller—Bad is good—Oils ain't Oils—The Beatles for sale—Roger, Roger—Shirley, you can't be serious—I join *60 Minutes*—Something fishy in Tokyo—Trouble in Thailand—Oh Meryl—I'm Michael's 'Best Man'—Sleepless in Sydney—I blow a fuse.

I haven't grown up. Grown-ups are closed-minded. They tend to be bigoted and narrow. I'm still a kid and I relate to all those kids out there who watch Countdown. *They have no fear of me because they know I like them and maybe even understand them.*
They treat me as their mad uncle.
Molly, *The Age*, 1983

One superstar never actually appeared live in the *Countdown* studios, but he was a big part of the show.

I was in the bathroom brushing my teeth when I first heard Michael Jackson. It was late 1969 and I was in London, getting ready to go to a reception for a group called Edison Lighthouse, who would top the UK charts with a song called 'Love Grows (Where My Rosemary Goes)'. *The Andy Williams Show* was on the telly and the sound was blaring through the apartment. Suddenly, I heard this fantastic song. I rushed to the lounge room and couldn't quite believe what I was seeing and hearing.

The song was 'I Want You Back' and the American group was The Jackson 5— five brothers, born and raised in Gary, Indiana.

It was an incredible performance and I knew that the band was destined for big things. Even in the taxi on the way to the Edison Lighthouse reception I was still humming the song. Unfortunately for Edison Lighthouse, they turned out to be just one-hit wonders. But not so The Jackson 5, because within a few months they had become one of the biggest groups in the world—remarkable, given their ages. When 'I Want You Back' hit, Jackie was eighteen; Tito, sixteen; Jermaine, fifteen; Marlon, twelve; and Michael was just eleven.

Four years after first hearing them in London, The Jackson 5 toured Australia. 'Jackson 5 Mania' was the headline of my *Go-Set* report. I raved:

> Not since The Beatles and The Monkees toured Australia have we seen the likes of such hysteria. I am still a little dazed by what I have just witnessed at Festival Hall in Melbourne. They are, in fact, just dazzling in every sense of the word. Ever since The Beatles first caused Beatlemania, critics and musos have knocked the screamers, but boy, it's good to see it back. 'Cause with scenes like that, you know that pop music is alive and well.

With my assistant Glenys, I attended a reception thrown for the group at a little nightclub at the top end of Swanston Street, which was owned by Brian Goldsmith (the father of Tottie), who was married at the time to Olivia Newton-John's sister, Rona. The Jackson 5 were presented with gold records, and also introduced to a group of young Aborigines.

The following day, Glenys and I went to the Southern Cross Hotel to interview the group and Mrs Rose Fine, who was their tutor on the tour. It was almost nine years to the day since The Beatles had caused riots outside the same hotel.

'Happy-go-lucky' was the best description of the band. I wrote in *Go-Set*:

> No egos to be broken through, no smart remarks, one of the easiest interviews I've ever had to do. They were willing to answer any question about their music and show business itself. To interview this group was one of the most pleasant and easiest tasks I've ever been set. One could hardly ever imagine them being a problem at any time.

Jermaine told me that Michael loved *The Brady Bunch*. I also remember that Glenys took notes in shorthand, and, as we spoke, the guys' little brother Randy, who was just eleven, stared at her pad for about five minutes before saying: 'Is that Australian you're writing?'

After the interview, I introduced the Jacksons to local teen sensation Jamie Redfern. I also gave them an Australian Rules football, which they took great delight in throwing at each other in the Southern Cross foyer and giggling every time they tried to bounce it like a basketball. We also took them to the Southern Cross bowling alley, where we had a great time.

Until The Jackson 5 came along, American culture had been so white it was like a detergent ad. All the sitcoms were the 'perfect' American white family—*Leave It To Beaver*, *Father Knows Best*, *The Adventures Of Ozzie And Harriet*, *The Partridge Family* and *The Brady Bunch*. Rarely was a black person seen, and if they were, it was usually in a subservient role.

I believe this had a profound effect on Michael Jackson. You have to remember, he never had a 'normal' childhood. He would go to school and then come home and rehearse. His father Joseph would not allow him to play with other kids. His only real connection to the outside world was television. He was also obsessed with the movie *Oliver!*, starring a British child star, Mark Lester, who will forever be remembered as the timid little boy who asked: 'Please, sir, I want some more.'

Michael grew up believing that if he was ever going to make it in the world, he had to be accepted by the white population.

The music world changed in 1977, led by a guy in a white suit, dancing to the disco songs of the Bee Gees. *Saturday Night Fever* was a blockbuster at cinemas and on the charts. And New York's Studio 54 became the hottest club in the world. Also in 1977, Michael Jackson started working with Diana Ross on the film *The Wiz*, which was an African-American remake of *The Wizard of Oz*, in which he played the Scarecrow. *The Wiz* was not a big hit at the box office, but during the making of the movie, Michael met record producer Quincy Jones, who was working on the soundtrack. A remarkable partnership was forged.

While Michael was working on *The Wiz*, I was in America on a *Countdown* trip with Grant Rule. Our major interview in New York was with Rod Stewart, but during our stay I was given the chance to hear a couple of tracks that Michael was working on. Impressed, I rang CBS Records and requested an interview, but was told he wasn't a priority for the label and I should forget about it.

After much persuasion and persistence, however, it was finally arranged that I would meet Michael at Studio 54. The interview was locked in for 5 p.m. It was a cold, wet and windy day in New York, and, as usual, we were running behind schedule. Grant and I were nearly an hour late, and I remember saying to Grant and the crew, 'Look, he'll probably be gone by now, and I don't blame him.'

Much to our surprise, when we finally pulled up outside

Studio 54, we saw a little figure huddled in the doorway. Michael was there by himself—no security people, no minders, no one from the record company. He was absolutely freezing, but very jovial.

We went inside and started setting up to shoot the interview. Michael even helped the lighting guys plug in their lights, and set up the microphones.

The interview lasted about fifteen minutes. He was shy, but I'll never forget the way he giggled when I asked about his 'funky little sister', Janet. 'She *is* funky,' he smiled. I ended our chat by thanking Michael for his patience and wishing him all the best for the film and a solo album he was planning to work on in 1978.

That album was *Off The Wall*, and Michael became a super-star.

Looking back, I consider that meeting with Michael one of the most important interviews I've ever done. And I wonder whatever happened to the CBS staffer who said Michael wasn't a priority.

Off The Wall, produced by Quincy Jones, provided us with three fantastic clips that we flogged on *Countdown*—'Don't Stop 'Til You Get Enough', 'Rock With You' and the title track. I even gave Michael a call during a *Countdown* episode in March 1980, when he promised he would return to Australia.

But the next Jackson to visit Australia wasn't Michael, it was Jermaine, who was the special guest at the 1981 Countdown Awards. He arrived a week before the big night, and we went camping in the Grampians—literally. Jermaine wanted an Australian travel adventure, so we went on a horse-riding trip for three days. Jermaine was an absolute delight. Down to earth and friendly. Mind you, the trip to the Grampians was not without its drama because on the first day my horse got spooked and took off at a million miles an hour, throwing me off. The result was a sprained ankle. Jermaine was very understanding and patient—I was like a peg-legged Molly, hobbling around and trying to keep up.

The following weekend we all went to Sydney for the Countdown Awards. Much to my horror, I was having major relationship problems and on the eve of the awards, my partner left me a note, saying he was going back to Melbourne. I was devastated. Jermaine and Lawrie Masterson, my great mate from *TV Week*, helped me make it through the night. Jermaine and I became very firm friends after that.

By the time Michael returned to Australia, he was the biggest star in the world. I will never forget the *Countdown* production meeting when we first saw the 'Billie Jean' video. We played it over and over and over again. Michael Jackson was the Fred Astaire of the '80s. With the *Thriller* album, he had created pure magic.

By the time *Thriller* arrived, MTV—which took a lot of its ideas from *Countdown*—had become a major force in the United States. Its influence was massive. Sadly, their playlists initially ignored African-American artists, so much so that Michael received little support. It was hard to believe that 'Billie Jean' was struggling to get onto MTV. But thanks to artists such as David Bowie, Elton John, Rod Stewart and Paul McCartney— who basically said, 'If you won't play Michael's videos, don't play ours'—MTV changed its policy.

In 1983, Michael appeared at Motown's 25th anniversary concert. After a Jackson 5 reunion, Michael performed 'Billie Jean', debuting his new dance move—the moonwalk. It was more Michael magic. The following week, I had a big party, and I recall some Aussie cricketers, particularly Rod Marsh and

Allan Border, loved Michael's performance—they couldn't stop watching it.

The only disturbing thing was I did notice that Michael was starting to look different. There was no escaping the fact he was changing physically. His nose seemed slightly smaller, and gone was the glorious afro that he had when we spoke at Studio 54.

In 1984, I travelled to Los Angeles to present Michael with a special Countdown Award for his contribution to the world music scene. I was whisked to the CBS offices under a cloud of secrecy and introduced to a Japanese/African-American lady named Shirley Brooks. Shirley, as it turned out, had Michael's complete trust and was a friend of the family. She led me to another area where we were to meet Michael. He finally arrived with a big entourage, though he was very hospitable and totally at ease, which was a surprise because he was still recovering from burns he received when the filming of a Pepsi ad went horribly wrong.

What also surprised me was that even though he'd received so many awards—including a record eight Grammys in one night—he seemed genuinely delighted about the Countdown Award. We took some photos, but Shirley told me it would take some time to receive the prints because Michael had to approve every shot. 'But we desperately need them to show at the Countdown Awards,' I begged. Shirley didn't let me down. She was a top operator, later leaving CBS to look after publicity and promotion for Julio Iglesias. We became great friends, and she is now the publicist for Julio's son, Enrique.

Incidentally, Michael at this stage was being co-managed by Freddie DeMann, who would later manage Madonna.

In 1984, The Jacksons, with Michael, released the *Victory* album, featuring a duet with Mick Jagger, 'State of Shock'—a song Michael had planned to do with Freddie Mercury. Michael wasn't keen to do The Jacksons' tour, but was reportedly persuaded by his mother, Katherine; some of the Jackson brothers were doing it tough and the tour would generate millions of dollars. I flew to the States to see the concert in Los Angeles with Shirley Brooks. It was an amazing spectacle. And I guess this set the benchmark for Michael—his concerts had to be bigger and better than anything else. Strangely, the *Victory* tour was promoted by boxing entrepreneur Don King.

My next rendezvous with The Jacksons was when we flew to Washington for another concert and interviews with Jermaine and Randy and Don King. We also went with Jermaine and Randy to a hospital, where they met and entertained young patients. I have to admit I did get into a fit of giggles when I interviewed Don King, because his hair looked so bizarre, standing straight up, almost as if defying gravity—so much so that he reminded me of someone who had just had an electric shock after having a toaster shoved up his bum. Totally weird!

Even though Don insisted it was a happy team, in reality, the tour was full of tension. Michael kept very much to himself and there seemed to be an assortment of different managers running around, trying to look important.

We raced off to do my report for *Countdown*. We didn't have much time because we were flying that afternoon to Pennsylvania to catch up with Bruce Springsteen. One of our locations was outside The White House. So here I was, ready to do my piece, completely frazzled. When the cameraman, my old friend David Etherton, yelled, 'We're rolling!', I said: 'Here we are outside The White House, isn't it fantastic, and look the flag is flying, which means the Queen is in the building—I mean, the President [Ronald Reagan] is in . . . um, er, oh shit, well he's probably a queen, anyhow.'

Talk about getting my locations mixed up! However, luck was on my side as the footage never made it to air. *Countdown* crew member Tony Vuat checked the tapes and rang to see if I wanted the piece to go to air. 'God no,' I said, 'they'll never let us back into America.'

> Travelling with Molly was always an adventure. I remember he was frazzled one day when we were staying at The Plaza Hotel in New York. We were running late for an interview, so we jumped in a cab and handed the driver the address. We drove about 40 feet and then stopped—we had arrived at the address. It was at this point that I realised an adult had to take charge.
>
> **David Etherton, cameraman**

In January 1985, I was staying with Roger Davies in Los Angeles. Roger managed Sherbet in the '70s, trying everything he could to break them in the States (including name changes to Highway and The Sherbs). He also looked after the Ted Mulry Gang. Roger then became one of the biggest and best managers in the world, working with Olivia Newton-John, Joe Cocker, Cher, Sade, Janet Jackson and later Pink. In the mid-'80s, he resurrected Tina Turner's career.

Roger had come a long way since writing Renée Geyer's first review, comparing her to a Greek goddess.

While I was staying with Roger, he received a demo tape from Lionel Richie's manager. It was a song that Lionel had written with Michael Jackson to raise money to fight the famine in Africa, called 'We Are The World'. It was some demo: they'd gone into Kenny Rogers' studio and done an incredible orchestrated instrumental version. The tape had been sent to Roger because they wanted Tina to be part of the recording session—at the A&M Studios on the night of 28 January, straight after the American Music Awards.

I have to admit, I felt very privileged sitting next to Roger's pool, listening to the demo.

Tina wanted to do 'We Are The World', but she didn't want to perform live at the American Music Awards. Instead, she would do a pre-record on the Saturday, two days before. As we drove to the venue, Roger, being the great manager he is, came up with an idea: 'Look, Tina respects you. Can you talk her out of this pre-record and get her to do it live? It will look stupid on the Monday night with the audience just sitting there.'

I swung into action, telling Tina many times: 'Come on, lovey, you don't want to look ridiculous on Monday night.' Finally, she relented. Roger was a happy man, as was the legendary Dick Clark, of *Bandstand* fame, whose production company was presenting the event. The producers also enlisted my help, handing me a photo of Midnight Oil and getting me to point out lead singer Peter Garrett.

'Why do you want to know?' I asked.

'Oh, he's presenting an award.'

I could not believe my ears. Back in Australia, Midnight Oil had refused so many times to do the Countdown Awards, saying they'd never 'sell out' by doing award shows, but here was Peter Garrett, presenting at the American Music Awards.

What a cheek!

Even though we'd had one major victory with Tina, Roger failed to convince her on another project. He wanted her to star in an upcoming Steven Spielberg film. But Tina wasn't interested. 'Look, Roger,' she said, 'he's a children's director. I'm not going to do kids' films.' Of course, Tina was thinking about Spielberg and *E.T.*, but this film was a little different. We couldn't convince Tina, so she never did *The Color Purple* . . . hello Oprah, hello Whoopi, hello Oscar nominations.

But Tina's performance at the American Music Awards was brilliant. And, sitting next to Roger, I had one of the best seats in the house—third row, right in front of the presenters' podium. The look on Peter Garrett's face when he saw me in the audience waving to him (or maybe I was giving him the finger) was something to behold.

After the show, if you had a special pass—and I was lucky enough to have one—you were told to be at A&M Studios within an hour. Believe it or not, Madonna, who was at the awards, had not been invited to be part of 'We Are The World'. I think the industry felt she was a one-hit wonder—how mistaken they were. 'Come on, lovey,' I said to her, 'I'll get you a pass.' But she gracefully declined. (I didn't offer Peter Garrett a pass.)

The scene in the 'green room' at A&M Studios was nothing short of amazing. We were greeted by a sign: 'Please check your egos at the door'. Bruce Springsteen, who had not attended the awards, arrived by himself; Bob Dylan was hanging out with Bette Midler; Huey Lewis, Billy Joel and Kim Carnes were swapping stories; Tina Turner was lying on the couch having a rest; Cyndi Lauper was entertaining everyone; and Stevie Wonder was rapping with Diana Ross. Stevie told the artists that if the song wasn't done in one take, he and Ray Charles would drive everyone home!

Cyndi asked everyone to sign her music sheet. I remember Tina said, 'Oh Cyndi, do I really have to? I'm so tired and you'll probably just lose it tomorrow.' Cyndi was mortified. 'No, I've still got every autograph I've ever got. I've even still got the first one, which was Peter Noone from Herman's Hermits. He signed it "Mrs Lauper, you've got a lovely daughter".' Tina and I burst out laughing.

Quincy Jones was in charge of the recording, and I was honoured to be asked to help sort out the microphones. The stars formed a horseshoe around the mikes and then came forward when it was their time to sing. All except Michael, who stood at the side of the studio with his arms folded, and with a make-up artist touching up his face.

At one point during the recording, they could not work out the source of an irritating noise. Quincy thought it was a technical fault, until someone realised it was Cyndi Lauper's jingling jewellery. As Cyndi removed the offending items, she said to Michael, 'Don't worry, they won't starve, they won't starve!'

Another distinctive memory I have from the session is Bette Midler looking a little sad and depressed, when she's usually loud and bubbly. I think she felt that maybe her career as a recording artist and performer was coming to an end. Little did she know that just around the corner was another hit movie— *Ruthless People*.

I've had many amazing experiences in the studio, but 'We Are The World' is hard to top. It was a night I'll never forget. One of the best.

When we returned to Roger's, there was a party going on. Now, it's not like me to say no to a party, but I was so tired, I just wanted to go to bed. The only problem was Roger's wife, Nanette, a dress designer, had the spare bedroom chock-a-block with clothes, so my bed was the couch in the entertainment area.

Without telling anyone, I slipped into Roger's office and made a bed under the desk, with my headrest being Roger's big dog. Because it was after midnight, it was now 29 January, and as I was falling asleep, I was thinking, 'This is the best birthday I've ever had!'

Mind you, Roger was in no mood for my birthday that day. He and his friends had spent half the night looking for me, even going back to the studio. Finally, when I woke up and explained to Roger and Nanette what had happened, they both laughed and Nanette said, 'Well, Molly, remember the old saying—if you sleep with dogs you wake up with fleas.'

Later that year, I received a very strange call from Channel Seven in Perth. The gentleman on the phone explained that Seven had an annual telethon and this year's special guest would be Michael Jackson. Would I be able to fly to Perth to look after Michael?

At this stage, there were many weird and wonderful stories floating around about Michael Jackson, from talking to animals, to collecting the bones of the Elephant Man . . . in fact, the English tabloids were calling him 'Wacko Jacko'. So I thought this phone call was just a stupid prank.

But after a couple more calls, I agreed to go. I doubted that Michael would be there, but it was all for a good cause, particularly the Princess Margaret Hospital for Children.

When I arrived in Perth, I went to the Entertainment Centre, where Michael was supposed to appear on stage. There was a huge crowd, but no Michael. About 30 minutes later, a limo pulled up and out jumped a little African-American man wearing a hat. I recognised him straight away—it was Bill Bray, Michael's personal bodyguard.

That's when I knew Michael Jackson was in Perth.

The telethon was the next day, but Michael's minders said he'd done his bit by appearing on stage and he was not going to go to the studio. But Janet Holmes à Court, the wife of Channel Seven's owner, Robert Holmes à Court, had other ideas.

Janet and Robert—who was Perth's first billionaire—had an afternoon party at their house. I was there, but there was no sign of Michael. I later discovered he was in the study watching tapes of Sammy Davis Jr performing at previous telethons. Michael was impressed because he loved Sammy.

Janet then asked Michael if he'd like to go out on their boat, which he did—leaving his minders back on shore. Janet suggested that he might like to go to the studio for the telethon. The Sammy Davis Jr trick worked—Michael said yes.

He arrived at Channel Seven with Janet, looking very nervous. He kept squeezing Janet's hand, whispering, 'This is so embarrassing.' Michael finally agreed to come onto the set and sit next to me and the telethon host, Peter Waltham. He also said hello to some of the children. It was a real treat for everyone. Michael then returned to Janet's side, again clutching her hand.

While in Perth, Michael met a group of young Aborigines, recording their didgeridoo playing on a tape recorder. Michael also spent hours at an antique bookshop, buying two nineteenth-century medical books on skin disease.

It was a surreal weekend.

As I flew home, I was still bewildered: why had Michael Jackson, the biggest pop star on the planet, agreed to fly all the way to Perth for a telethon?

Back home in Melbourne, I discovered the real reason—it was a business deal. Unbeknownst to me, Robert Holmes à Court had acquired ATV Music Publishing, which had a catalogue of more than 4000 songs, including 250 Beatles songs. Robert had no real interest in music publishing, so the catalogue was up for sale.

Michael Jackson and Paul McCartney were friends. *Thriller's* first single was a Jackson/McCartney duet, 'The Girl Is Mine'. And when they recorded 'Say Say Say', a duet for Paul's *Pipes of Peace* album, Paul and Linda had spoken with Michael about the importance of music publishing.

Paul and Yoko were keen to buy the Beatles catalogue. But Michael wanted it more. And when Robert Holmes à Court told Michael he'd do the deal if Michael did the telethon, Michael got on the plane. As my friend Michael Gudinski is fond of saying, if you want something badly enough, 'no flight is too long'.

Michael bought the publishing company for $47.5 million.

Another strange quirk in the deal was Robert kept one Beatles song. 'What's your favourite Beatles song?' he asked his daughter, Catherine. '"Penny Lane",' she replied. So Robert kept 'Penny Lane' and gave it to his daughter. What a wonderful gift!

Paul was not so happy. Years later, he told me he tried several times to buy the Beatles catalogue from Michael, but it got to the point where Michael wouldn't even return his calls.

In 1987, while holidaying in Noosa, with Michael Jackson's new album, *Bad*, on the stereo, I received another unexpected call. It was Gerald Stone, the boss of *60 Minutes*, asking if I'd like to be a *60 Minutes* reporter for a week and fly to Tokyo to interview Michael Jackson.

Me, someone who can't string two sentences together, a *60 Minutes* reporter? 'Um, er, um, yeah, that'd be great,' I told Gerald, who was probably already having second thoughts.

This was Michael's first solo tour of Australia, as part of the record-breaking *Bad* tour, but the tickets weren't selling as well as expected because of all the weird 'Wacko Jacko' stories. There was even one crazy rumour that Michael was so afraid of germs, he'd be performing behind a giant perspex screen. To counter these rumours, promoter Kevin Jacobsen, Sony's Denis Handlin and Michael's manager, Frank DiLeo, hatched the *60 Minutes* plan. And that's when I entered the story. Michael knew me from our past meetings, and also knew I was a good friend of Jermaine. And he'd seen my interviews with Madonna and Cyndi Lauper on MTV in America, which had been running *The Meldrum Tapes*.

Michael's publicist, Ginny Buckley, told the press: 'Molly is a good friend of Michael's sister Janet and brother Jermaine. Michael doesn't like talking to the press, but this is a special case because Molly can do it and Michael is about to go to Australia.'

And so, I was turning Japanese—for a week, at least. I went to Tokyo with Sony's Chris Moss plus the Channel Nine film crew, including Jana Wendt's producer, Gareth Harvey. We checked into the hotel where Michael was staying and went to the concert that night. *The Age*'s Peter Wilmoth was also covering the concert.

The show was spectacular. It left me breathless. I could understand why it had received rave reviews around the world. After the concert, Gareth took us out for dinner and the bill was also astonishing—it is very expensive in Japan. The next day was the big one—I was scheduled to do two interviews: one with Michael's producer Quincy Jones, and then, an hour later, with Michael. With Quincy, there were no restrictions, and he was a dream to talk to. Having been a record producer, Quincy is one of my heroes. Unfortunately, the chat with Michael was not as straightforward. Usually, if an artist places any sort of restrictions on an interview, I will say, 'No way'. But when you're the King of Pop and this is a world exclusive . . . well, we had no option.

Panicky publicists and meddling managers have become a problem in our business. I remember doing an interview with Keanu Reeves via satellite. I was told that I could ask him only about his band, Dogstar—who, to that point, had not even released a record. I was not, under any circumstances, to ask about his acting. This was so ridiculous that at the end of the interview I said, 'Thanks very much. I know I'm not to ask you anything about your film career. I guess there's not much to ask because you're not much of an actor.'

This was very out of character for me, but I was angry about such an absurd restriction.

Anyway, back to Tokyo and the interview with Michael Jackson . . . Five minutes before we were due to start filming, Frank DiLeo walked into the room and announced he wanted to sit in on the interview. 'What, you want to be in the room?' I enquired.

'No,' he replied, 'I want to sit next to Michael and be in the interview.'

Our chief cameraman whispered in my ear, 'No fucking way. We'd have to change all the lighting.' But we had no choice. I told Frank, 'Give us another fifteen minutes to re-set the lighting.'

Finally, Michael and the cigar-chomping Frank arrived with their entourage. Frank pulled me aside—there was another problem. He felt that his stool was too low. Frank was a big man, but short, kind of like a grumpier version of Danny DeVito. Frank, incidentally, was also an actor. If you want to see some of his work, he was a gangster in *Goodfellas* and the record company chief, 'Mr Big', in *Wayne's World*.

So we got a higher stool. I had to stifle the giggles because Frank's feet didn't quite reach the ground—he looked like Humpty Dumpty.

Without a doubt, this was one of the weirdest interviews I've ever done. I didn't know whether to look at Michael or Frank. When I posed a question about plastic surgery and whether all the strange stories hurt, Michael was about to comment, when suddenly Frank butted in and said, 'I'll answer that question, if you don't mind.'

'It hurts me, and if it hurts me, I know it hurts Michael,' Frank said. 'I find it very terrible some of the stuff that is written, particularly about plastic surgery. The majority of it—not the majority, *all* of it—is garbage and rubbish.'

This didn't really help to quash the rumours.

During the Japan trip, I saw the good and bad side of the Australian media. Peter Wilmoth's story in *The Age* was very honest. And the radio people that Sony sent to cover the concert loved the show so much they insisted on getting tickets to the second show. But would you believe that when they returned to Australia they did nothing but bag Michael and the concert on air? In 1987, it was uncool to rave about Michael Jackson, and of course they were the cool people . . . *not*.

Now, I know that Michael brought a lot of this on himself by being so introverted, but the media reports made me extremely angry because as an artist, he was a genius. All these crazy stories and negative reviews meant that many people in Australia were deprived of seeing a great performer. The *Bad* tour broke box-office records everywhere in the world, but not in Australia.

After the Michael Jackson shoot, the crew and I were all relieved. We were also starving, so we went to a flash restaurant. When we arrived, both the maître d' and the waiter could speak English. We ordered a mix of meat and fish dishes, but when the fish didn't arrive, the waiter's English seemed to diminish. Things were very fishy, indeed.

Finally, the fish did arrive, but not only was it cold, it looked as if rigor mortis had set in. We complained and suddenly the waiter could speak no English at all. Our crew went looking for another restaurant while I said to Gareth, 'Don't pay the bill until they give us a discount.'

The bill was more than $3000, which was simply outrageous. I called the maître d', who also now couldn't speak English. I snatched Gareth's credit card back and said, 'We're not paying this until you give us a discount.'

He finally agreed to revise the bill. And then I went right off: the 'discount' was just $20! Well, you could say I lost it, because I grabbed the credit card receipt and bill, went up to the maître d', whacked it in his hand and said, 'You can take this bloody bill and shove it up your silly ass.' I then started walking out with the rest of our group, stopping only when I saw one of the cold fish still on the plate. I scooped it up, turned around and said, 'And you can have your bloody fish as well!' It hit him in the head and dropped into the hand holding the bill. It was a very strange sight.

Unfortunately that wasn't the end of it. At the top of the stairs there was a big wooden beer barrel and Chris Moss said, 'Let's roll it down.' I needed little encouragement. As we proceeded to tip it over, Chris said, 'No, we'd better not.' Too late. I kicked the barrel and it started rolling down the steps. It was like thunder . . . boom, boom, boom, the barrel went down the steps. Then there was an almighty explosion. The barrel hit a mirror glass wall and brought it crashing down. Chris and I started running, as fast as we could. In fact, we ran past the rest of the group, and in the distance we could hear police sirens.

When we got back to the hotel, I was absolutely shitting myself, and so was everyone else. As our plane was not leaving until early the next day, we had to stay one more night. I was so scared, I made a bed for myself in the bath, with the curtain pulled shut. The next day, when we left for the airport, I was so worried I took off my cowboy hat and went in disguise. As I boarded the plane, I thought we'd gotten away with it.

Much to my horror, a few weeks later, Gerald Stone received a bill for more than $10,000—the restaurant had traced Gareth's credit card. I'm not sure who ended up paying for it.

On a brighter note, the show's ratings were huge. And I must say it was a buzz being a *60 Minutes* reporter. On the Friday before my story went to air, I flew to Sydney to promote the interview on *The Midday Show with Ray Martin*. After the chat with Ray, I was to go to another studio, sit on a stool and do a piece to camera saying, 'And I'm Ian Meldrum . . .' Ray told me it was one of the hardest things to do and that he and all the *60 Minutes* reporters hated doing it.

I remember saying to Ray, 'I know I um and er, but, surely, I can't muck up, "I'm Ian Meldrum".' He laughed.

Waiting in the wings were two of my dear friends, Jana Wendt and *60 Minutes* producer Gail Jarvis. I wondered why they had such suspicious smiles on their faces as they led me to the slaughter . . .

They called 'Action' and I said, 'And I'm Ian Molly Meldrum.' Then I was told, 'No, Molly, you look too serious, do it again.' Well, I did it again and again and again and again. I smiled, I frowned, I pouted, I was in tears, I was forgetting my name, and in desperation I think I blurted out, 'And I'm Dame Nellie Melba, so there!'

The Tokyo interview also taught me a valuable lesson—be careful what you wish for. I asked Michael, 'If I was the Fairy Godmother and could grant you one wish, what would it be?' Michael told me he wanted world peace and to make the world happy. He also added, 'I have lots of dreams and they usually come true.'

Nine years after the interview, I was cast in the pantomime *Hey Hey It's Cinderella*—as, you guessed it, the Fairy Godmother.

Shortly after the *60 Minutes* special went to air, Michael arrived in Australia. During the tour, a bizarre thing happened to me on a boat cruise.

Sony hosted a lunch for Michael on Sydney Harbour. Now, Sony loves hosting harbour cruises for visiting rock stars and the media—I think I've done hundreds of them. But this event was a little different—there was no media, apart from me, and Michael had asked for the Sony staff to bring their families.

I flew to Sydney with my close friend Heloise Pratt, who was very excited about meeting Michael. After Sony chief Denis Handlin did the platinum record presentations—including a surprise presentation to myself from Michael—I thought we could all relax. But Michael's publicist Ginny Buckley informed me that Michael wanted to have a private chat. She said that in ten minutes she'd walk by and give me the nod. Well, of course, I was talking and I missed the nod. But I then followed Ginny and Michael to the front of the cruiser. I thought we were going upstairs where a few people and their kids were playing, but Michael said, 'No, let's go down these steps.'

Much to my surprise, the steps led to the men's toilets, which comprised two cubicles and a urinal. Michael walked into one of the cubicles, obviously for the privacy, and said, 'Molly, why are the press so horrible to me? I've done nothing to them.' He then burst into tears.

I didn't know what to do. I just stood there, leaning against the door trying to comfort him. At that moment, one of the guests, Ian Duffell, the head of Virgin retail, walked into the toilet. He strode past me, said 'Hi, Molly', and then headed for the urinal, unzipped his pants and pulled out his old fella.

Then he spotted Michael inside the cubicle, crying his heart out. Poor Ian froze, didn't know what to do, and in the end couldn't pee at all. He sort of muttered something to me, put the old fella back in and stumbled up the steps. I was totally flustered by this stage.

We went back upstairs and, much to my horror, everyone was staring at us. 'I've done nothing,' I declared. 'I've done nothing to him!'

It was quite a tour. After the final show, in Brisbane, I presented Michael with a St Kilda football jumper and honorary membership.

Michael's 1987 Australian tour led to a funny encounter in New York several years later. As I was walking through Central Park, a woman smiled at me and said, 'You're Molly, aren't you?'

'That's right,' I replied, having no idea who the woman was.

'I met you in Melbourne at the Michael Jackson concert.'

'Oh yes, of course.' We then had a pleasant chat about how great the concert was.

'So are you still at Sony?' I asked.

The woman looked at me, perplexed. 'I don't work at Sony,' she explained. 'I'm Meryl Streep.'

Oh my God. This was Meryl Streep, one of the greatest actresses of all time. We had sat together at Michael's Melbourne show. Meryl had been in Australia, starring as Lindy Chamberlain in the movie *Evil Angels*. A dingo took her baby, but who knows what took my brain.

The next time I caught up with Michael was when I was flown to New York for an exclusive preview of eight of the tracks on his *Dangerous* album. The plan was to go to the studio to listen to the tracks, and then head to the office of Sandy Gallin, Michael's new manager, to tell him what I thought.

At the studio, the engineer sat me in front of the control desk, gave me a track listing and then pressed play. Looking out through the glass, I could see some people sitting in another part of the studio; one of them was Michael Jackson, which was a little unsettling. Now, I'm one of those people who likes to hear a track again and again, but this time there was no chance of that—it was one listen, and one listen only. Then I was ushered into a limo and taken to Sandy's office. 'What do you think?' he asked. 'It sounds fantastic,' I said. As I pulled out the track listing, an alarmed look spread on Sandy's face. 'Where on earth did you get that from?' He then grabbed it from me as he said it was totally confidential.

A few weeks later, I found myself in Michael Jackson's company when he attended his sister Janet's *Rhythm Nation* concert in Los Angeles. Roger Davies was managing Janet and I recall the hive of activity in his office because Michael kept ringing, wanting more tickets. In fact, I'm sure Roger's assistant, Lindsay Scott, felt more like a booking agent than a manager. As someone in the office remarked, 'You could almost fill a whole stadium with Michael's free list.'

Michael arrived at the concert with his entourage, including Arnold Schwarzenegger. When I was introduced to Arnie, I remember thinking, 'Gee, I thought he was a lot bigger than that.' But, nevertheless, he was a delightful person.

During the show, Michael would smile, clap his hands very gently and literally give the wave of approval. I got the feeling this was very unnerving for Janet. Halfway through the concert, I had to excuse myself, saying I wanted to check out other parts of the stadium, to get an overview of the whole show. In actual fact, I snuck into Roger's production office to ring Melbourne to check the footy scores. Janet was a winner that night, but—even more satisfying for me—St Kilda won as well.

In November 1991, I was asked by the Nine Network to put together a half-hour special on Michael because we had the Australian premiere of his eleven-minute new video, 'Black Or White'. Directed by John Landis, this was an epic, like 'Thriller', and it co-starred Macaulay Culkin and George Wendt. The video also showed off a striking new visual effect called morphing, with a black panther morphing into Michael.

The special got huge ratings and the public loved it. Michael was back on top again.

For the closing segment, I had to sit holding an actual black panther on a leash. I have never been more petrified in my life—especially when the trainer said he'd run out of meat to keep it happy. At one stage, the beautiful but fearsome animal leapt onto the couch, while I leapt over it. I immediately had to go to the loo to compose myself (and do a little cleaning up).

During that closing link, I tried to explain what I thought were the hidden messages in the clip's final four minutes:

I said the panther coming out of a cage and turning into Michael signified Michael being encaged in his own persona.

The smashing of the beer bottle on the street was his comment on drink driving.

The wrecking of the family car represented Michael's anger at the traditional family falling to pieces.

The trash can being thrown through the window signified what he thought of the press and the trash they'd written about him.

I said his raunchy dance moves were a direct stab at Madonna, who'd had a go at him for being too tame.

The Royal Arms Hotel dance sequence, which shows him stripping away his clothes as he's looking up at the neon sign crashing down, was Michael having a go at sister La Toya, because he was angry with her for posing nude for *Playboy* and for her biography, which dragged the Jackson name into the gutter.

How did this relate to La Toya? Well, would you believe I explained that you could also find the name 'La Toya' in 'Royal Arms Hotel'?

Needless to say, the press, especially talk radio, had a field day with me the next morning. Fortunately, I was in New York interviewing Mariah Carey, so I didn't have to answer their questions. I hardly wanted to tell them that I had an equally vivid imagination in my teens when my parents sent me to a psychologist and I would come up with the most fascinating explanations for what the ink blots were.

Without doubt, the biggest controversy was Michael's dance sequence where he touches his crotch. A lot of fans around the world were appalled, but it eventually became part of his image. I would even berate my adopted son, Morgan, for doing the same thing, and he would say, 'But it's the Michael Jackson dance!' I had no comeback to that.

During the *Dangerous* period, we did a series of Michael Jackson specials for Nine. One was for 'Remember The Time', which was an amazing video starring Eddie Murphy and David Bowie's wife, Iman. New Kids On The Block were touring Australia at the time, and they asked if they could come to my house to see the video. It was strange to see them turn from pop stars into fans. They absolutely loved the video's Egyptian theme, and they also loved my Egyptian-inspired house.

Again, the special notched huge ratings.

In 1992, Michael launched his *Dangerous* tour in Munich, and I flew to Germany with Richard Wilkins, Sony's Steve Millard and a film crew. It was absolute mayhem in the press area prior to the show. The print media were shunted to one part of the stadium, while the TV and radio people were herded into what was almost a barbed wire compound at the back of the stage.

With my film crew, I decided to go down into the pit area to film the support act, Kris Kross, a young duo from Atlanta who had a hit at the time called 'Jump', which sampled The Jackson 5's 'I Want You Back'.

After a brief interval, Michael's show started and I thought, 'Okay, let's go back to the pit area.' So the three of us started filming Michael's first number. After about a minute, bouncers came from everywhere and escorted us back towards the barbed wire area. Fortunately, the head security guy was distracted by someone else, and instead of returning to the press compound, we went into the audience. I guess you could say it was very naughty of me, but I told the crew to resume filming, and we actually filmed the entire concert. But, no, I didn't bootleg it. Like a gentleman should, I handed the tapes over to Sony.

After the concert, Michael's management informed me that I could say hello to Michael, without the crew, and we could have a photograph taken. With Steve Millard, I was escorted into the bowels of Munich Stadium, where I was finally ushered into a room that had been made to look like a photographic studio. I stood back, but was immediately told, 'Go and say hello to Michael.'

He whispered, 'Hi Molly, how's Australia?' I can't even remember what I said because I was a little stunned by the whole proceedings. He put his arm around me, and the photographer started snapping away. I laugh whenever I see those photos because I have a very serious look on my face. Just before the photographer snapped the pictures, I looked down at Michael's hands and was amazed to see how white they were. In fact, in the photo I look darker than Michael.

In 1993, I was scheduled to do another interview with Michael in Singapore during his *Dangerous* world tour. Michael was still the biggest artist in the world, and after the Asian leg, he was to return to Australia. A couple of days before leaving for Singapore, I was told we were going to Bangkok instead. I have to admit I was rather reluctant to go to Bangkok; I'd heard all the drug stories and just seen the mini-series *Bangkok Hilton*, which was a bit scary. But as usual with Michael, if you want the interview, you do what you're told.

We arrived in Bangkok around midnight on Sunday night, joining promoters Kevin Jacobsen and Michael Chugg, broadcaster Trevor Smith and his wife Jan, and photographer Serge Thomann for a late supper. After a couple of drinks, we all retired for the night because we knew we had a big day in front of us. Monday lunchtime, Michael would be holding probably the biggest press conference in the world at the famed Oriental Hotel. I have to admit I have never seen so many press people, video cameras and microphones packed into one room. It was very successful and Michael presented the Mayor of Bangkok with a cheque to help children in Thailand. He looked better than he had in years. He even looked happy.

That night, Kevin, Chuggi, Serge, Trevor and myself all went to dinner and on to various clubs. I was also getting myself prepared for the interview on the Tuesday afternoon and the first concert that night at Bangkok Stadium. At 5 a.m. on Tuesday morning the phone rang in my hotel room. It was a producer from Channel Nine's *A Current Affair*. The guy said, 'I believe you'll be filing a story for us at 1 p.m. today.'

I was a little confused. 'No, um, er, hold on, I'm here for *Hey Hey* and a special, not for *A Current Affair*.' The producer's reply floored me: 'Molly, I don't think *Hey Hey* will be interested in a story on child abuse allegations.'

He explained that news had just broken that the Los Angeles Police Department had raided Michael's Neverland Ranch, investigating claims made by Dr Evan Chandler that his thirteen-year-old son Jordan had been sexually abused by Michael Jackson. I held the phone in disbelief and mumbled, 'Um, I'm going to have to ring you back.' I went to the bathroom and threw cold water all over my face, thinking that maybe this was just a bad dream. I then picked up the phone and rang Kevin Jacobsen's room.

Kevin, who is a great Aussie bloke, answered the phone and said, 'Molly, what time is it?' When I said, 'It's ten past five,' he thought I was just getting in from the night before. 'Look, Kevin, this is urgent. I think I'd better come around to your room.'

I sat at the end of Kevin's bed and tried to explain the story. Kevin, in his naive way, looked at me and said, 'But these sort of things happen here, Molly.'

'No, not here, Kevin, it's in America, for God's sake.'

Needless to say, from that moment on there was no more sleep. As the day progressed, it became more frantic. For the press, it was a feeding frenzy. All interviews were cancelled, but it was announced that the show would go on that night. I went to the concert and I've got to say it's one of the strangest and saddest concerts I've ever witnessed. I was so pleased to get on the plane the next day—admittedly minus the interview—and fly home. Sadly, Michael Jackson's world had become a circus.

The second concert was cancelled, due to Michael collapsing from dehydration. The next day, Coca-Cola pulled off an amazing advertising stunt. Because Michael was sponsored by Pepsi, Coke took out full-page ads in the Bangkok dailies, saying, 'Dehydrated? . . . There's always Coke.' It was a telling shot in the cola wars.

Soon after, Michael cancelled his Australian tour— devastating his fans who had camped out to buy tickets. I felt Michael had let his fans down, so I wrote him an open letter, which was published in *TV Week*:

There are three adages I would like to refer to because they all apply to you.

They are: there's no business like show business; the show must go on; and when the going gets tough, the tough get going.

Firstly, there is no greater show than a Michael Jackson show, and your fans were understandably thrilled at the thought of seeing you perform. Now, due to circumstances beyond your control, you have had to cancel. But the reasons you have given will not, and should not be, accepted by your Australian fans.

Saying that logistically it is now not possible is rubbish. Either you were never going to come in the first place, or the promoters here had not done their homework overseas, which I know is not the case.

The last adage is really self-explanatory. No one can ever understand what your life has been like, or what it means to be the biggest superstar in the world. You are a unique performer. But Michael, as much as you can be vulnerable, you have to be tough as well and show some of the strength your Australian fans have shown in sleeping out to get tickets, then having the sales postponed, sleeping out again, and so on. You have left many of them feeling betrayed and very empty.

To finish, I can't believe in some ways that I am writing this column, because in all my life as a writer and commentator I have never criticised you before. Now I think there are a lot of questions that need to be asked.

Michael did return to Australia in 1996 for the HIStory Tour, jointly promoted by Paul Dainty and Kevin Jacobsen. By this stage he was back on top. Prior to his visit, I flew to California to do a special on Michael's Neverland Ranch. Even though Michael was not present, we got lots of great footage.

When the tour started, there was a feeling that I might get another face-to-face interview with Michael, but nothing had been confirmed. Nevertheless, Channel Nine scheduled a one-hour special, to be produced by Craig Campbell. The first show was at the SCG and I had to do some pieces-to-camera at the stadium, so I flew to Sydney to meet with Craig. He was staying at the same hotel as the Jackson crew, the Sheraton on the Park. When I arrived, I went straight to the Sheraton to meet Craig, who said, 'Look, we have to go out to the stadium now, so leave your bags here and pick them up after the concert.'

Our filming went off without a hitch and we arrived back at the Sheraton for drinks with Paul and Donna Dainty and some of the tour entourage. When we got out of our car at the bottom of the Sheraton steps, we were greeted by a huge press contingent. Everyone was taking photos and yelling, 'Molly, are you going to the wedding?'

'What wedding?'

'Michael Jackson's wedding.'

I laughed. I thought the press had completely gone mad.

As we proceeded to Paul Dainty's drinks, we chuckled about the madness that surrounded Michael. He had to put up with some wild stories—now we had a wedding.

As the night wore on, I decided to stay at the Sheraton. About 1 a.m., I decided to call it a night and I went to get my bag from Craig's room. Coincidentally, I walked to the elevators with Paul, bade him goodnight and then went to bed.

The next morning, 15 November, I got up early to catch a plane back to Melbourne. After checking out and heading down the hotel steps, looking for a taxi, I could not believe that the press were still hanging around. They were all yelling out things about Michael getting married, and, as we were driving off, I was sure I heard someone say, 'But you were the best man . . .'

At the airport, it was even more bizarre as people came up to me and asked what the wedding had been like. I seriously thought the whole city had gone nuts.

When I arrived in Melbourne, the story had developed. They were now saying that Michael had married Debbie Rowe, a nurse at his plastic surgeon's office, and that she was also pregnant to him.

My phone was running hot. The first major call I got was from CNN wanting to know details about the wedding. Then *Time* magazine was on the line. I was getting worried—was I having a breakdown? Maybe I'd had one too many and I just couldn't remember anything. It had happened before.

I realised it was real when I saw Richard Wilkins discussing the wedding on the *Today* show. But I was absolutely certain that I wasn't present, and that I was definitely *not* the best man!

It was like a bizarre flashback to Elton's wedding more than a decade before.

What was even more confusing was that when I switched on the telly, there was a news story on Michael with vision of his new bride—except it was Di Rolle, Paul Dainty's publicist.

Molly thought it was a great joke, telling everyone, 'God knows, we've been trying to marry her off for years. Thank God she's chosen someone like Michael.' I was on CNN. At the time, my mum was recovering from heart surgery. She saw the report and said, 'Oh my God, Di's run off and married Michael Jackson!'

Di Rolle, publicist

As the press kept insisting I was there, I finally gave in. 'All right, I was there, but I was the bridesmaid and I was furious that I wasn't given the role of flower girl.' I mean, what could you say?

Craig Campbell then rang and said, 'Look, don't say anything to the press. In fact, avoid them at all costs because this will only help the special on Saturday night.' This presented another problem—I was having a big party at my house that night to thank the media for their help in Peter Andre's recording success on the Melodian label! By Friday afternoon, I didn't know if I was Arthur or Martha. The world had indeed gone mad.

> A few days after the wedding, Michael made an appearance on the steps of the Opera House. Thousands of people were there and his fly was undone. I said, 'Oh Michael, your fly's undone.' He smiled and said, 'Only my wife could tell me that.' He was shy but he had a lovely sense of humour.
>
> **Di Rolle**

Prior to the supposed wedding, I had been asked by Sydney's *Daily Telegraph* to write a story about Michael Jackson. I wrote a sensitive article about how hard it was to be Michael, how no one else could understand, apart from maybe Prince Charles and his children. He'd never had a childhood, never enjoyed his teenage years, and had known nothing else but being in the public spotlight. 'Michael Jackson is strange,' I wrote, 'because he has never known a normal life. The world's greatest entertainer has been a superstar from early childhood and superstardom is a hell of a thing to handle.' The article ran in Saturday's edition.

Michael was a strange mix of man and child. I thought he was quite a sexy man. But other times he'd be in his hotel room, shaking a bottle of Pepsi and watching it splurt everywhere, saying, 'Oooh, look at that', like an eleven-year-old. Then his manager would tell him off: 'Someone has to clean that up, Michael.' And like an eleven-year-old, he'd say, 'Oooh, I'm sorry.'

Di Rolle

At 5.45 p.m. on Saturday, less than three hours before the one-hour special was to go to air, we received a call at Channel Nine, telling us that Michael had seen the *Daily Telegraph* article. He liked it so much that he wanted to do a live interview with me during the special.

This sent everyone into a frenzy, especially Craig Campbell, because he was still editing parts of the special. It was truly a world exclusive and we promoted it as such during the Channel Nine News and *Hey Hey It's Saturday*. After I'd finished my Melodrama segment on *Hey Hey*, I went to Studio 2 at Channel Nine to begin rehearsing the links and prepare for the interview.

At 8.05 p.m., they were having problems getting pictures from Sydney because as it turned out, the cameras of the crew travelling with Michael weren't compatible with Australian TV. So Channel Nine in Sydney had to race around and get their own cameras.

At 8.15 p.m., pictures came in from backstage at the SCG and we saw people gathering, including Richard Wilkins and his family, for a meet-and-greet with Michael. Things were going according to plan.

At 8.24 p.m., Michael appeared and I breathed a sigh of relief.

At 8.27 p.m., the Sydney feed lost power. A fuse had blown. This sent everyone into a panic at Channel Nine in Melbourne, and Archie, our floor manager, had to race around to Studio 9 where *Hey Hey* was being beamed live across the country. The plea was put to producer Pam Barnes and Daryl Somers: 'Can you please extend the show by another five minutes?' Being the professionals they are, Daryl and Pam somehow stretched it.

Meanwhile, mayhem was happening up and down the lines from Melbourne to Sydney. In the end, we were told that Michael would have to leave because they could not find an electrician, and he had to be on stage on time because of Sydney's noise curfew.

Back in Studio 2, I was sitting on a stool, trying to whip up a new intro with Craig Campbell. Then, much to my horror, I heard Archie say, 'Molly, ten seconds to go.' I said, 'What do I say?' and he said, 'Say anything!'

I know I've had many of them, but I think this was my worst TV nightmare.

Thankfully, Richard Wilkins hung around at the SCG and when we finally got power back he helped me get through the special, which eventually received a high rating. I could understand how some viewers thought the interview promotion was a hoax to promote the special.

It was the world exclusive that wasn't—all because of a $2 fuse.

By this stage, I was so over the Michael Jackson tour. But Michael felt so bad, he agreed to do an interview in Brisbane on the following Tuesday. As usual, I had to stick to the scripted questions, but this time Michael, and not his manager, answered the question about how he coped with all the crazy stories.

'It's very sad,' Michael said. 'I just want the fans to know and understand it's not the truth—99.9 per cent of it is not the truth . . . it's tabloid junk, they make it up for greed and money. Please don't listen to it, it's trash.'

When I asked, 'Does Michael Jackson ever relax?', he said he was a workaholic. 'I don't relax, really, I don't sleep a lot. My mind never stops, I'm always creating.' But he added that he loved 'a good water-balloon fight'.

I could certainly relate to the lack of sleep, especially during the past week, and that linked nicely to my last question, when I thought I'd be a little naughty—I strayed from the script.

'Now, there's one more question I have got to ask you . . .'

I could feel Michael's minders freaking out.

'This is about a personal friend of yours . . .'

I could sense Michael's growing unease.

'I am a Stephen King fanatic. Can I ask you . . . what is Stephen King like?'

Everyone breathed a sigh of relief. Michael had collaborated with Stephen on *Michael Jackson's Ghosts*, a stunning short film. 'Stephen King is a very gentle, sweet, kind man,' Michael said, smiling. 'The profile that we see and the books and his works, he's nothing like that, he's very humble. A lot of people try to judge me the same way. But I'm pretty simple—I love to create. I love to make magic. I love to create the unexpected.'

Michael then kindly signed my copy of Stephen King's *Insomnia*. A fitting end to what had been a sleepless fortnight.

After the Brisbane show, there was a bit of a party back at Denis Handlin's hotel. Denis then drove me back to my hotel. I pretended to be Michael Jackson and I said, 'I'm not riding with you lot' and I jumped in the boot. The poor bellboy got the shock of his life when Denis told him, 'The luggage is in the boot.' He opened it up and out I popped.

A couple of weeks later, Paul Freeman from Sony in Melbourne dropped around to my house. 'I've got your Christmas present,' he grinned, 'but you have to come out the front and get it.' Slightly concerned, I went outside. Freebs opened the boot and out jumped Sony's Melbourne boss Peter

Caswell—dressed as Michael Jackson. It was a fun end to what had been a stressful time with the King of Pop.

As I write this, Michael is, of course, no longer with us. But his music will live on forever.

I was getting set to go to London to see his comeback tour when I heard the news on 25 June, 2009. Even in death, Michael couldn't escape the crazy stories and wild rumours. I was stunned to see a story in the UK press about the former child actor Mark Lester, the star of *Oliver!* I remembered Michael telling me in the '70s how much he loved that movie. Now there was a story quoting Mark Lester: 'I gave Michael my sperm so that he could have kids.'

Michael never got to lead a normal life. He loved going to the movies, but to do so, he had to wear elaborate disguises. 'I have incredible disguises,' he told me in Tokyo. 'I can fool my own mother. I enjoy it, because I can get to see the way life really is sometimes.'

The Jackson family invited me to his funeral in Los Angeles. I was worried it was going to be a media circus, but it was actually a moving, dignified memorial service.

So many memories came flooding back: the fun I had with The Jackson 5 in 1973, the CBS staffer who told me Michael wasn't a priority, the buzz Michael got by being at Studio 54, the dramas in Bangkok, the wedding in Sydney, and, of course, the incredible music.

It struck me that I had done more face-to-face interviews with Michael than anyone else in the world, which is a great honour. Sometimes I think about those first two meetings, in 1973 and 1977, and wonder what happened to that relaxed and normal Michael Jackson.

But he achieved what he told me he wanted to do.

Michael Jackson created magic.

At the end of one trip to Hong Kong, Molly was heading to Bangkok. He said, 'Would you be able to take a bag back to Australia for me?' Reluctantly, I said I would, as long as the bag didn't contain any gay magazines.

Well, the bag contained a heap of bodybuilding magazines, as well as weights and tins of bodybuilding supplements—Molly was working out a lot at the time. I got the bitch from hell on the check-in counter, and the bag was over by about a ton.

'Is this your bag?' she asked. 'Can you please open it?'

I was as astounded as she was. There were so many tins of powder, it looked like I was running an importing business.

'Is this your bag?' she asked again. She kept looking at me. 'Did you buy all these bodybuilding magazines?'

Then she looked at me again. 'It's not working, is it?'

The Hong Kong customs guys were all standing around, laughing at me. I wanted to kill Molly.

Steve Millard, former recording executive

12: POWER AND THE PASSION

1971–1989: The record company people through the years—
Handcuffs, hits and hot tubs—Boz and The War Of The Words—Married
to Michael—Blues over Barnesy—A woman called Michelle Higgins—
Not so Hot For The Orient—In good Hands.

*John Teerds: Many parents have been critical of your method of delivery
on Countdown.*

*Molly: Well, I can only be myself. I get the negative saying, 'You really
can't string a sentence together sometimes', and, on the other hand, I get
parents saying to me, 'We much prefer you to be that way—being yourself
and no bullshit about it—than putting on a supercilious front.' I can only
be me on television. You either like it or lump it. I can't alter that.*
The Age, 1980

When EMI promotions guru Michael Matthews moved to
Melbourne in 1980, his first job was to forge a relationship with
Countdown. He got in his company car and drove to my house
in Alfred Street, Prahran.

It's a tiny street and Michael was driving slowly, checking
the numbers, when he saw a dishevelled guy in his late-twenties
handcuffed to a gate.

I thought to myself, 'I hope that's not the house.' But, of course, it was. I'd heard that Molly was a little weird, but handcuffing someone to the gate?

Michael Matthews, EMI

Michael walked in and greeted me: 'Do you realise there's a guy handcuffed to your gate?'

'Yeah,' I replied, 'he's got a demo tape and he won't leave until I listen to it.'

'What are you going to do?'

'Nothing. He can get stuffed.'

Around 1979–80 I had added a record label and small-scale distribution arm to my record store, Missing Link. We'd never had much luck getting any of the punk/new wave acts I handled on *Countdown*, so I made a suggestion to a guy called Ron Rude—who had already tried being on a hunger strike in the window of the store for a week as a means of promoting his independent album to radio (he got some TV coverage, but the council and police made us stop as the crowd were blocking traffic in narrow Flinders Lane in Melbourne). Anyway, I suggested he chain himself to Meldrum's front fence in Prahran to force his way onto the show.

Ian came around the corner in his car, spotted Ron chained to his fence and sent out word that he wasn't going home until Rude was removed from the premises. Naturally, Ron Rude never got onto *Countdown*.

Keith Glass, Missing Link Records

That Alfred Street house was the centre of the universe when I was a promo person at RCA and then Mushroom in the late-'70s and early-'80s. The door was always open and anyone came in at any time. Some people would have the courtesy of ringing the bell before they went in, but you would never stand on the doorstep waiting for someone to come and get you. I'll never forget my first visit. It went something like this:

'Molly, where are you?'

'I'm in the bedroom, lovey, come in.'

Molly was in bed with his boyfriend, whom everyone called 'Mum'.

'I'll wait outside.'

'No, come in, lovey, show me what you've got.'

'Where shall I sit?'

'On the bed, lovey.'

I handed Molly the new Amii Stewart single. I cannot recall the title. It was the follow-up to her one and only hit, 'Knock On Wood'. Molly passed it to his friend. 'What do you think of this, Mum?'

'Well, she looks quite glamorous, I think you should put this one on.'

I quickly realised that Molly didn't have a conventional office. All the business seemed to be done in the bedroom or in the spa.

Peter Caswell, record company executive

My spa seemed to take on a life of its own. Years later, it would become the subject of many jokes by John Blackman on *Hey Hey*.

He used to love that spa bath. It was a nice, leafy backyard and he would just plonk himself in it. You'd go over to present him with the latest records and he'd be in the spa, saying, 'C'mon, get in.' You'd strip down to your undies and then he'd say, 'Well, what have you got, lovey?'

Peter Caswell

I had to laugh when Merrick and Rosso walked on stage at the 1999 ARIA Awards and said: 'We're here to induct Molly's hot tub into the Hall of Fame . . . it's seen some action.'

I've worked with some great record company people over the years. One of the best was Denis Handlin, who's still going strong as the head of Sony in Australia, New Zealand and Asia.

When Denis became CBS's national promotions manager in 1977, his boss, Mr Smith, gave him a simple instruction: 'Look, son, we've got to get film clips on *Countdown*.'

> I flew to Melbourne to see Molly. I caught a taxi to the ABC, expecting to find Molly at the *Countdown* office, but I was redirected to his Alfred Street house. From his bed, Molly welcomed me to his house.
>
> 'Oh, you're from Brisbane, lovey,' Molly said. 'Well, we do things a little bit differently here.'
>
> **Denis Handlin, Sony**

Denis' first major promo campaign was for Boz Scaggs' *Silk Degrees* album. CBS released a double A-sided single, 'What Can I Say/Lido Shuffle', and they came up with a great publicity slogan: 'Boz Is The Buzz'.

Despite selling more than 500,000 copies of the album, the Boz campaign went horribly wrong. CBS had a party at the Opera House to welcome the American star to the country, but Mr Smith admonished him for being a bad role model to the poorly dressed crowd by wearing casual clothes instead of a suit and tie. He then gave Boz opal cufflinks. Boz was not impressed.

The tour got worse in Melbourne.

The tour publicist, Patti Mostyn, organised a big party for Boz at the Hilton. I turned up and I was not in a good mood. In fact, I was fuming. *Countdown* had done so much to promote the album, and I found it outrageous that Boz was refusing to appear on the show.

> Molly was being vile to me. He was blaming me, and it probably was my fault because I knew that Boz would hate *Countdown*. Boz came over and said to Molly, 'You've been rude to my publicist!' He basically pushed Molly out of

the room and raised his fists. Molly complied and a scuffle followed. Molly was later found sobbing outside the hotel.

Patti Mostyn

After the run-in with Molly, Boz was like, 'Who is this maniac? I'm not talking to any more media.' It was grief from hell.

Denis Handlin

When Boz released his *Middle Man* album in 1980, the cover showed him lying down, eyes closed, with smoke coming out of his mouth. On *Countdown* I cheekily said, 'Now, here's a photo of Boz Scaggs after I knocked him out, and he's still fuming after the argument.'

Patti really ruled the roost in the '70s. We had a run-in during The Beach Boys tour and she banned me from entering the venue—the Myer Music Bowl. All of the bouncers were told not to let me in, so I climbed a tree outside and had a perfect view of the stage. The branch I was sitting on came crashing down and landed inside the fence. I was in, and there was nothing Patti could do about it.

Denis Handlin also did a great job with Boz. We all did. What first impressed me about Denis was his passion and persistence and his love of music. If Denis was promoting an album, it was a case of 'whatever it takes'. He would never give up. An example was the launch of Jeff Wayne's *Musical Version Of The War Of The Worlds* at the Hilton in 1978. Denis had organised a huge sci-fi presentation, with thunder and lightning. I arrived at the function, where I had a disagreement with a journalist, so I decided to leave before the presentation. Denis chased me towards the lift, screaming, 'You can't leave!'

As I pressed the down button, Denis threw himself on the

floor, in front of the lift. I started to run down the fire escape. Denis chased me. I pushed him; he pushed me. Eventually, he calmed me down and I stayed.

Denis' dedication to the project paid off. *The War Of The Worlds* was a massive record in Australia. And Denis has become one of my best friends in the business.

> Molly stayed at my house in Sydney and we had a blinder. He had to get up early the next day to fly back to Melbourne. The only problem was we forgot to tell our housekeeper. Molly walked into the kitchen in his underpants and his hat. She screamed. Molly thought she was going to have a heart attack, so he grabbed her to try to calm her down. Then she thought she was being attacked. It was the scene from hell.
>
> **Denis Handlin**

Another passionate record company person was Mushroom's Michelle Higgins. Michelle had started at Mushroom in 1979. Before that, she was working for Festival Records in Adelaide, who distributed the Mushroom releases.

> Molly had some tremendous arguments with Michelle. Those two were born to fight. If something wasn't going on *Countdown*, she'd say, 'I'm going around there!' Within the hour, I'd get a call from Molly: 'Can you come and get this woman out of my house?!'
>
> **Peter Caswell**

One of our fights is famous at Mushroom Records.

> I rang Ian and said we really need to get Christie Allen on *Countdown* a second time. I knew that if we did, 'Goosebumps' would be a hit single. I was saying, 'We've nearly done it, it's your success, it's our success . . .' But Molly was saying there was no room on the show. He was screaming at me, *'Can't you understand?!'* And I did understand. I knew it was only a 55-minute

show. But I got so angry with him: 'This is really unfair—this is Australian music and you're ignoring it.'

Michelle Higgins, Mushroom promo manager

During that phone conversation, I also thought I heard Michelle call me 'a little poof', which I didn't appreciate. 'Can you hang on,' I said to Michelle, 'there's someone knocking on my door.'

Five minutes later, as Michelle still had the phone to her ear, my Jag pulled up outside Mushroom's Wellington Street office. While I was supposedly answering the door at my Alfred Street house, I was actually driving to the Mushroom office to confront Michelle.

I remember Molly came stomping in. I went to hide in another office. I was getting very nervous. At the same time, the Skyhooks were in Michael [Gudinski's] office, breaking up. Molly was screaming, 'Where is she? How dare she say that to me! Get rid of her, Michael. I'll never deal with her again!' The whole building could hear it. He was so powerful, it was my job. If I couldn't deal with Molly, I didn't have a job and this was my life.

I went home that night thinking it was all over. I got into the office at 7 a.m. the next day and there was a note on my desk from Michael [Gudinski]. I'll never forget it—I've still got it somewhere. It said: 'You'll never lose me for believing.'

Five minutes later the phone rang. 'Is Christie Allen available for *Countdown* this week?' I knew it was Molly. I said, 'I believe so.'

He said, 'Well, check with the staff what time she'll be due. Goodbye.' And that was that.

The fight actually brought us together. He then understood that I was a player and a believer.

Michelle Higgins

Michael Gudinski is my closest friend in the music business. I love him, but we do fight a lot. It's like we're married. In the end, I'll always defend Michael, no matter what, even though at times I've wanted to kill him.

Over the years, it has been like a marriage. We've both supported each other. I probably haven't got the patience that he would like, but if I had enough patience for Molly, I never would get anything else done.

If there's been a third party in our 'marriage', it's probably been Jimmy Barnes. There's always been a very funny relationship between Molly and Jimmy. I think a lot of this had to do with Cold Chisel taking the piss out of the Countdown Awards. I think Jimmy stood for a lot of things Molly didn't like. Together, they were always okay, and I'm sure that Molly respects him as a singer and as an artist. But he was like a jealous wife; he thought I was spending too much time with Jimmy.

Michael Gudinski

Barnesy was inadvertently involved in one of our biggest fights. Mushroom's Denise D'Sylva had organised a party at the Warehouse nightclub in South Yarra for Melodian Records, the label that Michael and I had started together. The Melodian artists were all there, including Roxus, Jo Beth Taylor and No Justice. It was a fun night, but I kept waiting for Michael to arrive for the speeches.

Michael's label boss, Warren Costello, kept saying, 'Come on Molly, we should just get on with it.' But I said, 'No, no, wait for Michael. I'm sure he'll come.'

By 1 a.m., I realised that Michael was going to be a no-show. We tried ringing his house, but no one answered. I had no idea where he was. Then I found out he'd been at a Jimmy Barnes gig. I was livid. Michael was obsessed with Jimmy Barnes. Now, I've got nothing against Jimmy, but how many times can you go see him?

So, I went to a Jimmy Barnes gig? The guy was staying at my house, I was managing him and I went to his gig. There were enough people to handle the Melodian thing, as far as I was concerned. I didn't know I was required to make any speeches.

Michael Gudinski

By 3.30 a.m., my fury had turned into blind rage. I decided to pay Michael a visit. I leapt over his fence, bypassing the security cameras, and rang the doorbell. No one answered, so I just kept my finger pressed on the bell. Finally, Jane Barnes opened the door. 'Move over,' I barked, 'I don't need to talk to you.'

Michael's wife, Sue, then appeared. 'Where is he?' I yelled.

Michael then came roaring down the stairs. 'What the fuck is going on?'

It wasn't time to mince words, so I thought I'd get straight to the point: 'You are a selfish fuckwit!'

'I won't have you in my house doing this!'

Michael then grabbed me and started shaking me. 'Stop it,' Sue said, 'he's enjoying it.'

The only way Michael could shut me up was by shoving my head into the microwave oven. Then he threw me out.

Jimmy slept through the whole thing.

When I appeared on Michael Gudinski's *This Is Your Life*, I said:

Basically, Michael and I have had more dramas than Shakespeare and more laughs than *Seinfeld*. I could go through a lot of the stories—him shoving my head in the microwave oven. But, no, I'm going to be very nice tonight because we really are like Walter Matthau and Jack Lemmon in *Grumpy Old Men*. I love him as a friend, I totally admire him for what he's done in this business. I love you, mate.

Now I can hate you for the next 10 years!

Molly loves a fight. He would get really upset, terribly animated, scream and burst into tears, and he'd aim it all at you. It took a while to realise that it probably wasn't about you, it was about something that had happened the previous night, on the phone to Elton. He'd always come into the office after a major outburst and say in his own way, 'I love you.' And you knew you were going to get a hug or a kiss.

Ted Emery

You never heard the word 'Sorry'—sorry seems to be the hardest word with Molly. But you got an acknowledgement.

Stephen Jones

I went with Molly to Michael Gudinski's office for what was supposed to be an amiable meeting. Ian was very tired; he'd been up for two days. He caused this ridiculous argument with Michael, throwing things and screaming that he hated him and that Michael owed him. As we left, I said, 'Ian, you caused that argument intentionally, didn't you? Tell me the truth.'

And, for once, he was honest. 'Yeah, I did.'

'Why?' I asked.

'Because I'm really fucking tired and I needed a boost. I needed my energy level to go up. And now I feel great.'

Russell Morris, 'The Real Thing'

Michael Solomon Gudinski was born in Melbourne on 22 August, 1952, the youngest of three children to Russian migrants. At the age of seven, he was renting out parking space at his parents' Caulfield home when it was race-day at nearby Caulfield Racecourse, charging two bob a car. He could get eight cars into the yard.

The Gudinski archetypal story is that a schoolteacher once asked him: 'What is ten per cent of $2000?' Young Michael replied, 'Exactly. What *is* ten per cent of $2000?'

At seventeen, three months before his final exams, Michael took a job with a promoter. His dad threw him out of the house, but he has since achieved more than anyone else in the Australian music business.

> Molly and Michael Gudinski almost single-handedly created the Australian music industry in the '70s.
>
> **Alex Smith, Moving Pictures**

Not surprisingly, our relationship is rooted in friction. In 1971, Michael Gudinski and his then business partner, Michael Browning, had a booking agency, Consolidated Rock, but they decided to start a music paper in direct opposition to *Go-Set*, called *Daily Planet*. Gudinski believes that Mushroom Records would have started a couple of years earlier if not for a bad review of Billy Thorpe in *Go-Set*.

> Michael [Browning] was managing Billy Thorpe and the Aztecs and they did a gig in Sydney and got a shocking review in *Go-Set*. Michael was crazed. I wanted to start a [record] label, but Michael came back and said, 'I'm sick of fucking *Go-Set* and their monopoly, we're setting up a magazine!'
>
> **Michael Gudinski**

> I have a slightly different memory. Molly would bag us every week in *Go-Set* for having a monopoly [with the booking agency]. I thought, 'Fuck you, Molly, we'll start our own newspaper and put you out of business.'
>
> **Michael Browning**

Daily Planet was launched with a poster campaign, trumpeting: 'The People Shall Have An Honest Music Paper'.

> Neither one of us knew anything about the newspaper business, it was really just to get up Molly's nose. To that extent, it worked. Molly was very pissed off at us. I think the posters really hurt him. I remember getting very irate phone calls from him.
>
> **Michael Browning**

But it was an expensive point to prove. The *Daily Planet* sent Michael Browning broke. He sold his share in the agency to Ray Evans, went overseas with Billy Thorpe, and later managed AC/DC. And Michael Gudinski finally got to start his record label.

Mushroom's first releases were singles from the bands Madder Lake ('Goodbye Lollipop') and Friends (a cover of Little Richard's 'Lucille') on 8 February, 1973. An ad in *Go-Set* heralded 'a label with a new concept'. Soon after, Mushroom signed Mackenzie Theory and announced they would be releasing albums from Madder Lake and Matt Taylor, as well as a triple live album of Sunbury '73.

By mid-1973, Mushroom, based in Wellington Street, St Kilda, boasted a roster of acts, including Madder Lake, Mackenzie Theory, Chain, Matt Taylor, Sid Rumpo, and Friends. By year's end, Gudinski started to show an interest in the pre-Shirley Strachan version of Skyhooks. I convinced him to see the band, then fronted by Steve Hill, at Michael Browning's Sebastians nightclub in the city. We used to haunt Sebastians, and I just loved the band's songs; they were really unusual.

> Molly will tell you that he discovered Skyhooks . . . that's a good myth. Anyway, he loved them because they were glam and colourful and different.

He blamed me for creating grungy blues. He would snigger, 'You and your muso mates . . . what's happened to entertainment?'

Michael Gudinski

Skyhooks signed to Mushroom Records in April 1974. Their debut album, *Living In The 70's*, was released in October 1974. By March 1975, it had become the biggest-selling album in Australian rock history. But when Skyhooks turned up to record their second album, *Ego Is Not A Dirty Word*, the studio wouldn't let them in—because Michael hadn't paid the bill for the first album!

It was ludicrous running an Australian label back then. If an accountant had come and looked at Mushroom before Skyhooks succeeded, they would have shut it down and said, 'What are you doing? Are you crazy!' Everyone thought that Mushroom was making a fortune, but all we were doing was paying off all the debts that we had before Skyhooks happened. They were fantastic for Mushroom; we would never have got there without them. I appreciate Greg Macainsh's quote that 'Mushroom would have done it with a band, whether it was us or not.' But they were the right band and it was the right time.

Michael Gudinski

The Hooks' hits happened at the same time as *Countdown's* success.

It's the chicken or the egg: did *Countdown* make the hits, or did the hits make *Countdown*? Did Skyhooks make *Countdown*, or did *Countdown* make Skyhooks? It was all serendipitously around the same time.

Stephen Jones, *Countdown* producer

Skyhooks' Greg Macainsh came up with a song that summed up the time—'Party To End All Parties'.

The parties always had an incredible mix of people. One thing you can say about Molly is he's no snob—if you were a two-bob shit-kicker, but Molly liked you, you were there. We'd buy $200 worth of Bodega, at 80 cents a bottle—I still can't look at champagne because of it—and $100 worth of KFC. Molly used to be able to stay up later than all of us. I don't know how he did it because he was never someone to take something to stay up.

One morning, I got up to get the Sunday papers and I found Molly's green Celica wrapped around a pole outside the house. I rushed to his bedroom and said, 'Are you all right?' He replied, 'What do you mean?' He had no memory of the car running into the pole and him leaving it there. It summed up his life at that time.

Michael Gudinski

Cars, Michael and me—it can be a volatile mix.

When Mushroom Records was still in Wellington Street in St Kilda, one of my partners, Philip Jacobsen, had just bought a brand-new car and he was really proud of it. Molly came rushing into the office, and, of course, he'd forgotten to put the handbrake on his car. We heard this huge bang—Molly's car had run straight into Philip's car. He nearly had a stroke.

Michael Gudinski

Michael and I share a passion for the St Kilda football team. Michael even became vice-president of the club. Fortunately, Moorabbin, St Kilda's then home ground, wasn't far from the ABC studios, so I could usually see at least half a game before heading to the *Countdown* taping. One day, the game was close, so I stayed until well into the third quarter. A message came across the PA system: 'Molly Meldrum, could you please leave the ground and head to the ABC, because if you're not there in ten minutes, you're fired.'

Michael Gudinski has always surrounded himself with great

With the King of Pop in 1984, when I presented him with a special Countdown Award for his contribution to the world's music scene. (Molly's collection)

One of the greatest artists of all time. It's an honour being Madonna's friend. (Herb Ritts © 1989 Sire Records)

When I talked to Madonna about Australia, she said, 'Well, I've heard about the surfers.' I smiled and claimed, 'I haven't noticed them.' 'You lie!' Madonna laughed. (Molly's collection)

It was a privilege to spend time with Princess Diana. Her beauty made me nervous and I introduced her as 'Princess Charles'. (Molly's collection)

Egypt is my spiritual home, and it's a big part of my actual home in Melbourne. (Photograph by gregnoakes.com)

Sheikh, rattle and roll! (Photograph by gregnoakes.com)

A man is not a camel—get me another drink! (Molly's collection)

What a talented family! When this photo was taken, Janet Jackson was being managed by Australia's Roger Davies, the best manager in the world. (Molly's collection)

Ricky Martin is one of the nicest guys in showbiz. And I'm still buzzing after seeing Ricky, Kylie, Joel Madden and will.i.am sing 'The Real Thing' on *The Voice* in 2014. (Molly's collection)

My good friend Amanda Pelman signed Kylie Minogue to Mushroom Records. Who knew that Kylie would become one of our greatest pop stars? When Michael Gudinski and I presented Kylie with an Outstanding Achievement Award at the 2002 ARIA Awards, I said: 'When you look at the career of Kylie Minogue, we all know how hard it was in this country at times to be recognised, how the critics slammed into her, and yet she stood tall.' (Molly's collection)

Oils ain't Oils—doing my Peter Garrett impersonation with John Farnham at the final *Countdown*. (Photograph by gregnoakes.com)

He drives me crazy. I drive him nuts. We yell, we scream, we fight ... and I love him. And no one has done more for Australian music than Michael Gudinski. (© Newspix)

Nearly three decades after the end of *Countdown*, I'm still close friends with 'The Countdown Sisters', who rarely missed a show in the '80s. Here I am with Karen and Linda Freedman at a Christmas party at my house. (© The Countdown Sisters)

I was honoured to be the Melbourne Storm's number one male ticket-holder, alongside Julia Gillard, the club's number one female. Julia achieved so much for Australia—history will show she was a great Prime Minister. And she and her partner Tim are lovely, down-to-earth people. (© Newspix)

Some players are true Saints. Lenny Hayes retired in 2014 after 297 courageous games. Lenny laid 1496 tackles in his career—an AFL record. With us is another Saints' champ, Farren Ray. (Molly's collection)

Back on the throne. I'm a Moomba monarch for a second time, in 2010, alongside the beautiful Queen, Kate Ceberano, and my trusty aide-de-camp, Ziggy. (© Bill Strong)

Catching up with The Countdown Sisters, Linda and Karen Freedman, and former *Countdown* executive producer Grant Rule. (© The Countdown Sisters)

The love of my life, Ziggy, meets the bane of my life, Dickie Knee. Ziggy is wearing some Melbourne Storm ribbons in his hair. (© *Hey Hey It's Saturday*)

My dear friend Daryl Somers also appeared on *Countdown*. In 1981, he came on the show to perform his single, 'What's Forever For'. I can't wait to write about my *Hey Hey* years! (© Newspix)

The amazing medical team that put me back together again after my accident in 2011.
When we took this photo, I asked: 'So did I behave myself in here?'
'Well, Molly,' one of the team replied, 'we know you love St Kilda and the Melbourne Storm
… and what happens on the footy trip stays on the footy trip. We're not saying anything.'
'Oh my God,' I thought, 'what did I do?'
Words cannot express my gratitude to these wonderful people. (© Newspix)

I fondly call my maintenance man 'No-Show Joe'. But fortunately, Joe Galjar was there
when I fell from the roof in 2011. Put simply, he saved my life. (© Newspix)

One of my most prized possessions. This is the only item in the world signed by John & Yoko, Paul & Linda, and Julian and Sean Lennon. (© Newspix)

I miss the great Chrissy Amphlett so much. When she died in 2013, I told *Sunrise*: 'She had it all … she was fearless. She just had everything.' (© Newspix)

God bless, Alana Patience. Her last name is apt—she was very patient with me on *Dancing With The Stars*. But sadly, unlike Leif Garrett, I was not made for dancin'. (© The Seven Network—*Dancing With The Stars*)

I was so awestruck when I met Dame Joan Sutherland on a plane, I asked for her autograph. She signed it 'To Ian & Molly'. (Molly's collection)

My dear friend Jan and her son, Morgan, who I adopted in the late-'80s. We are family.
(Molly's collection)

I've never been happier than when I met my grandson, Jason, at the start of 2014. Morgan and his wife, Crystal, are wonderful parents, and I'm a very proud grandfather. (© Newspix)

Ian Alexander Meldrum meets Jason Alexander Scholes. Just call me Grandpa Guru. (© Newspix)

people. Michelle Higgins was the prime mover in getting Paul Kelly and Jo Jo Zep and the Falcons signed to Mushroom.

> I get on these crusades, and once I'm on a crusade, I don't stop until it is done, until I have over-publicised the band so badly I have ruined their career—as did happen with the Uncanny X-Men.
>
> **Michelle Higgins**

One story sums up Michelle's passion. After Mushroom released his *Post* album in 1985, Paul Kelly was out of contract. His manager, Stuart Coupe, told Michelle that Paul planned to leave the label to sign with Regular Records. 'Over my dead body,' Michelle said. She called Mushroom boss Michael Gudinski and demanded, 'What is the fucking situation with Paul Kelly?'

She then went to see Paul Kelly. She burst into tears. 'Paul, you can't leave.'

She locked herself in a room at the Sebel Townhouse and told Michael she wasn't leaving until Paul was re-signed. She stayed for nearly a week, running up a drinks bill of $4000 (with a little help from her buddy, The Saints' Chris Bailey). She called me in a furious state. 'Michael has to do the deal!'

Eventually, Michael rang Michelle and said, 'We're going to do it.' Still, she refused to budge until she saw Paul's signature on the contract. 'Please get out of that damn Sebel,' Michael pleaded.

A few months later, 'Before Too Long'—the first single from Paul's landmark *Gossip* album—was added to radio, and Michelle's faith was rewarded.

Michelle loved Paul Kelly. She also did a lot for the Falcons. Part of her job was ensuring that sax man Wilbur Wilde didn't get too drunk when the band appeared on *Countdown*. And then there were the dying days of Skyhooks . . .

I criticised the band's final album, 1980's *Hot For The Orient* (which had Tony Williams replacing Shirley Strachan on vocals), on *Countdown*. I didn't want to do it, but Michelle forced me. She just wanted me to talk about the album. 'It doesn't matter what you say,' she told me, 'just do it.' So I did. And I was blamed for their demise. And then things turned ugly. I was at Yarrawonga on a golf course when eight guys with golf clubs were ready to lynch me because they said I'd killed Skyhooks. It simply wasn't so.

I just didn't think *Hot For The Orient* measured up to other Australian albums of the time. I said: 'If anyone can prove that *Hot For The Orient* is anywhere as good as albums like [Cold Chisel's] *East* or [Mi-Sex's] *Space Race*, then I'll eat my words.'

The *Hot For The Orient* cover featured a photo of a Japanese geisha girl taken by Hideki Fujii, whom Hooks guitarist Bob Starkie called 'the Japanese Andy Warhol'.

It was such a beautiful cover that I felt that if we could get it on the screen then 10 million Australians would rush out and buy it because the cover was so extraordinary. But I think we all knew in our hearts what was going to happen. We were just trying to stall it [Skyhooks' demise]. Molly bagging the album didn't help.

Michelle Higgins

I had another run-in with Michelle when Neil Finn joined Split Enz. Festival and Mushroom were having a conference in Ballarat and the finale was a Split Enz performance at the Ballarat Town Hall. Unfortunately, it was smack-bang in the middle of winter and Ballarat can be a very cold place. I informed Michelle that I would give the Ballarat gig a miss and see Split Enz when they next performed in Melbourne. But Michelle had other ideas, insisting I go to Ballarat. Her nagging wore me down. 'Okay,' I conceded, 'I'll bloody well go.'

The night started with a Festival Records dinner, which, frankly, was more like a wake at a religious convention. We then proceeded to a very cold Ballarat Town Hall. I guess I was such a fan of Tim Finn that I wasn't quite ready for Neil to take such a leading role in the vocal department. I just didn't enjoy the performance—more fool me because Neil became a major part of the band.

I went on *Countdown* that weekend and bagged the gig.

To say the shit hit the fan is an understatement. Michelle was fuming. And the normally reserved Neil Finn threatened to knock my block off a few nights later at the Muso's Club. It was a difficult time.

Of course, when you are rarely critical, any negative comment—as in the case of *Hot For The Orient* and Split Enz—is usually blown out of proportion.

> People used to always say to me, 'But Molly likes *everything*, he has no credibility.' I would explain to them that he has only X amount of space and he'd rather be positive instead of negative. Why do a shitty review when you can use that space to talk about something you *do* like? It's all about utilising the space.
>
> **Michael Matthews, EMI**

Michael Matthews is also one of the great music people, and I'm pleased that he's still working in the industry, even though we've had our battles over the years.

> I remember a fight after the *Xanadu* Dance Competition. Molly asked me what I thought of it and I told him I thought it was dreadful. He ended up poking his finger into my chest, saying, 'How fucking dare you!' I hate being touched, so I pushed him over. It was pretty nasty stuff. But the thing I love about Molly is he never holds a grudge. Two weeks later, everything was fine.
>
> **Michael Matthews, EMI**

Michael was instrumental in the success of bands such as Australian Crawl and Savage Garden, while Peter Caswell introduced me to INXS.

> INXS were on the Deluxe label, which was distributed by RCA. From the Deluxe label, we were pushing The Numbers and The Dugites as well. In many ways, INXS were the least likely to succeed. I remember they were staying at Macy's in South Yarra. Six of them in the one room. I asked them if they wanted to go get something to eat. They said, 'Yeah, that'd be great, but would you mind paying because we've got no money.'
>
> **Peter Caswell**

Cas came to my house to play the video for INXS's second single, 'Just Keep Walking'.

> More than anything, Molly was taken by Michael, the star potential he had. Though I knew that nobody would be there, I took Molly to see the band play at Macy's. Molly was riveted by Michael. I introduced him to the band and it was a big thrill for them to meet Molly. And then he put them on *Countdown*.
>
> **Peter Caswell**

After INXS's first *Countdown* rehearsal, producer Robbie Weekes went to Cas and said: 'You've got to get these boys going a bit. We need lots of colour and movement, like Devo.' So, like a footy coach, Cas gave the band a pep talk: 'You guys have got to lift. You're not animated enough. When you were on stage at Macy's you were full of energy.' Then the show started. And INXS were jumping all over the place! It was nothing like the rehearsal. Cameras were going everywhere.

With about ten record companies all saying, 'Play this video/ Interview this act/Come to this function/See this gig', sometimes the pressure became ridiculous.

I was there during the *Countdown* days when Molly would be in the toilet having a shit and people would be shoving cassettes under the door for him to listen to. Other people would go screaming mad, but he'd handle it. He'd flush the toilet, come out with the tape and put it on.

Jim Keays, The Masters Apprentices

The record company visits were more fun than any structured industry function. The mid-morning meetings frequently turned into lunchtime, incorporating bands, managers, neighbours, sports people and journalists.

Molly lectured me one day that it was getting completely out of hand and that he had no privacy. He decided the business was going to be done on a more formal basis. He insisted that each record company have a set appointment and write out a list of what acts we had available.

I decided to wind him up by giving him a real list—a four-foot by six-foot advertising sign listing Mushroom's new videos parked on a trailer outside his house. Molly was really good about it and appreciated the humour, even posing for a photo for the paper.

But the next day he got slightly pissed off when I couldn't find a car with a tow bar to move the sign. He blasted me, saying it had gone beyond a joke. He claimed it drew attention to where he lived—not that everyone in Melbourne didn't already know.

Rodney Woods, former record company executive

So what makes a great record company person? Someone who really believes, who can appreciate releases that aren't on

271

their label, is willing to go out and see bands, and can survive frustration and disappointment. I couldn't handle the job. To be continually knocked back by radio, without even getting much of a hearing, would be devastating. But somehow they manage to pick themselves up and keep going.

I have known some excellent record company people over the years. Two of the great ones have been Peter 'Iris' Ikin and Steve Millard. My travel travails with Iris and Steve are documented elsewhere in this book.

Cas went on to work for my beloved Melbourne Storm, while Michelle Higgins became an organic gardener two hours north of New York. Another fantastic promo person was Steve Hands, who worked for Warner Music. Steve—who looked like Robert Plant—helped to break the big 'West Coast' acts in Australia, including the Eagles, Jackson Browne and Fleetwood Mac. The Eagles were such a fan of Steve's work, they tried to convince him to relocate to the States to work for the band.

Steve was the first promo person to come to my house and say: 'Sit down, Molly, and shut up, you are going to listen to these records!' He pioneered the process that still exists today. Probably one of the most outrageous things Steve did was when he invited me to go fishing. He loved that sport with a passion. I thought, 'Oh, how nice, this will be lovely and relaxing.' We left the Mordialloc Marina in Steve's boat and puttered out into Port Phillip Bay.

On this particular day, there were warnings of late storms, and I must say I became a little nervous when we could no longer see the coastline. Steve pulled out a couple of beers and a scotch and coke for me and we waited for a bite. But the bite was not quite what I expected, because Steve also pulled out a Sony Walkman. He handed me the earphones and thrust a list in my hand. 'Now,' he ordered, 'listen to this product.'

'Come on,' I begged, 'I'm not going to do this.' But Steve was persistent—he even had the album covers in the bait box.

As the ominous black clouds started to roll in and with talk of me becoming shark bait, I had no choice but to listen to the new releases from Richard Clapton, Billy Field and Swanee. I was caught hook, line and sinker.

Steve was brilliant with local artists, and was instrumental in breaking Cold Chisel. Sadly, Steve died of cancer in 1999. The music industry misses his uniqueness, his power and his passion.

Our lighting guy at one of our gigs at Billboard in Melbourne came up to me afterwards and told me that Molly had tapped him on the shoulder and told him to turn the bass up. Remember, he's the lighting guy! Not too sure what to do, he pushed one of the sliders up, and this orange light came on. He looked over to Molly, who gave him the big thumbs up.

Darren Danielson, Roxus

13: PLEASURE AND PAIN

1978–1997: Run-ins with three of our biggest and best: Chisel, Oils and INXS—No-shows and low blows—My turn to cry—Fight, baby, fight—Reconciling with Mr Nice.

It's an unusual characteristic—Molly likes to fight with his friends. I guess you have to take it as a compliment if you have a big fight with Molly. People really close to him always cop a serve.
Michael Gudinski

Cold Chisel were booked to make their first appearance on *Countdown* on 10 June, 1978. They rehearsed 'Khe Sanh' at Studio 31, and Michael Shrimpton told the band they had to change the lyrics.

Two parts had caused controversy: 'And their legs were often open/But their minds were always closed' and 'the growing need for speed and Novocaine'.

The band discussed the situation and decided they would leave. As they walked out the door, Michael said, 'You've no idea how difficult you've made things for us. But, by God, I admire you for your principles and I wish you every success.'

Countdown could make or break you, but the song was too important to change.

Jimmy Barnes

Even though it is viewed as an unofficial national anthem, 'Khe Sanh' didn't crack the Top 40 until 2011—33 years after it was released.

> We wanted to be an albums band, but the radio stations talked us into releasing 'Khe Sanh' as a single. And then it was banned. But within three years, Cold Chisel had become the biggest band in the country.
>
> **Jimmy Barnes**

Chisel were competing with Australian Crawl and Split Enz at the 1981 Countdown Rock Awards, and they dominated, winning seven awards—Most Outstanding Achievement in Australian Rock Music, Most Popular Australian Group, Best Australian Album (*East*), Most Popular Australian Record (*East*), Best Songwriter, Best Producer (Mark Opitz) and Best Record Cover.

But much to my annoyance, the band failed to collect any of the awards. They did, however, close the show with a live performance of the album track 'My Turn To Cry', changing the lyrics to attack the Awards' co-presenter, *TV Week* magazine: 'I never saw you at the Largs Pier Hotel/I never saw you in Fitzroy Street,' Barnesy spat. 'And now you're tryin' to use my face to sell *TV Week*.'

Chisel had behaved immaculately during rehearsal. But when it came to showtime, they switched to the alternative version of 'My Turn To Cry'. They'd also gone out and bought cheap Japanese copies of all their instruments, so they didn't mind smashing them.

As Barnesy grabbed his bottle of vodka and stormed off stage, Mossy tried to smash his guitar. That was the most amusing thing for me, Mossy trying to smash his guitar and it just wouldn't break.

Hendrix and Pete Townshend made it look so easy, but I just couldn't break it. The strings were cutting into my hands. I don't know what the timber was, it weighed a tonne and it just wouldn't break.

Ian Moss

Cold Chisel's record producer, Mark Opitz, was representing the band in the ABC's outside broadcast truck. Just before the performance, he warned the crew, 'Guys, in one minute's time, everything's gonna change. Just stay with me, please.' When the stage started getting trashed, the squawk box was going with Robbie Weekes yelling, 'Bring it down, we've gotta bring it down!'

'Stay with me, guys,' Mark responded, 'We can't hear that, can we?'

Eventually, the screen came crashing down. The heavy wooden base hit Mossy on the shoulder. The final scene showed his guitar flying through the screen, as I returned to the stage, a little stunned, and mumbled: 'I told you they were a great band live.'

By that time, Mark Opitz had leapt out of the truck, and the band had exited a side door. They jumped into a couple of waiting vans and headed to their own private party.

We laughed our heads off all night.

Mark Opitz, record producer

It was certainly one of my most memorable moments during the *Countdown* era. I was standing side of stage at the Capitol Theatre, not quite believing what was going on. In fact, I had to turn around to watch the television monitor, just to make sure it really was happening.

The person who probably had the most fun was Robbie Weekes, who was directing the show. Robbie was a unique director who never really blocked his shots during rehearsal; he worked totally on instinct. Once the Chisels broke from their rehearsed routine, Robbie was in his element. He loved it.

It was reported that I was fuming following the band's performance, which is not true. I ended up at the Chisel party. Admittedly, I'd spent an hour before at the *TV Week* party, where the magazine's executives were not so happy. But it certainly made great television. It was a watercooler moment before offices even had watercoolers.

But, to be honest, the band's protest seemed rather silly to me. Through my column in *TV Week*, as well as other pages in the magazine, we had literally raved about the band since they started. It wasn't our fault that Jimmy and the boys felt that *TV Week* was lightweight. The magazine was selling more than 800,000 copies at that stage, whereas the highest-selling music magazine was lucky to sell 30,000 per week.

We were a well-balanced band—we had a chip on both shoulders! We had this aversion to *Countdown*. As much as it did really great things for Australian music, they tended to dictate to the bands and try to remove creative control.

Bands like Chisel and the Oils didn't like miming, we wanted to perform live. *Countdown* didn't like that because it was then out of their control. And the other thing was *TV Week* did nothing for any band until you had the number one album and then suddenly you were the pin-up boys.

We knew we were going to win a lot of awards and Cold Chisel wasn't really an awards band. We said we'd only go on if we could close the show—we didn't want to trash the set for everyone else. And we said we'd only go on if we can play live, which was our protest at the miming thing, and we had this devious plan to trash the place.

Jimmy Barnes

I actually had mixed feelings about doing it. Looking back, it really was just a publicity stunt, and it did us the world of good. I remember feeling like a naughty kid and feeling a bit guilty. A lot of people didn't like it, it really tore the country up. I've still got mates in Alice Springs, where I grew up, and one or two guys still say, 'We still don't like what you did.' I can't really understand why they took it so seriously.

Ian Moss

I got stuck into the band in my Humdrum segment on *Countdown* the following week, saying Chisel didn't deserve to win the Most Outstanding Achievement Award.

'First of all,' I said, 'let me point out that in my opinion—and I've stated this in the papers and it's only my opinion and not the opinion of *Countdown*—one award that I didn't think deserved to go to Cold Chisel was in fact the Most Outstanding Achievement Award.'

I said Air Supply would have been more deserving, given they had three Top 5 hits in the United States in 1980 ('Lost In Love', 'All Out Of Love' and 'Every Woman In The World').

'I might add that the boys also agree with this, including their manager Rod Willis. Rod, if you're listening tonight, what would be a really nice thing, because you do honestly believe in that fact, it would be nice to send the award across to Air Supply and say there's been a grave mistake.'

I was clearly on a roll, so I turned my attention to the price of albums and concert tickets.

'If they [bands] do care for the people . . . at the moment I'm sure you're aware albums are very costly, and the way you could bring down album costs, and I'll use Cold Chisel as an example . . .'

Holding up a copy of the band's *Swingshift* album, I said:

If you put this in a brown paper bag, you'd bring down the cost of an album by at least a dollar.

If you appear at concerts—and you must realise there are over 250,000 unemployed in this country under 25—why not at your Festival Hall concert, instead of taking a lot of money, why not, in fact, take as much as people on the dole do—$50 a gig or $56 a gig—and let the rest of the money bring down the concert tickets and that way you could get in for $2.

While we have a think about all those things, I'd also like to add that I think Cold Chisel are still one of the finest rock 'n' roll bands in the country.

If I may just finish off, to everyone, including Flowers, who didn't come up to accept their awards . . . one of the greatest comedians in the world—also he was a songwriter and a musician in his own right—was Charlie Chaplin. He went through hell in America during his early days when they kicked him out of the country. When he finally came back and they presented him with an Academy Award, he said this: 'For me not to accept this award with pride would be wrong, because when I was literally run out of America in my early days, it was not what the American people did to me, but the chosen few who held the power. By not accepting this award tonight would be an insult to the public who obviously believe in me. There is no dignity lost in accepting any award, especially this one.'

And that was Charlie Chaplin. All right, enough of that.

Phew, what a speech!

A decade after the Awards, Melbourne radio DJ Billy Pinnell asked Chisel's chief songwriter Don Walker why the band behaved as they did. 'We felt we were in an awkward situation,' Don explained. 'These awards had always been a very sort of King of Pop thing, [which had] nothing to do with us. So we thought we'd go on and do a performance that held something of the violence that people could expect in a live show from time to time.'

Ian Moss also did an interview in Detroit, saying: '*TV Week* is a small, almost offensive TV magazine that decided to jump on the bandwagon of rock 'n' roll. We saw the whole thing as genuinely phony.'

TV Week discontinued its association with the Countdown Awards after the Chisel incident. And at the 1982 Countdown Awards, Air Supply won the Most Outstanding Achievement Award.

After the set-trashing, *Countdown* had a bit of a cold war with Cold Chisel.

After much persistence by Steve Hands and Peter Ikin, Molly relented and decided it was time to play Chisel on the show again. Now, everyone called Peter 'Iris', but he was becoming a serious executive at this time, so there was a corporate Warner memo: 'Please be advised that all correspondence must now be addressed to Peter Ikin, not Iris.'

After introducing the Chisel clip on *Countdown*, Molly looked straight at the camera and said, 'And I hope that makes you happy . . . *Iris!*' I was at home, watching the show, and I nearly fell off my chair. Only a handful of people would have realised how funny it was; the rest of Australia would have been thinking, 'What's going on here?'

Bill Duff, WEA Records

When Cold Chisel came on *Countdown* on 25 July, 1982, to perform 'When The War Is Over', I said, 'I have a feeling they might be talking about this show.' But the war wasn't over. My Humdrum column in *TV Week* on 14 August, 1982 had a sting in its tail: 'P.S. Cold Chisel, if you happen to be reading this story, I realise you don't need television. Then again, we don't need you.'

I look back at those days and the things that I wrote and I think, 'What a little bitch I was.' Still, in defence of *TV Week*, the magazine did give Cold Chisel a lot of publicity, whether they liked it or not, and as far as *Countdown* was concerned, Chisel got some of the best sets, the best lighting and best direction. In fact, our set designers took great pride in recreating the band's album covers and artwork.

The show was responsible for a lot of the great hits that happened in this country. People like to bag it, but if it wasn't for that hour on a Sunday night, half of Australia wouldn't have known about the music that was happening. We've had our ups and downs, but Molly is one of my favourite people. He's been responsible for some of the best music in this country. A lot of people forget about the incredibly good stuff Molly does. He's a great man and I've got a lot of time for him. Whether as a journalist, a producer or a TV presenter, he's always been a champion of Australian music, someone who stands up and says, 'Listen to this.'

Jimmy Barnes

Before Cold Chisel trashed the *Countdown* set, another one of Australia's biggest bands made a statement by *not* appearing on the show.

Ted Emery was the *Countdown* producer who said no to Midnight Oil. The drama started when the band was late for rehearsal.

We had this regular thing of bands turning up late, and Michael Shrimpton got sick of it. He said, 'I don't care who they are, the next band to do it is off the show.' The next band to do it was this band that Molly had gotten on the show, Midnight Oil. I simply said to them: 'You're not on.'

Ted Emery, *Countdown* producer

The Oils had done a gig the night before at the Bondi Lifesaver with Rose Tattoo and had to catch an 8.30 a.m. flight to Melbourne. They went straight to their hotel, the Majestic in St Kilda, for some sleep, while their manager, Gary Morris, went to the *Countdown* studios.

When Ted told Gary the band was being bumped, a furious Gary yelled, 'We don't fucking need you guys, we're going to make it without you.' Midnight Oil never did appear on *Countdown*, seemingly wearing their non-appearance on a 'pop show' as a badge of honour.

I was not on set when the Oils were kicked off the show, but I pleaded with Michael Shrimpton to drop the policy. 'That's rock 'n' roll, Michael,' I explained.

But Michael disagreed. 'This is television,' he replied. 'It's expensive and you don't keep a crew of 30 people waiting because some bastard can't get out of bed.'

I still don't know exactly what happened with Midnight Oil. I do remember Ted calling me at home the day before the taping to tell me there were problems with the band because they wanted to do their own sound and lighting. This was impossible—the ABC was heavily unionised at the time and such a move would have led to a strike. I can even recall getting into trouble on set one day because I helped move a podium. I was told, in no uncertain terms, that this was not my job. So I have a feeling that when the Oils' management was refused permission to take charge of the sound and lighting, they were purposely late for rehearsal, knowing what the end result would be.

As Ignatius Jones, lead singer of Jimmy And The Boys, explains, it was a different work environment back in the *Countdown* days.

When we launched our last single, a cover of the Stones' 'Get Off My Cloud', we created this fabulous sort of apocalyptic 'Heaven' set on

Countdown, all cotton wool and white grand pianos, with plaster cherubs hanging from the ceiling. We'd given all the cherubs these long cigarette-holders, with cigarettes in them naturally, as a kind of decadent touch, and we were all dressed in schoolboy uniforms I'd completely trashed with a blow-torch.

We were just about to start filming when someone remembered you couldn't show cigarettes on television before 7 p.m. or something—and pulled the plug. We all thought this was rather amusing, and rather than wait around for a stagehand, I climbed up on the piano and removed the offending fags from the cherubs' cigarette-holders.

The place went nuts—I was a *performer*, I couldn't touch the sets! I'd broken every union demarcation rule, and the crew downed tools and went on strike!

More than three decades later, radio company MCM Entertainment requested a 'career retrospective' interview with Oils singer, Peter Garrett, then a minister in the Gillard Labor Government. Peter was happy to talk about the band's hits, his lack of hair, and whether he was a good songwriter. But he was not forthcoming about the band's *Countdown* no-show.

The interviewer, Christopher Hollow, said: 'We'd love to get your take on why Midnight Oil never appeared on *Countdown*.'

Peter: Too long and boring a story.

Christopher: C'mon now, Peter, we need to push you on this.

Peter: Can't even remember.

Christopher: Was it because you were initially booted off the show for being late?

Peter: No. It honestly is too long ago to even dig out of my cobwebbed closet.

Peter wrote in a newspaper column in 1986: 'Flown to Melbourne, placed on a studio set and required to mime in front of a crowd of twelve-year-old girls certainly wasn't where we were at.'

I smiled when I read that particular statement because I really think Peter underestimated what the *Countdown* audience was. Yes, indeed, there was a young audience in the *Countdown* studios, but the show was going out to millions of people a week, covering all age groups. Surely Midnight Oil wanted their political messages to reach a young audience?

A journalist for *The Australian* later wondered if the reference to 'the music of middle-aged queens' in 'Stand In Line' on the Oils' 1979 album, *Head Injuries*, was a dig at me and *Countdown*.

Midnight Oil later went into the *Countdown* studio—to appear on the ABC's Saturday morning music show *Recovery*.

> *Recovery*, to its eternal credit, loved experimentation. It's incredibly attractive, loose and spontaneous, whereas *Countdown* was heavily formatted.
>
> **Rob Hirst, Midnight Oil**

Midnight Oil were a great band. And, to their credit, they had a hugely successful career without appearing on *Countdown*. But I let the band know—in no uncertain terms—what I thought of their attitude when I did an interview with Glenn A. Baker in *The Australian Magazine* in May 1989:

> I've always found most major overseas acts to be a delight. The most difficult artists to work with sometimes are our own Australian artists. They can be so up themselves that someone should shove a bomb up there. If I could do it to Peter Garrett, I would. He's so intent on expounding his own ideas that he doesn't know what music is about. I actually like Midnight Oil, but for a band that's always about issues like nuclear disarmament and Aboriginal rights,

well, I've been to their concerts and they're the most violent you could go to. My God, people smash chairs over each other.

I was also disappointed by the band's double standards. I think as far as Midnight Oil were concerned there was one rule for Australia and another for the rest of the world. I had to laugh the night of the American Music Awards in 1985, where I waved to Peter Garrett as he presented an award. Why was it okay for him to present an *American* music award, but not collect any awards at Australian shows? I thought it was hypocritical, because in America the Oils seemed to discard their 'moral' values—suddenly they were happy to appear on television shows, award shows and do radio IDs.

Peter Garrett also deigned to give me a lecture when I turned up backstage at one of Midnight Oil's Sydney concerts. He bailed me up and said, 'Molly, being a city boy, you don't understand the plight of the Aboriginals.'

'Peter,' I replied, 'you might not know my history. I grew up in Quambatook, Orbost and Kyabram. I went to school with Aborigines. My brother Brian played in a band in Kyabram called The Shades with a couple of Aboriginal guys . . . so you're right, Peter, I'm a city boy and I don't understand.'

Midnight Oil were not the only politically charged band to boycott *Countdown*. Redgum also never appeared on the show.

When we signed with CBS and did our second album, the record company told us they'd have a crack at getting us on *Countdown*. We told them we'd think about doing the show, but we wouldn't mime and we wouldn't perform in front of the flashing *Countdown* sign.

John Schumann, Redgum

There was a standoff with the *Countdown* producers, and Redgum decided they would never do the show. They even wrote 'The Countdown Song' (set to the tune of 'April Sun In Cuba'), which sent up the show and became a highlight of their live set (complete with the band and crowd waving their hands in the air, like the *Countdown* audience).

When Redgum's 'I Was Only 19' hit number one, we asked the band to appear live. They refused. We then asked to show the video for the song. Again, the band said no, so we cut our own clip, without featuring the band.

But *Countdown* didn't hold a grudge.

I remember sitting home watching *Countdown*, knowing we were 'persona non grata', and yet I saw one of our gig posters adorning the set. Molly also awarded Redgum—none of whom was present, of course—a Countdown Award for '19'. Molly spoke well of the song, declaring it was an important song and that it deserved to take its place among the other award-winners.

Given Redgum's response to all things *Countdown*, Molly's statement that night was generous and sincere. It was appreciated by me and earned Molly my respect.

John Schumann

Nearly 25 years later, John surprisingly became part of the Countdown Spectacular tour, saying, 'I thought it would be churlish not to go and play "I Was Only 19". This is in the context of a celebration of that era. People want to see that song, and it would be silly not to do it.'

It was great to have John on the road. Though I have to say, towards the end of *Countdown*, it annoyed me when Australian acts refused to appear live on the show. It was the rise of music video, and many acts, having spent thousands of dollars on a clip, would say, 'Why should we go on the show? Just show the video instead.'

INXS was one Australian band making amazing videos, but I think viewers still preferred to see them live in the studio.

At the end of 1991, when INXS did a satellite cross at the Australian Music Awards, I assumed they were overseas, but they were actually in Sydney. They claimed they were busy recording, but they always seemed to find time to do the American Music Awards.

I had a go at the band's no-show and their live album, *Live Baby Live*, on the final *Hey Hey It's Saturday* for 1991, arguing that the album relied on studio overdubs. This is what I said:

> I don't often criticise acts, certainly Australian acts, but I feel I have the right to do this. I think that INXS not appearing or not taking the time to appear at the Australian Music Awards last week was inexcusable. They were up in Sydney. The year before, when they were overseas, they could not do a satellite link into Australia for Ausmusic Day, which is very important for the Australian music scene. Quite frankly, way back through the *Countdown* days, in the last four years of the program, they couldn't even appear live in the show, and, after all, we were a live show.

I then said that *Live Baby Live* was 'about as live as that link'.

> It's a very boring album. It's hardly live. It's hardly live. Boys, if you are going to give us a live album, give us a live album. And please give us the time for the Australian music industry.

The band was not happy. In fact, INXS's management group, MMA International, sought legal advice and considered suing me for defamation.

Keyboard player Andrew Farriss responded: 'To see somebody come on national television to say you have not recorded a live album is extremely annoying. It was a grand statement by Molly. It's not true, it's offensive.'

Saxophonist Kirk Pengilly added: 'More than anything, it hurts you. It's a shame someone with the power can get on national television and kill an album you are proud of.'

I refused to back down. 'I make no apologies,' I told Channel Nine's *Today* show. 'The only thing I may apologise about is the ferocity at the way it was delivered. I would love to love this album. But I don't find it an inspiring live album and I have said as much.'

I made it clear I was bagging the album and not the band, stating, 'INXS are one of the finest live acts in the world, and the best Australian live act since The Easybeats'.

Live Baby Live was INXS's least successful album in eight years. It peaked at number 72 in the United States, and number three in Australia.

It wasn't just the band that was angry at me. At a Jimmy Barnes reception in Sydney, the then wife of INXS's producer, Mark Opitz, threw a glass of champagne over me. Which really is a horrible waste. Also, I had to laugh at that because it was through the Mark Opitz association that I learnt that the INXS album had serious overdubs. Mark was the producer of the Roxus album and during that time in the Sydney studios, Juno Roxas saw the overdubs being done and couldn't help but tell me.

I think Molly had a pretty toxic outlook on the whole situation, which had as much to do with me as INXS. Two shows into a Roxus tour, I decided to go home to Melbourne. On the way to the airport, I dropped into Rhinoceros [Studios] to see Mark Opitz, who was doing some stuff with INXS. Molly was angry with me about blowing out the tour, and he obviously had some issues with INXS, so he turned.

Juno Roxas, Roxus

I love Molly and respect his passion, but in this case, he got it wrong. Seriously wrong. Aside from two overdubs, which we did at a Glasgow studio to fix up the Wembley technical problems [a microphone had collapsed just as Kirk started his sax solo in 'Never Tear Us Apart', and two or three bars of bass were lost when one of the bass DI's had briefly gone down], everything was live on *Live Baby Live*.

Several of the songs were, indeed, recorded live in three or four places around the world, but everything was in sync. For example, if there were mistakes in a song, I might have used the drums from Philadelphia, with the guitars from Rio, and the bass from Chicago. To me, that's a good thing, not a bad thing. We were trying to give people the best live performance. Molly alleged we were doctoring the songs, mixing live tracks with studio overdubs. But this never happened.

I've done a lot of albums over the years, but, strangely, my two favourites are probably the albums where I've had the least input—Cold Chisel's live album, *Swingshift*—no overdubs; and *Live Baby Live*—two overdubs. Others may disagree, but I believe they're both killer live albums.

Mark Opitz

Two years after the drama, Michael Hutchence was still angry, telling *The Herald Sun*'s Nui Te Koha:

I do think people should be informed before they come out with statements. Journalism is essentially investigation, and if a guy like Molly, who should be responsible . . . his criticism of *Live Baby Live* pissed me off a lot. It pissed me off a real lot.

As a consequence, the album died here. It cost us, purely in money terms, hundreds and hundreds of thousands of dollars, over one stupid statement. And that's just money.

Unfortunately, I just didn't think it was a good album. But it was wrong to blame its failure on me—the album also flopped in the United States, where I have no influence.

> Molly's long suit is enthusiasm, and you gotta love somebody with enthusiasm. When he slags somebody, it actually seems to hurt him. I don't think he likes slagging people. I think he genuinely likes getting behind people. Maybe his tastes aren't as long as his enthusiasm, but you can't hate Molly Meldrum, because he is the ultimate rock 'n' roll fan.
>
> When a band releases an album that disappoints a fan, a fan doesn't leap upon it with glee like a nasty rock critic and go, 'At last, I get to slag these bastards!' A fan leaps upon it with disappointment: 'Fuck, that's not as good as I wanted.' And that's what you've got to love about Molly.
>
> **Ron Hitler-Barassi, TISM**

Still, I'm glad I made my peace with Michael.

In 1995 my friends ganged up to shock me with an episode of *This Is Your Life*. Michael kindly offered this tribute:

> Before MTV, there was *Countdown*, and *Countdown* gave many, many, many bands such a great chance. Molly, thank you very much. You're the most wonderful old queen of a groupie in the world and that's what makes you fabulous.

In August 1997, I found myself booked into the same Los Angeles hotel as Michael. He was under the name 'Mr Nice', with Paula Yates, their baby daughter Tiger, and his mum and step-dad. I wrote about the meeting in my *TV Week* column on 16 August—twenty years to the day after the band played their first gig: 'I haven't seen him so relaxed in years. INXS's American tour is going well, and he said he was hoping the band would play some Australian shows before the end of the year.'

Michael said to me: 'Molly, I've never been so relaxed and happy.' But there was a dark side to his contentment. Michael was locked in a battle with Paula's former husband, Bob Geldof. Paula and Bob had three children together, and Michael and Paula wanted the kids to travel to Australia with Tiger. But Bob apparently said no. At the hotel, I could tell that Michael was desperate. 'Bob's a friend of yours,' he said, 'could you please call him?'

I agonised about Michael's request on the plane flying home, but I decided I couldn't intervene in what was obviously a personal, family matter. That chat with Michael has haunted me ever since. I often think, 'What if I'd made the call to Bob? Would things have turned out differently?'

On 22 November, Michael Hutchence was found hanged in a Sydney hotel. He had called Bob twice in the early hours of that morning, pleading with him to allow Paula to bring her kids to Australia.

That day is a blur. When news broke of Michael's death on the Saturday morning, Rebecca Barnard and Shane O'Mara from Melbourne band Rebecca's Empire were due at my house for an interview.

We walked in and Molly was distraught. I gave him a big hug and we left soon after.

Rebecca Barnard, Rebecca's Empire

I was to have met Michael in Sydney the day before he died, but I had to postpone the meeting. Talking about his death was the hardest Melodrama I've ever had to do on *Hey Hey It's Saturday*.

In 1981, the year of the Cold Chisel episode, Molly owned a Jaguar and transported it to Sydney on a train for the Rock Awards. The morning after the awards, as we were checking out of the Gazebo, I asked Molly if I could put my daughter Danielle's toys in the boot.

We opened the boot to find it was occupied by a sewing machine. Molly couldn't believe it. He thought that someone staying at the hotel must have put it in the wrong car, or that we were winding him up. He said, 'Let's just get rid of the thing.' So we lifted it out of the boot and just left it in the hotel car park.

A few days later, Molly was on the phone to me, frantic, wanting to know where we'd dumped the sewing machine. The owner had turned up at Molly's house, inquiring about the antique sewing machine worth thousands of dollars.

It turned out a neighbour had borrowed Molly's car and put the sewing machine in the boot. Molly insisted I keep his name quiet because it would look bizarre in the Sydney gossip columns. I rang the hotel and, after a lot of explaining, I retrieved the sewing machine.

Rodney Woods, former record company executive

14: THE WILD ONE

1984–2014: Who's that girl?—Australia takes a Holiday—Footy at the Forum—I'm on MTV—Sean snaps, the Penn is not mightier than the horde—Lynne says 'Ciao, baby'—Mugged in Florence—Dreaming in LA.

The whole reason I got into this business is because I want to be near people. I want to communicate with people. I don't want to have a separation, I don't want to hide from people. I want to be approachable. I want people to see I'm a human being with the same faults and the same problems and the same fears. I don't think that I'm better than anybody else.
Madonna to Molly in 1985

'Who the fuck's Madonna?'

'What the fuck is a Molly?'

And so began a great showbiz friendship.

It's the start of 1984 and I'm in America on a *Countdown* trip, primarily to interview Van Halen, who are huge at the time. I remember David Lee Roth telling me a joke: *How many people does it take to change a light bulb at a rock 'n' roll gig?* Answer: Twenty! One to screw in the bulb, two to hold the ladder, and seventeen on the VIP guest list.

In New York, one of my favourite acts, Eurythmics, are doing five nights at the Roxy, supported by Australia's Real Life, whose single, 'Send Me An Angel', is a Top 30 hit in the States. At the end of each Eurythmics show, a huge screen descends on the stage and they play videos. One of them catches my ears and eyes. It's a song called 'Burning Up'.

'Who is that?' I ask the person next to me.

'That's a new act called Madonna.'

When I find out she's on the Sire label through Warner Music, I say to my travelling companion, Peter 'Iris' Ikin, a Warner executive: 'Look, I really want to do an interview with this Madonna chick.' His reply is blunt: 'You haven't got time to do an interview.'

But I manage to squeeze it into the schedule.

On this particular day, I have to do five interviews and by the time I get back to the Warner office for Madonna, I am running horribly late. At this stage, you weren't meant to be calling Peter 'Iris', because he was trying to be very corporate. But I was walking down the corridors of the Warner office, screaming, 'Iris, where are you, Iris?!'

He appeared, barking, 'How dare you! You are so late!'

Feeling a little cheeky, I said, 'Look, I don't care, who the fuck's Madonna anyhow?'

Then, around the corner, came a voice: 'I'm fucking Madonna, what the fuck is a Molly?'

It's not the best start to an interview.

It's obvious that this girl has got attitude. You can feel the tension as we sit down to start the interview.

'Madonna, welcome to *Countdown* and welcome to Australia.'

'Thanks,' she says tersely.

'Look, I've got to ask you: who the fuck's Madonna?'

She laughs, and from this point on I know that we're going to be good friends.

During the interview, I tell Madonna how much I love her 'Holiday' single. 'This is a really good song,' I say, 'a potential number one.'

'Well, why don't you make it into one?'

'I will.'

'How long will it take you?'

'Five weeks.'

I went home, and we did it in four.

It's Madonna's first number one anywhere in the world.

My first mention of Madonna on *Countdown* was on 8 April, 1984. I introduced her as a 'great chick from New York', saying: 'Tell you what, watch out for her because I think she's going to be really big in Australia on the charts over the next two to three months.'

Three weeks later, as the 'Holiday' clip ran in the background, *Countdown* played part of the Madonna interview:

Molly: Um, reading the press coming from England and America and Europe, they describe you as the new—the female Michael Jackson. Have you read that?

Madonna: That's nice, that's flattering.

Molly: Not bad, is it? So who is Madonna?

Madonna: Me.

Molly: And where do you come from? Detroit?

Madonna: Right.

Molly: And how did you start off?

Madonna: In the music business?

Molly: Yeah.

Madonna: Well, it was kind of roundabout how I got into the music business. I came to New York to be a dancer. I was a dancer, and I came to New York to dance in a company professionally. I did that for a while and I got tired of it. And I wanted to sing as well because everyone would hear me sing and say, 'You have a great voice, you should do something.' So I decided I would try to get into musical theatre. I'd still be dancing, and singing live on stage. I went to an audition for a world tour for Patrick Hernandez. Have you heard of him?

Molly: 'Born To Be Alive'.

Madonna: Yeah. He was doing a world tour and looking for girls to do back-up singing and dancing and to go around the world, and I thought that would be great to start off in the music business. I went to the audition and their producers saw me and they thought I should come to Paris, that I was too good to be behind Patrick Hernandez. So I went to Paris and that's basically how I got involved in music. Nothing happened to me there, of course, because that sounds too good to be true, doesn't it?

I wrote about Madonna in my Humdrum column in *TV Week* on 21 April, 1984, in a piece headed 'New York's Madonna The Rage!'

I returned to America in 1984 and that's when I really cemented my relationship with Madonna. I hung out with her, and her then boyfriend/producer Jellybean Benitez. She played me songs from what would later become the *Like A Virgin* album. We also spent a lot of time with Madonna's publicist, Liz Rosenberg, who also became a great mate.

Years later, Molly and I were in Miami with Shirley Brooks. We went to the hot club in town, but there was a huge queue, and I hate lines. Jellybean was playing there that night and he walked out to have a cigarette. His face lit up when he saw Molly. 'Molly, how ya doin'!' We went straight in, were introduced to the owner, got the best table in the house and had French Champagne all night.

Steve Millard, former recording executive

After the album was released, I went to the MTV Awards with Roger Davies, Sherbet's old manager, who was now living in the States and managing Tina Turner. I was actually Tina's date. We were sitting near the stage when Madonna came out of a wedding cake, dressed as a bride. When she started crawling around the stage, Tina had a look of absolute horror. I remember she said to me, 'What is this woman doing?'

To top it all off, Madonna spotted me in the audience, gave me a wave and said, 'Hi, Molly.' I had to confess to Tina: 'Actually, I know her.'

I also went to see one of Madonna's concerts at the Forum in Los Angeles, sitting two seats up from Paula Abdul. The only problem was St Kilda was playing Footscray that night, so I had to watch the concert while hearing the game broadcast from Australia on a mobile phone. It was a very stressful game and we ended up losing. After the concert, Liz Rosenberg came down to get us. 'Come on, Madonna wants to speak to you now.'

I walked into the dressing room and Madonna said to me: 'What did you think of the concert?'

'It's totally fucked!' I said, reflecting on the game.

Jaws dropped. Everyone stopped talking. Most eyes stared straight at the floor. Liz had a horrified look on her face. 'What, what did you say about the concert?'

'Oh my God, *the concert*! Sorry, I loved it!' Thinking quickly, I added, 'I just thought it was totally fucked that Paula Abdul spoke through the entire performance.'

Madonna's eyes grew wider. *'What?!'*

'Yeah, spoke through the whole concert, it was outrageous.'

The next night on stage, Madonna absolutely destroyed Paula Abdul. And I'm not sure if they've spoken since—all because the Saints lost.

In 1985, MTV America wanted to do a special with Madonna. She said she'd do it—if I was the interviewer. This was a big interview for me. I flew to Los Angeles, where we were going to do the interview at Liz Rosenberg's apartment. I was in a state of shock when I arrived because it was like a movie set: there was a crew of about twenty people running everywhere. I was like, 'What is all this?' I was used to a cameraperson, a soundperson and me. Anyway, after the set-up took hours, we finally got into the interview. It was going great, until Madonna's boyfriend, Sean Penn, arrived. It was then I realised how much she was in love. Once he was there, I'd lost her.

That night, we all went out to dinner at the Columbus Restaurant. Madonna's manager, Freddy DeMann, asked how the interview had gone. 'Actually, not so well,' I said. Then I had an idea. 'After dinner, why don't we go back to my hotel and with my crew we can cover the things we haven't got?'

Liz and Freddy were like, 'Dream about it!'

Anyway, later during the dinner, Sean also asked me how the interview had gone. I said, 'Well, you love birds, it was going all right until you arrived.' Then I put my proposal to Madonna: 'Look, this is a really important interview, why don't we go back to the hotel after this and wrap it up? You know my cameraman, David [Etherton], you trust him, so how about it?'

Madonna looked to Sean for approval. 'Is that okay with you, Sean?'

Sean said, 'Sure', and soon we were back at my hotel, shooting another 90 minutes. The MTV special ended up being about 80 per cent David's stuff. The cost of this was about $1000. The cost of the production earlier in the day was $46,000.

I asked Madonna about her relationship with Sean.

Molly: Seeing you with Sean, where he can really faze you . . . I mean, the love, you can see it.

Madonna: What are you talking about? This is personal stuff, right?

Molly: Well, it sort of is . . . where another person can actually put Madonna second.

Madonna: In other words, I actually care about what somebody else thinks about me? Well, yeah, that's what happens when you're in love with somebody. You give up a certain part of yourself. That's the trade-off—you also get a certain kind of security that you don't have when you're not with somebody.

They were deeply in love, there's no doubt about it. But Sean always had a private side, and that was disturbed by his relationship with Madonna. And he became explosive. At restaurants, waiters would slip away to ring the paparazzi. Then Madonna and Sean would be met by a barrage of cameras. I was with them one night when photographers jumped out of the bushes. It's very off-putting, and Sean didn't like it. He was always very protective of Madonna. He always worried that someone would try to hurt her or kidnap her.

It really is a strange thing to experience. If you're in a crowd of people all yelling 'Molly, Molly, Molly', you don't know what to do. It can be embarrassing and very scary. People ask me how I handle it, and the thing is, I got used to it way back in the *Kommotion* days, when we would be mobbed at shopping centres and dances. Then I would go to the footy on Saturday and I would become the fan, so I had a really nice balance. The only time the attention annoys me is if it affects people around me and they get stressed. In a crowd of people yelling 'Molly, Molly, Molly', 98 per cent of the people will be really nice. But there's always a couple of dickheads, and sometimes my friends will want to belt them. But I always say, 'Don't worry about it, just forget it.' The only time it really annoys me is at the footy or the cricket. I don't mind kids asking for autographs, but occasionally yobs will focus on me instead of watching the game. But public attention has never stopped me from going out. I have to admit that I love being in London or New York because over there, I can catch buses and trains, and I really love doing things like that. Still, being recognised in Australia is really satisfying in a sense. Young and old people all come up to me and say, 'Hi, Molly'. It's like I'm part of the family, and that's nice.

When Sean Penn married Madonna, he took out his rifle and shot at the helicopters circling above. In 1987, he served 34 days in jail for punching an extra who tried to take his picture on the set of *Colors*.

Madonna and Sean were divorced in 1988. I know that deep down Madonna will always love Sean. They were genuine feelings. And I'm sure he has the same.

In the mid-'80s, my personal assistant, '60s pop star Lynne Randell, took a call from Kids In The Kitchen's manager, Neil Bradbury. He wanted a letter from me saying how much I liked the band, because they were on the verge of signing a deal with Sire Records, the label run by legendary recording executive Seymour Stein, who signed Madonna.

> For some reason, Molly never got around to doing it, so I decided I would do it and put Molly's name to it. I sent it to Neil, they got their deal with Sire, and I said to Neil, 'Get me out of here, you owe me.' I'd reached the end of my time with Molly. I didn't like certain people he did business with and the way they treated him, and I also wanted to be closer to my son in New York.
>
> **Lynne Randell, former personal assistant**

On a Sunday afternoon, Lynne wandered through Wattle Park in Melbourne, looking to God for guidance. She owed money to the bank and she wanted to go to New York. That night, she went to the Chevron. A couple of hours after she got home, the phone rang. It was 6.30 a.m. Annoyed—thinking it was me, or one of her drunken friends calling from the Chevron—Lynne picked up the phone.

'Hello, this is Seymour Stein . . .'

'Oh yeah, right.'

'I've been meaning to call you for weeks, but my mother's been ill and she died. We buried her today.'

'Oh, that's a bummer.'

'Well, I have it on very good authority that you are a very good PA.'

'I'm the best, the best in the universe,' Lynne said, gearing up to give her 'friend' a serve.

'Didn't Neil Bradbury tell you I was going to call?'

Suddenly, Lynne woke up. Neil *had* been leaving messages for her. This *was* Seymour Stein.

'I would like you to come and work for me, but I don't want Molly to be angry with me.'

Lynne's prayers had been answered.

Australians would be astounded at how revered Molly is overseas. When it comes to 'We need a hit in Australia', no other name is spoken. Having worked for him, I know how much money record companies will spend just to get 30 seconds on air. Australians don't understand what a power he is. He can get in doors in America that no other person in the Australian industry can get in. I know, I worked for Seymour.

Lynne Randell

While working for Seymour, I had a dinner with Lynne, Madonna, Seymour and Liz Rosenberg.

Molly and Madonna were as thick as thieves. They both love a good gossip.

Lynne Randell

As we were leaving that dinner, Madonna went into the kitchen and then reappeared with a doggy bag, asking me: 'Would you mind giving me a lift?' She was going to visit a friend, Michael, a 21-year-old dancer who had AIDS.

Madonna was in the middle of making *Who's That Girl*, but whenever there was a break in filming, she would go to New York and nurse Michael. This was a very special thing to see, and the public never saw any of it. Some people say 'Madonna's heartless'. That's rubbish. Yes, she's ambitious and driven. But she doesn't ignore her own personal life. And, at times, she can be petulant like a child, but she's also a very caring person.

In 1987, just after the end of *Countdown*, I went to Italy to do a concert special with Madonna for Channel Ten. It was an eventful trip—I was mugged in Florence. The day after the show, I was in the Florence Square, looking at a map when, bang, this guy grabbed my wallet. A woman saw it and she tried to stop him, but he hit her and broke her arm. I ran after him and was just about to grab him when another guy came from nowhere and knocked me to the ground.

At the end of the '80s, I went to Los Angeles to interview Madonna about her new movie, *Dick Tracy*. When I arrived at the Mondrian Hotel, Liz Rosenberg called to see if I would like to go out to dinner with Madonna. 'Which restaurant?' I asked.

'We haven't worked that out yet. The car will pick you up at 7 p.m. and take you to wherever we're going.'

The car arrived and we went driving up into the hills. 'Which restaurant is this?' I asked the driver, who replied, 'No, no, sir, we are not going to a restaurant, we are going to Mr Beatty's house.'

I was going to have dinner with Warren Beatty, a man I'd

idolised ever since I saw *Bonnie and Clyde* in 1967. As Warren Beatty served the salads, I sat there speechless.

After dinner, we went downstairs, where Warren had his own cinema. He put on a movie, but I was so tired I fell asleep and started snoring. When I woke up, Madonna was demanding to see *Bonnie and Clyde*. 'I haven't got a good print of it,' Warren said. But Madonna insisted.

You don't say no to Madonna.

Half an hour into the movie, Madonna declared, 'I want some popcorn.'

Warren left and reappeared a few minutes later with popcorn for all of us.

'I am dreaming,' I thought to myself—I'm watching *Bonnie and Clyde* with Warren Beatty and he's cooking me popcorn!

In 1990, I saw Madonna's Blond Ambition tour, which the Bishop's Conference in Italy campaigned to ban, stating: 'Her new show, with the symbols it uses and the values it expresses, is an offence to good taste.' This was Madonna's most controversial tour. Italian television refused to air her 'Like A Prayer' video, deeming it blasphemous. All of the drama led to Madonna losing her lucrative deal with Pepsi.

In 1991, we were in Hollywood. In the next studio to us was Madonna, who had just signed a $1 million exclusive deal with MTV. She walked out and saw Molly, and then she did a piece for us for *Hey Hey*—the MTV people wanted to throttle Molly.

Daryl Somers

So who the fuck's Madonna?

When I talked to her about the *Ray Of Light* album, I remarked: 'Your mood changes on this album all the time.'

Madonna: Well, I'm a very moody girl.
Molly: God, you don't have to tell me that!

Yes, she can be moody at times. She can be bitchy and, sometimes, she wants to be the centre of attention. But I think she's wonderful, one of the most important artists of all time, without a doubt. She's had more than 70 hit singles and that's amazing. Who would have thought this woman, dubbed a 'Pop Tart' after the release of her first album, would have lasted so long? I even recall that when her name was mentioned at one of the Countdown Awards, the audience booed. Only true superstars rise above their critics.

I have been lucky enough to have seen every Madonna tour—including the Virgin Tour, the Who's That Girl Tour, Blond Ambition and The Girlie Show—and all of them have been spectacular. She's single-minded and I admire her for that. Though it's very disappointing that she has come to Australia only once, for 1993's Girlie Show. Her Australian fans—and there are lots of them—deserve better.

Bette Midler introduced Madonna at the Philadelphia leg of Live Aid as the 'woman who pulled herself up by her bra straps'. And she has endured some pretty hurtful publicity.

Madonna is strong—in will and in body. And, like Debbie Harry in the '70s, Madonna has inspired female performers around the world. She's fearless, ambitious and daring. ('Listen, everyone is entitled to my opinion,' she said to a sound technician in 1990.)

I like singer-songwriter Liz Phair's description: 'Madonna is the speed boat. The rest of us are just the Go-Gos on water skis.'

I'm proud to call her a friend. I smiled when Mike Munro told the tale of going to Cannes to interview Madonna for *60 Minutes*. He accidentally met her in the hotel pool before the interview. 'I introduced myself and said I'd be interviewing her that afternoon. Luckily, I said the magic words: "Molly Meldrum says hello." Once I mentioned his name, she was charming and trusted me a lot more.'

I haven't always agreed with everything Madonna has done. I thought the *Sex* book, in 1992, was going too far, and I told her that, which I don't think she appreciated. And, of course, a lot of her movies have been duds. But 1996's *Evita* was a triumph, which proved what Madonna was capable of on the big screen. The *Evita* saga started in 1988, when it was tipped that Madonna had the Eva Perón part. Then it was reported that Meryl Streep had the role. In 1993, Andrew Lloyd Webber said Madonna was too old for the role. She ended up doing the movie while pregnant with the love of her life, her daughter Lourdes.

I know that her kids have given her more joy than any of her musical achievements. She's the Material Girl who became the devoted mum. In one interview I did with Madonna, we talked about demons. She said she still had a few more to exorcise from her soul. I asked her if the past fifteen years had been hard.

Madonna: Being famous? It's taken me fifteen years to deal with it gracefully. In the beginning it's a rush, you don't know what you're in for. Then you go through the 'Oh, my God, no privacy, no anonymity'. You become bitter and want to tell everybody to fuck off. But now I feel like I've come out on the other side of it. I've accepted it.

Molly: If you stripped away the Madonna character, what would there be?

Madonna: The person you're looking at. [*Long pause*]. That's me, you know.

When I was in New York with Molly, we went to a Madonna revue with Liz Rosenberg, put on by a group of drag queens. Molly commented very loudly throughout the entire show, and when one of the drag queens came out as Liz Rosenberg, Molly jumped on stage.

'If you want to see the *real* Liz Rosenberg, she's here tonight—stand up, Liz!'

The place was packed. People were calling out, 'It's the gay Crocodile Dundee!'

Steve Millard, former recording executive

15: ABOUT THIS HAT

1980–2014: Hats off, step lively—Hat tricks, bad hair days
and gongs—Wherever I lay my hat.

Molly: There's the fashion and the music and suddenly it becomes old hat.

Andy Taylor, Duran Duran: It's about time you got a new one, isn't it?
Countdown, 13 November, 1983

The hat is no big deal.

Olivia Newton-John gave me a hat, a Stetson, in the early '80s, and I wore it a few times on *Countdown*. When I stopped wearing it, people wrote into the show asking, 'Why doesn't he wear the hat again?'

My friend Lindsay Fox, the trucking magnate, brought me a hat back from America—a 'Billy The Kid' Stetson. In his kitchen, I remember folding it and tying it because I didn't like the strap hanging around my chin.

That was the hat.

A couple of years later, Stetson stopped making the 'Billy The Kid' style. My manager at the time, Ray Evans, came up with the idea of getting the hats made. He found some hat makers in Queensland, called Mountcastle, and they recreated the Billy The Kid. It's now a totally Australian hat, but it's not for sale—the company is not allowed to sell them.

A lot of people call me 'The Hat'. When Elton sees me, he always says, 'Oh, she's still wearing that dreadful hat!' And I guess it has become as much a part of me as the name Molly. And it has helped the image of Molly Meldrum.

From an overseas point of view, when I do interviews, the hat sets me apart from the crowd, as well as the fact that my name's Molly and I'm from Australia. The hat has its own character. It intrigues people. And you certainly can't be missed in a crowd. The only time I get lost is when I'm in Memphis or Nashville— where everyone's wearing a hat! In those areas, people wear hats all the time. It's part of their personality.

The hat is part of Molly Meldrum's personality. There is a difference between Molly and Ian Meldrum. Molly is the TV and public person. Ian is totally different at home and with friends.

Sometimes I take a deep breath when I go out my front door: 'Okay, right, here we go . . .'

When I'm doing a television show or appearing at a club, I basically have to be Molly Meldrum. It's a different person in the sense that I don't wish to be Molly Meldrum all the time. In my house and with my friends I am not like that. I enjoy doing the ironing and sweeping the floor and walking around in my underpants.

That sounds strange, but it's not. For example, Red Symons is not what you see on telly. He's actually a real pussycat, but when he becomes Red Symons the TV personality, he can be downright rude to people. It's all part of the act. When I see it, I often go into shock—but that's Red and people love it. I've heard people say: 'Isn't that wonderful, Red was rude to us!'

I have to say I laughed when I appeared in the annual Country Music Awards in *Truth* in 1983. Under Best Attired Artist, columnist Peter Olszewski wrote:

A special mention must be made to Ian Meldrum who insists on wearing a cowboy hat and has consequently traumatised all serious urban outlaws.

Is the hat associated with hair loss? No. I had a full head of hair when I started wearing it. It's just become part of me, and that's that.

Do I wear it to bed? No.

Do I wear it in the shower? Sometimes, depending on how drunk I am.

Do I feel like something's missing when I take it off? Yes and no. I wouldn't take it off in public; that's not something that Molly Meldrum would do. I have had offers to take the hat off, but I wouldn't do that. It's theatre. I always remember a producer saying you should never let an audience come backstage—you don't want to destroy the illusion, the mystique.

I don't place any big deal on the hat. The hat is just me. And it makes dressing a lot easier. I'm very basic with my dressing: the hat, R.M. Williams boots, and usually something black. It would be a pain in the neck if I had to wear something different every time I went on television, so I don't bother!

When I'm out, I tend to wear the cowboy hat, though if I'm at the theatre, I'll usually wear a beanie—because there's nothing worse than being stuck behind a person wearing a big hat.

People associate me with the cowboy hat. If I'm wearing a baseball cap, they'll say, 'Where's the other hat?'

Would Molly have been Molly without the hat?
Amanda Pelman, agent and former housemate

I had a funny meeting of hats in London a few years back. I was waiting for a car at the side entrance of the Regency Hotel, when I saw a group of people talking next to me, also waiting for a car. I spotted a guy in a baseball cap.

'Garth?'

'Do I know you?'

'Molly.'

'Molly!'

It was the biggest country star in the world, Garth Brooks. But, initially, we didn't recognise each other because we were both wearing baseball caps.

In March 1992, I was at the 121 Bar in Melbourne when the hat was ripped from my head. The thief later sent an anonymous message to a newspaper columnist: 'We have the size 58 black Akubra. Molly Meldrum's was the Hawthorn of hats, it was there to be knocked off.' It was the second hat to be swiped in two weeks. The first thieves actually wanted a $200 ransom.

The Go-Betweens were a great Australian band. I caught up with them in London and took them out for four hours of drinking pina coladas and champagne. The meeting ended with singer Robert Forster leaving, wearing my hat, with me chasing after him.

The hat has been kidnapped several times, which, of course, I try to discourage. Every year, I'd probably go through twenty hats, thirty if I go on a few benders and they keep rolling into gutters.

The hat has proved to be a problem on some occasions. I remember being at the Oyster Bar at The Plaza Hotel in New York. A waiter said, 'Sir, you'll have to remove your hat.'

'Excuse me,' I replied, 'I'm Muslim.'

'What?'

'I have to have my head covered.'

In a Jewish area of New York, they probably thought, 'Let him leave it on, we don't want any trouble.'

On 30 May, 1986, I was honoured to receive the Order of

Australia for my work on Live Aid, presented by the Victorian Governor, Dr Davis McCaughey. Greg Kerr wrote in the Melbourne *Herald*:

> Australia's most famous urban cowboy, Molly Meldrum, committed the unspeakable at Government House today. He and his beloved cowboy hat parted company—for a total of 25 seconds.
>
> Government House officials stood somewhat red-faced when Meldrum arrived 20 minutes late, wearing that hat. However, seconds before receiving his award, Molly whipped off the cream hat—to reveal a thick mop of black hair.

I received the award for services to youth, and for my involvement in Live Aid.

'I don't mind taking my hat off for my country,' I told the press.

When I got the Order of Australia, I was doing a breakfast show at RRR, so I was pretty tired, and treated it like another gig. It didn't hit me until I was sitting at Government House, next to a nun and some charity workers, just how proud my mother and grandmother would have been.

The award meant a lot to me—even if I did leave it under my seat and wondered where it was for two days, before calling Government House.

Bert Newton: You've been lucky with the hat—you never have a bad hair day.

Molly: Yes, but sometimes when I've not been able to get into the house and I've fallen asleep on a park bench, the poor old thing gets a bit crushed . . .

I was living at Molly's house, but I decided to leave. It was three in the morning and he was playing a record over and over. I went upstairs and started packing. I had my suitcase on the waterbed. He was jumping up and down on the bed, and, as I put things in the case, he'd throw them over the balcony and into the pool. So basically I left with nothing. I jumped into my car and he grabbed the door handle. For the length of the street, he held on, screaming, 'Come back, come back, I'm sorry!' I went back.

Amanda Pelman, former housemate

16: BEDS ARE BURNING

1984: Everything's on fire—Meeting Miss Mod—U2, Boy George, Billy Idol, Meat Loaf, Luxor—Lemonade and Stolis—Burning down the house.

Molly developed a way of living in the 1960s and he has stuck with it. His life has always been incredibly hectic. It's as if he is too frightened of what would happen if he stood still. He is always on the move, always right on the edge of not being able to cope because so much is going on. That's the way he lives.

Lee Simon, radio programmer, *The Age*, 1983

In October 1984, I went to London to interview Boy George. Culture Club were about to release their third album, *Waking Up With The House On Fire*. Meanwhile, my friend Lynne Randell was looking after my house in Melbourne. Our favourite album at the time was U2's *The Unforgettable Fire*.

Lynne was Australia's biggest female singer in the mid-'60s, when she was known as 'Miss Mod'. Her recording career started in 1965 with a cover of Lulu's 'I'll Come Running Over'. She was 16 when she first appeared on the cover of *Go-Set*. Soon after, Lynne relocated to the United States, where she went on tour with The Monkees and Jimi Hendrix. Hendrix told an English newspaper: 'There was a fantastic girl singer on the tour—Lynne Randell. The world will be hearing a lot more of her.'

Thousands of young girls tried to mimic Lynne's hairstyle, wondering, 'How do the side bits seem to stick in her mouth when she sings?' They didn't know Lynne's secret—she went to bed every night with two large rollers on the top of her head, and hair sticky-taped to her face. Being fair-skinned, she'd wake up every morning with 'Xs' on both sides of her face, as if she'd been cursed by the Devil.

Lynne had her biggest hit, 'Ciao Baby', in mid-1967. Her last single was a cover of Cat Stevens' 'I Love My Dog' at the end of 1969, which Jo Beth Taylor also recorded, nearly three decades later. Lynne married and stayed in Los Angeles until 1980. In the early '70s she did a column for *Go-Set*, Lynne Randell's Stateside Scene.

I met Lynne when she literally kicked sand in my face at the beach at Lorne. 'Hey,' I yelled, before stopping, surprised. 'Aren't you the sheila who sang at the Lifesaving Club?'

'Yes, I am,' Lynne replied, proudly. She'd won a talent quest at a school fete and first prize was a pearl necklace and a gig singing for a week in Lorne, with a band called The Spinning Wheels.

When she moved to the States, I visited Lynne and her husband, Abe, in Los Angeles. It was my first time in the city. Apparently, before I landed, Lynne warned Abe: 'There is something you need to know about this guy—wherever he goes, so goeth chaos.'

> He was supposed to let us know when he was arriving, but, of course, he called us from the airport. And he stayed two weeks longer than he was going to. I took Molly to see Joe Cocker, and Abe took him to his first gay porno movie. And then I didn't see him again for years.
>
> **Lynne Randell, former personal assistant**

When she finally returned to Australia, Lynne was greeted by people who would say: 'Didn't you used to be Lynne Randell?' She struggled to readjust to life back in Melbourne.

In America, I could be as full-on as I wanted and they loved it. But back home, people were like, 'Who is that woman? What's her problem?'

Lynne Randell

Lynne had been a child star and then a party girl in Los Angeles before becoming a mum. What were her career options? She thought about starting a Groupies School. It would have been a weekend school, where girls could learn the essentials:

Always have money in your sock for a cab home.

Never give your phone number or ask for a phone number.

No teeth.

And it wouldn't hurt to have a school uniform in your carry bag.

I never met one guy in the music industry who thought it was a bad idea.

Lynne Randell

Lynne put a band together in Melbourne, doing Springsteen and Ted Nugent covers.

It rocked and I had some great players, but it was not meant to be. I wasn't comfortable in that skin because I'd shed it so many years before. And if you're not comfortable, the audience will always know. You can't stand in front of the public and expect them to accept you unless it is your total and complete mind-set. And it wasn't. I couldn't go back. But I didn't know how to go forward.

And then a white knight appeared, the strangest white knight you'd ever want to meet—Ian 'Molly' Meldrum. I was totally lost and disoriented, and Molly gave me back my identity, validated me as a human being.

Lynne Randell

Lynne started helping me in the garden, and answering my phone. Then one day, when Culture Club were in town, I announced: 'Come on, grab a notebook, we're off to the Hilton to interview Boy George.'

Then it was Lynne's job to get Boy George to appear in Adelaide. The City of Churches had been left off his touring itinerary, prompting 45,000 South Australians to sign a petition demanding he go there. George ended up appearing in Rundle Mall, singing an impromptu version of 'Karma Chameleon'.

There was certainly no job interview—Lynne had simply become my personal assistant, a role she later described as my 'nagging wife'. For four years, Lynne ran my life.

I did everything for him, except about three things, and you need your own hands to do those.

Lynne Randell

When the phone rings at my place, you never know who's going to be on the other end.

'Hello, Lynne speaking.'

'Can I speak to Molly?'

'Who's calling?'

'Madonna.'

'Yeah, right. Who is this?'

'It's Madonna.'

'Okay . . . Ian, it's fucking Madonna on the phone!'

The only problem was it actually *was* Madonna.

Lynne also took charge of my house. She was dismayed every time I returned from Egypt with more knick-knacks. Once she said to me: 'My God, I didn't know they had CopperArt in Cairo.' She was very cheeky!

Lynne's obsessive cleaning drove me nuts. 'I'd never take you to Egypt,' I told her, 'because you'd want to clean it.'

We did, however, share a wicked sense of humour.

I remember Molly would call from overseas, demanding that I phone Michael Gudinski *right now*.
'But, Ian, it's 4 a.m. Michael's not going to like it.'
'That's why I want you to call him.'

Lynne Randell

One Saturday morning, we were watching *Hey Hey It's Saturday* and the show was joking about how country people weren't very smart and they wore hats. I spat out my toast. 'Hey, I'm from the country and I wear a hat—come on, Lynne!'

We jumped in my Rolls-Royce, which had an EON-FM sticker on the back, and drove to Channel Nine—a man in a cowboy hat and bathrobe, and a short, mad, blonde woman. And we walked straight onto the set.

Daryl Somers' mouth was wide open as I walked past, exclaiming, 'I'm from the country, I wear a hat, and I'm not dumb!'

You never knew what was going to happen at Molly's place, or who was going to turn up. One day, at the height of Duran Duran's success, Molly kept Simon Le Bon waiting because he had to go see the Archibald Prize painting of himself. We arrived home to find Simon waiting at the front porch.

Lynne Randell

In 1983, I had a big party for Duran Duran and the Australian cricket team. It also saw Lynne renew acquaintances with John Farnham and his wife, Jill.

Everyone told me what a hoot Jill was but, for some reason, she'd always been a little cool towards me, so I cornered her in the toilet: 'Why do you not like me, Jill?'

'Well,' Jill said, 'I don't hate you, it's just when I met you in Los Angeles . . .'

I couldn't actually recall meeting Jill and John, but apparently we had met when the Farnhams were on their honeymoon.

'Well,' Jill continued, 'when we met, you said, "Nice to meet you, I'm Lynne Randell, I give the second best head in LA."

I laughed. 'Jill, I'm really sorry. What I meant to say is I give *the* best head in LA.' We both cracked up.

Lynne Randell

The day after the party, there was a knock on my door. It was the young Christian couple who lived next door.

'Excuse us,' they politely said to Lynne, 'we don't want to be a bother, it's just that there were people on the footpath until 5.30 in the morning, saying, "We love Duran Duran."'

'Oh, sorry,' Lynne replied, 'that was Dennis Lillee.'

'Oh well, um, it does tend to keep us awake, so when you're going to have another big party, could you perhaps tell us a week before, so maybe we could go and stay somewhere else?'

Unfortunately, not everyone was as polite as the Christian couple. Other disgruntled neighbours would throw rocks at the house and pour battery acid on guests' cars. One night, the guy I hired to cook a spit roast in the backyard was hit in the head by a flying rock.

The annual cricket party, which coincided with the Boxing Day Test, was always a big night. One year, the Test team turned up wearing pink T-shirts.

'Why have they all got pink T-shirts on?' I whispered in Lynne's ear.

'They think they're sending you up,' Lynne explained. 'They think it's funny, you know, pink, camp . . . geddit?'

'Oh, okay.'

Another time, Lynne was forced to reprimand a New Zealand Test cricketer who she caught urinating in one of my pot plants. She went to the kitchen, got a wooden spoon and whacked him on the dick.

While working with me, Lynne got to meet Rick Springfield's wife, when Rick, his mum, and his wife came over for lunch.

'Thank you for getting my husband's ear pierced,' Rick's wife said to Lynne.

'You are very welcome,' Lynne replied.

I thought the whole scene was very amusing, knowing that Lynne had an affair with Rick. I nudged Lynne in the back and whispered, 'Good thing she doesn't know what else got pierced.'

Lynne cooked a big lunch, not knowing that Rick had become a vegetarian.

I think he just wanted to get out of there. He seemed rather nervous. I don't think he knew that I was going to be there—Molly loves surprises.

Lynne Randell

The next surprise . . . I didn't love so much.

In October 1984, I had to go overseas to do some interviews for *Countdown*. First stop was London. Just before I left, I decided to do some work on the house, repainting the kitchen and entertainment area. My manager at that time, Ray Evans, also convinced me to install a security alarm system. He also urged me to update my insurance, but I dismissed him, stating, 'Look, Ray, if the house gets robbed they'll only take records, stereos and televisions. It's not worth it.'

I asked Lynne to look after the house and oversee the workmen while I was overseas. She said, 'Ciao, Baby!' as I walked out the front door.

As I was 13,000 miles away, an old flame of mine—as my mate Gavin Wood would later put it—was about to jump out of the closet.

Here's how Lynne recounted the story . . .

The young carpenter looked up as Lynne brought him a cup of coffee. 'I don't want to work on these shelves anymore,' he said.

'Why not?' Lynne asked.

'Because the power points are humming.'

(It reminded Lynne of an old roadie joke: Why are the amps humming? Because they don't know the words.) She also made a mental note, to get an electrician to check the wiring.

The electrician arrived the following day. After walking around the whole house, touching everything with his screwdriver, he said, 'When your boss comes back, tell him that if he doesn't have this place rewired pronto, he won't have a place.'

That night, a friend, Mitch Clark from Mushroom Records—who had been dog-sitting my dog, Ziggy, while the tradesmen were at the house—arrived. U2's new album, *The Unforgettable Fire*, was blasting through my new $5000 speakers, which Lynne bought because she was sick of me blowing up every set of speakers.

Lynne told Mitch about the electrician's comments, before popping down to the pub to buy some lemonade. As she walked out the door, she added, 'I think I should start asking for danger money.'

(I always smile when I think about Lynne claiming she was going to buy some lemonade. I think this was actually code for vodka. Not that I don't mind the occasional lemonade myself.)

The pub is less than 100 metres from my place. Mitch ran after Lynne, yelling, but Lynne couldn't hear her. Mitch could detect a strange, burning smell.

When Mitch walked back into the house, she was met by flames shooting out of the linen cupboard.

Lynne stayed at the pub for about ten minutes because something on the telly caught her eye. As she walked back to my place, she saw fire trucks racing down the street and thought something dreadful must have happened to the neighbours.

Then Mitch grabbed her arm. 'Lynne,' she screamed, 'Ziggy is still in there!'

Lynne tried to run into the house, but a fireman put his arm in front of her. 'No one's going in there, lady,' he ordered.

It was all over in twenty minutes, but it was horrendous. Fortunately, the dog and cat survived, but the firemen walked me through the house, and what wasn't damaged by fire was ruined by water and soot. It was awful. But you know what was untouched? Molly. There was only a small scorch mark on the Archibald Prize portrait, which you can't even see. And with the other portrait of Molly, which is in the bathroom, the frame and glass fell away, but the painting was fine. I've always thought that was kind of strange.

Lynne Randell

I was about to chat to Billy Idol in an interview room at the Marble Arch Inn in London when an urgent phone call was put through to me. It was my manager, Ray Evans. He asked if I was sitting down.

'Why?'

'I want to know if you're sitting down because I've got something serious to tell you.'

'Look, Ray,' I said, annoyed, 'I haven't got time for all of this shit. I'm just about to do an interview, so stop mucking around.'

'Stuff you then, I just wanted to tell you your house has burned down.'

And then he hung up.

I returned to the chat with Billy Idol, but Ray's words were ringing in my ears. 'Can you hold on a second, Billy, I need to make a phone call.'

I rang Ray, who calmly revealed what had happened. I resumed the interview with Billy, but he sensed something was wrong.

'What is it, Moll?' he asked.

'Um, my house has just burned down.'

'Well, man, forget the interview, let's go and have a drink!'

Meat Loaf was scheduled as the next interview, but he joined Billy and myself at the bar. Those two guys got me through a very difficult day.

Ray and Lynne decided it was best if I didn't see the house in such a state, so I stayed in London. David Bowie heard about the fire and called from Switzerland. He asked me to come and stay with him. I said, 'No, I'll be fine,' but it was a beautiful gesture from a lovely guy.

After a sleepless night, I had to interview Boy George, who had also become a good friend. But George couldn't help but see the funny side—his new album was called *Waking Up With The House On Fire*.

'Thanks, Molly,' he smiled. 'Some people will do *anything* to publicise an album.' I had to tell him it would be the most expensive promotion he'd ever have. To add to the act, I set fire to the album during the interview. George's eyes nearly popped out of his mascara!

Later that day, I had to do a satellite interview with Bert Newton for Channel Nine's *Tonight With Bert Newton*. I was a regular on the show in 1984. During the chat, the London studio was engulfed in smoke. Bert kept a straight face, but when he saw the horror on mine, he burst out laughing. It was all good fun.

The fire caused more than $200,000 damage. It was one time I wished I'd listened to my manager, because my house was grossly under-insured.

Luckily, The Beatles' *White Album*, which John, Yoko, Paul and Linda had signed, was on loan to a museum at the time. But I lost a lot of priceless, irreplaceable Egyptian pieces and a heap of rock and sport memorabilia, including my precious cricket bats. It was devastating, but it made me understand the pain of people who lose everything in bushfires. In fact, my loss was minuscule compared to so many tragedies.

Growing up in the country, I had seen many bushfires. I even worked as a volunteer fireman in the '60s in the Dandenongs. But to personally experience fire was something else. With the things I lost, I had to almost wipe them from my mind, pretend that I never owned them. Only then could I get on with my life.

I'll never forget coming home. The stench of smoke lingers. From the front, the house looked the same, but when I opened the door, all I could see was charcoal.

'I just can't rebuild it,' I said, as I buried my face in my hands. But you do.

I lived in the back room, next to the garage, for four weeks while I found another house to rent. Every morning, I woke up to the sickly smell of smoke. It was horrible.

But times of devastation can also bring moments of genuine joy. With the kitchen ruined, Lynne took to washing the dishes in the outside spa. One afternoon, the spa was otherwise engaged, so Lynne screamed out to me while I was on the phone: 'What the hell will I do with these dishes?'

'How the hell would I know,' I yelled back, 'I'm on the damn phone. Chuck the bloody things in the pool for all I care.'

And Lynne did just that.

I had to spend the next couple of hours diving in the pool, recovering the plates, cups and cutlery.

After that little drama, we sat in the garden, had a good laugh and sipped on a lovely glass of cold lemonade.

When I was living with Molly, often I'd wake up and see that his Jag wasn't out the front. I'd say, 'Where's the car?' He'd just look confused and say, 'I don't know, lovey.' Then it would be my job to ring just about every club in Melbourne and ask: 'Is there a red Jag parked outside?'

Amanda Pelman, former housemate

17: THE QUEEN AND ME

1954–1997: Rockin' the Royals . . . in more ways than one—The
King and I—A call from Ronald McDonald—Working with a rampant
leftie faggot—The death of a Princess.

In your search to find out 'why' with Molly, you probably won't find it.
There is no why. There's just an 'is'.
Mark Holden

My interview with Prince Charles in 1977 wasn't my only right
royal blunder.

In the early '80s, I flew to the United States to do some
interviews. I checked into the Bel Age Hotel in Los Angeles and
went through my messages. Much to my surprise, there was a
call from John Reid's office, giving me details about his birthday
bash, which was being held that Saturday. The message said
Mr Reid (Elton's manager) was staying at the Sunset Marquis.

'Oh, no,' I thought—I'd forgotten all about the birthday
invitation I'd received a few weeks before. I was going to have
to tell John I couldn't attend because I had to be in New York
for three major interviews.

The problem is, John doesn't like taking no for an answer.

With my tail between my legs, I headed over to the Sunset
Marquis to catch up with John's entourage, including publicist
Patti Mostyn, Australian recording executive Ken East and his
wife, Dolly. John was delighted to see me and very excited about

his party. I managed to muster the courage to diplomatically tell John I couldn't make it. Patti turned on me, calling me the rudest person on earth. But I explained that John wouldn't be happy if I cancelled an Elton interview. He calmed down and insisted that I delay my New York flight for at least one day, because he was having a dinner party.

The dinner was at one of the most exclusive restaurants in Los Angeles—Le Dome on Sunset Boulevard.

Unfortunately, I arrived at Le Dome about an hour late because of a busy interview schedule. I was shown to a private room at the back of the restaurant. I was duly berated, and sat in the middle of the table next to Dolly East. The conversation was lively, as always, and the gentleman sitting opposite me, David—whom I assumed was an American friend of John's— started chatting to me. I kept referring to him as 'mate' because I thought I'd met him before.

As the party wore on and guests started to leave, we all moved towards one end of the table and it was then that I realised I didn't actually know David; he just reminded me of someone. 'I'm sorry,' I said, 'I thought I knew you, but I actually don't know you at all.'

Still thinking he was American, I told him he bore an uncanny resemblance to the English Royal Family. 'What I mean by that is the Queen of England's sister, Princess Margaret, was once married to Antony Armstrong-Jones and you have an uncanny resemblance to him.'

At this stage, I didn't realise there was a hushed silence around the table. I went on and on. 'What happened was that Princess Margaret got divorced . . .' I then provided a potted history of the Royal Family.

Finally, I took a breath and John Reid stood up and intoned: 'Molly, have you met Viscount Linley?'

I sunk into my chair. David was Princess Margaret's son.

'I am so sorry,' I said meekly.

'No,' he smiled, 'I am very impressed—you seem to know more about my family than I do.'

I must say I was furious with John Reid, who hadn't told me he was managing Viscount Linley in his furniture-making business. To this day, John thinks my faux pas is hilarious.

Viscount Linley is a lovely bloke, very down to earth. I saw him again when Elton John and Eric Clapton performed at Wembley. During the interval, I was standing at the bar with Viscount Linley when the Duchess of York, Sarah Ferguson, bounced up and said hello. He ignored her, literally turning his back, as Fergie went bright red. She muttered an apology and walked away, as we returned to our conversation. I must say I was flabbergasted.

After the show, Bernie Taupin was having a private party at a very fashionable restaurant in Covent Garden. Viscount Linley pulled me aside. 'Molly, I really must apologise for my strange behaviour at Wembley. You may or may not understand, but at the moment we are having some private family problems.'

'Oh, that's all right,' I said, 'we all do.'

I have always been fascinated by the Royal Family, and, at times, I have been a real royalist. But I became a republican in the '90s. We are our own country. And I find it offensive that as an Australian I am always caught in a huge line at Heathrow Airport, while Europeans just walk straight through. It always hits me that even though we have the Queen on our coins, we still have to stand in line. I also have strong views about our flag. I don't think the Union Jack should remain. Having it replaced by the Aboriginal flag would be a good alternative.

For England, however, I think they must keep the Royal Family. I cannot imagine England without royalty, and, of course, it adds so much to tourism.

My first brush with royalty came at the start of 1954 when Queen Elizabeth II made her first visit to Australia and came to Shepparton. I was a student at Shepparton High School. I was so excited that I was going to see the Queen, I threw up the night before she arrived. Mind you, it was so packed at the Shepparton footy oval, it was hard to see her as her grand black Rolls-Royce drove around.

I also remember going to Melbourne at that time and seeing the dome on Flinders Street Station done up like a royal crown in lights. To that point in my life, it was the most impressive thing I'd ever seen.

The next time I bumped into royalty—literally—was during my first trip to London in 1968. I was sharing an apartment with promoter Kenn Brodziak in a mews off New Bond Street, which is a rather exclusive part of London. One afternoon, as I was racing to collect Mr Brodziak's dry cleaning from a shop, I accidentally crashed into a man on the street. We both fell to the ground. As I picked myself up, I realised I'd knocked over The Duke of Kent.

I was so stunned, I couldn't even mumble an apology.

In 1985, I had another round of rock 'n' roll royalty.

At the end of 1984, while my house was being rebuilt after the fire, I moved into a place just off Victoria Street in Richmond. I shared the house with Lynne and a good friend of mine, a rather wild man named Darren Wright. They really helped me get through some tough times, as did my girlfriend, Joy, who I was unofficially engaged to at the time.

In January 1985, I was due to fly to Cairo to meet Joy, who had spent Christmas with her parents in Perth. Unfortunately, I partied a little too hard in Melbourne and missed my flight. The following day, when I went to check in, I discovered I'd left my passport at home. Joy, who had never been to Cairo, was stranded on her own and not happy. Fortunately, I was able to board a plane on my third attempt, landing in Cairo only to find that my luggage had gone missing. By the time I got to our hotel, it was 2 a.m. and Joy wouldn't let me into our room. Through the big wooden door, I explained to her about the luggage and she finally relented. As I collapsed on the bed, I was overcome by an intense garlic smell. Joy was suffering from a cold and had turned to a diet of garlic pills. There was no doubt this trip was turning into a disaster. But, once Joy saw the magnificent beauty of the great Pyramids and the Sphinx, all would be forgiven—or so I thought.

I had to spend the next day trying to track down my luggage, and the Cairo dust was doing nothing for Joy's cold.

We took an overnight train, up the Nile to Luxor. We checked into the Winter Palace and headed to the Valley of the Kings. Joy's cold wasn't getting any better and I have to admit it was a very hot day, and the garlic smell was making me a bit nauseous. To me, the Valley of the Kings is one of the world's most fascinating places, and I could spend weeks there, wandering from tomb to tomb. But for Joy, clambering down tombs in hot conditions was not exactly her cup of tea. She loved the Tomb of Tutankhamun and also the Tomb of Horemheb. She was patient when we clambered down Ramesses I, she looked a little impatient when we took on Ramesses III, and she'd had enough when it came to Ramesses IX.

I guess it was the old saying, after you've seen one tomb, you've seen 'em all. And I knew that if I kept insisting, she would willingly bury me with one of the Ramesses. Trying to calm her down, we went to a restaurant overlooking the Valley of the Kings and sipped on a delicious Egyptian Bloody Mary.

I remember her sitting there saying, 'You really love this place, don't you?'

'Yes,' I replied, 'one day we'll hopefully come back and live here for six months each year.'

The look on her face was one of dread. At that moment, I realised the engagement was over, but we'd always be friends.

When we returned to our Cairo hotel, there was another urgent message from my manager Ray Evans. 'Oh, no,' I thought, 'surely, we haven't burned down the house we're renting?'

When I finally got hold of Ray, he revealed that I'd been asked to be King of Moomba. 'No way,' I said. But Ray explained why I should do it, explaining how it would be good for *Countdown*. And Joy convinced me it could be a lot of fun. So I finally agreed to do it, flying home from the land of the Kings and the Pharaohs to become the next King of Moomba.

Moomba is a major Melbourne festival, and it was absolutely massive in the '70s and '80s. I can't say I didn't know what I was getting into, because my good friend Daryl Somers had been King in 1983. 'Mollice,' he warned me, 'you'll have a lot of fun, but, believe me, it's a lot of hard work and they'll own you for that month.'

Daryl wasn't wrong. I got off the plane and my royal duties had started. They even put an ex-Army officer in charge of my day-to-day commitments. The first event was a Town Hall reception, where I was crowned. Everyone was wondering whether I would wear a crown instead of my hat; well, I had a special crown made that sat on *top* of my hat. I must admit it looked a little bizarre.

A Queen was also crowned, Anne Erikson, and she was an absolute hoot. After the coronation, there was a press conference and, of course, a member of the press couldn't help himself:

'And so Molly, what is it like to be the Queen—oh, um, I mean the *King* of Moomba?' The room burst into laughter and I couldn't help but have a little giggle myself. The Queen looked a little bewildered.

Juggling my royal commitments with *Countdown* was a nightmare, but working for charity is very rewarding and can be a lot of fun. I did get frustrated with my minders at a few events. Kids would be asking for autographs, but I'd be told, 'No, you haven't got time to do that, you'll be late for your next appointment.'

'Too bad,' I'd say, 'you've just got to do these things.'

It's good to be King.

I appointed Gavin Wood as Court Jester and decreed that Derryn Hinch had to wear a tie to any official Moomba function. And John Blackman and Shirley Strachan faced charges of treason if they continued to send me up during my reign.

I remember one incident at Flemington Racecourse. When the Queen and I arrived, we were ushered up to the hallowed members' area. Let me tell you, they're a stuffy lot up there. Snobbish and bordering on boring. One of the committee men's wives—who looked like some crazed relative of the Royal Family—came up to me: 'Oh,' she sniffed, 'you're the Queen of Moomba, they tell me.' And then she laughed with her friends. I was so furious I felt like asking what number she was in the next race.

The Queen and I were driven around the racecourse. When the car stopped in front of the main grandstand, I was mobbed by a group of kids, scrambling for an autograph. I stopped in the middle of the track and started signing. The officials were flustered. 'Molly,' they informed me, 'you've got to get off the track, we're about to start the next race.' But I stood firm. I was still smarting from the remarks of the committee man's wife, and I didn't want to disappoint the kids. The race was delayed for seven minutes, which is unheard of. God knows what it did to the TAB. Afterwards, I felt a little guilty and was hoping that my brother Brian, a racing writer, wouldn't cop any flak—this could really be a case of Hard Luck Harry.

The Moomba commitments climaxed with the parade down Swanston Street. Instead of the usual float, the organisers allowed me to have a St Kilda float, decked out in red, black and white, with some of the St Kilda team sitting at my feet. It was a blast—and a far cry from the Batmobile Gavin Wood and I were in the year before, which we had to push when it ran out of petrol.

I really did feel like the King of Melbourne for a day.

Shortly after Moomba, Lynne and I returned to the newly built Luxor. We had built a second storey and installed all the mod-cons, including a huge air-conditioning/heating system. The only problem was we couldn't work out how to turn down the heating, so it often felt like we actually were living in the Sahara.

About a week after returning home, the phone rang.

'Hello, this is Ronald McDonald,' Lynne thought the caller said.

'Yeah, very funny,' she replied as she went to hang up.

'No, no. This is *Ranald* Macdonald. I would like to speak to Ian Meldrum.'

'Well, he's not here.'

'Could you please tell him that I called?'

'Yeah, sure.'

When Lynne gave me the message, I knew it was important. Ranald was a member of the Syme family (who owned *The Age* newspaper from 1856 to 1983 when they sold it to Fairfax) and a former managing director of *The Age*.

Lynne rang Ranald back. 'What would you like to speak to Mr Meldrum about?'

'Their Royal Highnesses are coming to Melbourne for Victoria's 150th celebrations, and there is one royal request— Princess Diana would like to see some rock 'n' roll bands.'

It was my job to organise a gig for Prince Charles and Princess Diana.

My heart sank. This'll be a laugh-a-minute, I thought . . .

Lynne Randell

Lynne made an appointment for Ranald and his assistant to meet me at my house. She told me and, of course, I forgot all about it.

Three days later, Ranald and his assistant arrived at 9 a.m. 'Molly, get up!' Lynne yelled, before offering the guests a cup of tea. She then realised I was out of milk, so she excused herself and raced to the 7-Eleven.

I eventually woke up. With the heater still broken, I desperately needed a glass of water. I staggered down the stairs in my underpants and headed for the kitchen, not even noticing the two people sitting on the couch. As I gulped the water, I looked up and was surprised to see two strangers. 'Who the fuck are you?' I asked.

It was not the best introduction.

Ranald and his assistant explained the Prince Charles and Princess Diana visit to Melbourne and how, at Diana's request, they would like to stage a rock concert. I agreed to organise the show. The first thing I did was contact the man who helped out when I was King of Moomba, Graeme Stephen.

Graeme is a leading member of Melbourne's gay community. He likes to call himself 'a rampant leftie faggot'. He was surprised when asked to work on the concert.

> In my youth, I was involved with revolutionary organisations, Irish organisations. And I didn't give a fuck about them [Charles and Di]. They were just wasting taxpayers' money.
>
> **Graeme Stephen, events coordinator**

The Bicentennial Authority once sent Graeme out to buy a suit. He returned with a new pair of jeans and a denim jacket and explained, 'Well, that's a suit—a denim suit.'

We made quite a team: the royalist and the anti-royalist. He took great delight in calling me 'comrade' and referring to me as 'the dude who grew up in the country and was still impressed by the ruling class'.

> I think Ian was always a bit blown away by my 'fuck off' attitude. He would say, 'Graeme, you can't say that to people.' I would reply, 'Why not?' Ian, I think, was always amused by my stupidity.
>
> **Graeme Stephen**

It was decided to call the event, after much deliberation in Ranald's office, 'Rocking With The Royals', and it was scheduled for the Melbourne Concert Hall on Tuesday 4 November, 1985.

But who was to be on the bill?

I desperately wanted INXS as the headline act. I also pitched for the Models, and I'm Talking with Kate Ceberano. I quickly confirmed that the Models and I'm Talking were keen, but INXS's manager, Chris Murphy, gave a simple reply: 'No way.'

I then begged Chris's assistant, Gary Grant. 'They're in

the country, for God's sake. What's stopping them from doing it?' Gary explained they were in the middle of recording commitments and the band was unavailable.

I tried a different pitch a day later, but got the same answer—forget it.

> I remember Molly being so taken aback and furious that Chris Murphy could be so pig-headed. But Molly never takes no for an answer.
>
> **Lynne Randell**

I set Lynne a task: get the phone numbers for Michael Hutchence's mother and Mrs Farriss, the mother of Andrew, Tim and Jon.

I then called the mums. 'We're organising a fantastic event in Melbourne with Prince Charles and Princess Diana,' I revealed. 'If INXS were to perform, would you like to come to the show and sit with the royals? Yes, that's right, you'll be in the same row as Princess Diana.'

Two days later, Chris Murphy's office called. 'Fuck, Molly, they'll do the show.'

I also added another one of my favourite bands, Kids In The Kitchen.

The show sold out quickly, so I decided that, for $2, members of the public would be admitted to the underpass next to the venue, where they could watch the show on giant video screens. Afterwards, the bands and the royals would wave to the crowd. A security nightmare, but a great public relations exercise.

The Concert Hall was barely half-full when Kids In The Kitchen hit the stage—Melbourne had been hit by a downpour a couple of hours before the show, which caused traffic chaos.

Kids In The Kitchen did just one song, 'Current Stand', backed by a 40-piece choir. As they left the stage a few minutes after 8 p.m., bass player Craig Harnath decided to 'hit the drink rider'.

Lynne, who sat with the royals as I compered the night, later told me that Diana said she loved Kate Ceberano and I'm Talking, but she added, 'I'm not sure I got the next band [the Models].'

Unfortunately, the Models were not happy with their performance, because James Freud had some gear problems.

> What happened was James's monitor system was wired the wrong way. He always wanted to hear just his voice in the mix when he sang, but on this night, he had just me—my guitar and vocals, so he had a major tantrum. Being the Concert Hall, there was an orchestra pit in front of the stage, so he kicked his monitors into the pit, and he threw his bass across the stage, snapping the neck. It was one of the biggest onstage dummy spits I've ever seen. I imagine that Prince Charles would still remember it.
>
> **Sean Kelly, Models**

When the Models were introduced to Diana, she said to James: 'I noticed you seemed to have a little bit of trouble with the public address system.'

At interval, the royals were escorted to a private function, where they were introduced to members of the Red Cross. Lynne accompanied the royals, along with Lee Simon, the program director of EON-FM, and his wife, Jan.

During the break, Princess Diana asked Lynne if she would mind accompanying her to the toilet. Lynne's reply was: 'I certainly *do* mind.' Thankfully, Jan Simon came to the rescue and she escorted Diana.

The second half of the show featured INXS.

Wearing a leather jacket over a 'Watch the world argue' T-shirt, Michael Hutchence looked like the archetypal rock star.

This was a band at its absolute peak, about to break worldwide. 'Good to see ya,' Michael told the crowd. 'Great to be back in Australia. Let's have a party.'

The INXS set included 'The One Thing', 'This Time', 'Listen Like Thieves', 'What You Need' and 'Original Sin'.

It was a mesmerising performance.

Pointing to the crowd before the band launched into 'Don't Change', Michael smiled and said, 'Hey, the Royals are rockin'!'

After their performance, I had to dash out the back entrance to get to the underpass balcony. Looking down to the underpass disco was amazing—thousands of people were dancing and the noise was deafening.

Earlier in the day, Lynne and I decided it would be best if we were to introduce the royals to the lead singer of the respective bands and they would walk with us and introduce the rest of the members. Lynne's responsibility was to look after Prince Charles, while I was to take care of Princess Diana. Unfortunately, Lynne got lost trying to find her way to the balcony, which left me rather flustered.

'The royals are about to walk down the stairs,' I was told. In a panic, I whipped off my hat and half-bowed and half-curtsied at the same time. I then tried to introduce Princess Diana to Scott Carne, lead singer of Kids In The Kitchen.

'Your Royal Highness, I would like you to meet the lead singer of Kids In The Kitchen, Scott Carne. Scott, this is Princess Charles.'

She giggled and whispered, 'No, I'm Princess Diana.'

'Oh yes, you're right,' I stammered, 'that's Charles behind you.'

The band's bass player, Craig Harnath, also made an impression on the royals.

I had no idea we were going to meet the Prince and Princess. When we were lined up afterwards, Prince Charles said to [guitarist] Claude [Carranza], 'I think your friend's had a little too much to drink.'

Craig Harnath, Kids In The Kitchen

As I walked down the line, thousands of people in the underpass were screaming, 'We want Di! We want Di!' I presented the royal couple with four cowboy hats: two big hats for Charles and Diana, and two miniature hats for Princes William and Harry.

'Oh, heaven forbid,' Diana shrieked. 'I'll have to take them back to the children and they'll want to *wear* them!'

I then gestured to the couple to go to the front of the balcony and wave to the crowd. Diana insisted that I join them. It was a magic moment. I thought I was on the balcony of Buckingham Palace. I just wondered if maybe down there Christopher Robin was with Alice.

A documentary on the event—produced and directed by *Countdown*'s Karl Steinberg—ends with Michael Hutchence, sitting in the passenger seat of a big white car. The window is wound down and Michael is tapping his hands on the door. 'Rockin' the Royals,' he beams. Spotting a friend in the crowd, he waves. 'See you at the party!' And the white car drives off into the distance.

A few months later, the INXS special was shown on the BBC, which helped break the band in the United Kingdom. And a song from the show, 'One x One' ended up on the *Live Baby Live* album, which I've already said enough about.

After the concert, with the royals safely tucked in bed at Government House, the crew and I staged a big party at the Melbourne club Inflation. We presented the band members with special commemorative medallions. I know they were all blown away by the night. And there were some very proud mums as well.

The day after the concert, I accompanied Princess Diana as she visited the Royal Children's Hospital. I was in awe of how she related to the sick kids. The following day, I flew to Canberra for lunch at The Lodge, with the royals and Prime Minister Bob Hawke and his then wife, Hazel. The PM had invited twelve notable Australians—how I got a guernsey, I'll never know.

For once in my life, I was actually the first to arrive. I was led into a drawing room and asked if I'd like coffee or tea. About ten minutes later, I was surprised by a loud voice: 'Molly, where the fuck are you?' I nearly died. It was Bob and Hazel's daughter Rosslyn, who was staying there with her two children. For the next half-hour, we sat in the garden and had a great chat.

Finally, the royals arrived and were introduced to the twelve guests. Princess Diana burst out laughing when she was introduced to me. 'What do I call you, Ian or Molly?' I told her that after what I'd done the other night, she could call me anything.

I was seated next to Diana at lunch, with golfer Jack Newton on her other side. For once, I was 'out-Mollyed' by Jack, who lost his right arm when he walked into the propeller of a light plane at Sydney Airport in 1983. As the guests tucked into a traditional Australian dinner—roast lamb with gravy, peas and potatoes—Jack said to Princess Diana: 'Doesn't it give you the shits having to do all these things and meet boring people like us?'

He then added, 'You're sitting on my good side, so I'll be able to play with your leg under the table.'

Princess Diana giggled, 'Oh, you're terrible, Jack.'

I was so stunned, my fork slipped on the roast lamb, sending some peas flying towards Hazel.

Jack would later explain his comments, 'Being yourself is the only way to be.' Which is very true, and how I've tried to live my whole life.

Twelve years after Rocking With The Royals, I was rocked by Diana's death, in a car crash in Paris. My mind hurtled back to the concert, where Graeme Stephen and his creative crew had organised for a smashed car to be hung in the overpass. Shaken, I called Graeme and asked, 'How on earth did you ever come up with an idea like that?'

Graeme was blunt, as usual: 'It was just a wanky artist who wanted to create a way-out disco scene.'

I placed a candle in the underpass for Diana.

Diana was a big music fan—she loved Duran Duran, Sting, Elton, Michael Jackson and many others—and she was a wonderful mum and a lovely lady. I felt numb for days after her death. My beloved St Kilda had just finished on top of the AFL ladder, but even that didn't seem to mean much to me.

I was struck by Diana's charm and aura. People, including many pop stars, try to have an aura, but with Diana it was natural. She truly was an English rose and as brave as a candle in the wind.

I was having a '40s party sometime in June 1985 and, as was my custom, I flew Molly into London to stay for the week. It happened to be Derby Day the day he arrived (it must have been the first Wednesday in June), and I had tickets for the Royal Enclosure, which required morning dress. I had secretly contacted Molly's assistant and got his measurements.

We picked him up from Heathrow about 10 a.m. and took him back to my house, where I told him he had an hour to get ready to go to the Derby. He was totally confused and couldn't understand how on earth we could get there in time for the first race. We just told him to shut up and drink the champagne. Twenty minutes later, poor jetlagged Molly thought he was in Vietnam when two helicopters descended on my lawn. I was able to pull off a miracle and get the second helicopter especially for Molly and I. We were in the Royal Enclosure with Her Majesty 25 minutes later. The biggest piss-off for me was Molly knew more people than I did!

A year later, I was in Australia for the Melbourne Cup and the Adelaide Grand Prix. I tried everything to get an airline ticket and a hotel, without success. Molly called me on the morning of the Grand Prix to say he had secured two tickets on an airline, and a hotel room for the night. I arrived in Adelaide about an hour before the race and was met by a police car at the airport. I rushed to the hotel and realised that not only did I have a room, I had the Presidential Suite. The police waited and took me to the VIP stand, where Molly was waiting.

After much hugging, Molly casually introduced me to his friend Bob, a very nice gentleman, whom I spoke to for the next fifteen

minutes. I then asked someone, 'Who is Bob?' I was told that he was the Australian Prime Minister, Bob Hawke.

   Molly got his one-upmanship.

**Billy Gaff, former manager of Rod Stewart
and John Mellencamp**

18: TURN UP YOUR RADIO

1981–1987: Living in the '80s—Radio Ga-Ga—Docker shocker—
Mi-Sex, Pseudo Echo and Incredible Penguins—A funking disgrace—
Some really heavy sex—I win a Logie—Live Aid—Waking up
the Neighbours—Jack comes back—The Countdown Sisters

It was a story unfolding every week. It was a lot harder to access
entertainment news back then, and Countdown *told us what was going*
on. Even though I was more of a fringe dweller, there were many times
when I saw it first on Countdown.

Joe Camilleri

As if I wasn't busy enough, I got a new job in 1982.

On 5 October, I started a breakfast radio shift with John
Peters on EON-FM, arranging not one, but five, wake-up calls
to make sure I got there on time.

On our first show, we interviewed James Reyne, Duran
Duran's John Taylor and Derryn Hinch. I told the press: 'The
station has given us the go-ahead to do whatever we like, as
long as we don't go overboard.'

Michelle Higgins—who worked for EON after leaving
Mushroom Records—and program director Lee Simon were
instrumental in me joining the station. The offer came out of
the blue. I thought I was way too mainstream to work for EON,
which was a progressive station when it started.

Michelle influenced my life in another way, encouraging me

to go on the Beverly Hills Diet. The health kick was so successful that I decided to ride my bicycle to EON. I did Tuesday and Thursday mornings at EON. The Thursday shift was the hardest because Wednesday was a big night at the Chevron and often I would go straight from the club to the station.

My assistant, Lynne Randell, would often get frantic calls from John Peters: 'Where is he?!'

'I don't know,' Lynne would be forced to reply, 'and I can't call him on the car phone because he's on his bike.'

John Peters moved to a night-time shift, pioneering the popular listener request show, The Top 8 At 8, and I was joined on air by my *Countdown* buddy Gavin Wood in July 1983. It was two hours of wacky radio, including a segment called Batman and Robin: I was Batman and Gavin was Robin. Gavin referred to me as 'Batsy Watsy', and, in a butch voice, I would often say, 'Robin, for God's sake, pull yourself together.' We also did the voices for the supporting cast, including Damian Featherbottom, who used to be Duran Duran's personal hairdresser, Lady Farquhar and receptionist Tita Miena. But the segment was curtailed when the publishing company that owns Batman and Robin complained to EON's management, and I think we ended up as 'Super Bruce and Randy'.

The 'Holy Copyright Infringement!' drama was nothing compared to the trouble that was to happen at the end of 1983.

Gavin had an excellent radio philosophy: 'If you can't go on air and have fun, you shouldn't be there.' Good advice for any would-be FM broadcaster. But on 1 December, 1983, at 7.20 a.m., we decided to get serious.

Bad move.

Molly: Listen, there's a bit of a worry in the papers this morning on a report. You know that guy that's doing the Royal Commission into the Painters and Dockers?

Gavin: Ah, Mr Costigan?

Molly: Yes.

Gavin: Yeah.

Molly: He has been paid—and this is apparently official—$1,003,750 since his task began in October 1980. He began on a daily fee . . . Wait for this, hold on. He began on a daily fee of $1200 a day, which means he went up, you know, which went up to $1300 in July 1981, and to $1500 last February, minus a hefty tax slug.

Gavin: Goodness me, that's about $330,000 a year.

Molly: Now, quite frankly, Mr Costigan, I don't care a damn what the Painters and Dockers are doing anymore, if you're getting paid this money, with all those people unemployed, I think there should be an inquiry—a total Royal Commission—into you. Now, if we get sued, I'll still say it . . . He shouldn't be paid that much money. *[I was starting to dig a very big hole.]*

Gavin (announcing The Clash's 'Rock The Casbah'): Same here. It's ridiculous! Twenty-one past seven, EON-FM, Rock the QCs everywhere. 'Rock The Cashbah' . . . Now, you were saying about Costigan and all that ridiculous money the man is getting paid, right.

Molly: Look, we are fools! No, we are fools! *[At least I got that bit right . . .]*

Gavin: Yes, I know, he . . .

Molly: Oh, not another report.

Gavin: People could argue that he is a very learned man and all of that, but, still, that money is not . . . it is ridiculous money and he shouldn't be paid that much money.

Molly: $1 million . . . I mean, look, I'd prefer to go down and see the Painters and Dockers . . .

Gavin: In the Odd Spot . . .

Molly: Probably getting a slug from them anyhow.

Gavin: Well, speaking . . .

Molly: Oh! I shouldn't have said that, 'slug'.

Gavin: Ah, speaking of stupid expenditure . . . well, expenditure which is quite reasonable, I suppose, when you really get to the seat of the problem—toilet paper costs.

Molly: Now, this is more like the Costigan report.

Gavin: Yes, yes. The State Government last year paid $59,345 for toilet paper.

Molly: You're joking!

Gavin: But that figure doesn't include the toilet paper used by schools, police stations or law courts.

Molly: Which just goes to show how much bull goes on in parliament.

Gavin: And can you imagine if there was no toilet paper at the police stations, the police would have nothing to go on.

It was a mix of music, serious political comment and lame jokes. And the result was we were all hit with a Supreme Court writ from Mr Costigan's lawyers, who said that the report alleged that Mr Costigan was:

    (a) Corrupt.

    (b) Had conducted the Royal Commission solely for the purpose of personal gain.

    (c) Had conducted the Royal Commission in an unprofessional and partial manner.

    (d) Had accepted bribes from painters and dockers.

    (e) Had presented reports to Parliament and/or would present reports to Parliament worthy only as toilet paper.

EON worked out a settlement with Mr Costigan, and Gavin and I were forced to read out an apology on air.

Then we had to apologise for the apology.

The girl in the office typed up the apology. Instead of writing, 'We unreservedly apologise to . . .', she wrote, 'We reservedly apologise to . . .'

Of course, we didn't pick up on it. And the shit hit the fan again. The lawyers went crazy.

Gavin Wood, radio host

In a separate incident, we locked ourselves in the EON studio for 27 hours.

In 1984, after many lean years, Tina Turner was back on top of the charts with the single, 'What's Love Got To Do With It' (co-written by former Twilights member Terry Britten), and album, *Private Dancer*. But Tina honoured commitments made before her comeback, including performances at McDonald's sales conventions, and shows at Hilton hotels in Australia. As well as the Hilton shows, I thought Tina should do a show at the Melbourne Entertainment Centre, so her fans could see her at a more affordable price. But the entertainment union said she wasn't allowed because her work permit had expired.

I hatched a plan. At 8.55 a.m., as Gavin was signing off for the morning, I announced, 'We're not going anywhere . . . you and I are staying in this studio until we get word from Roger Davies [Tina's manager] that she will be doing a show for everyone.' Gavin thought I was joking, but I said, 'No, Gavin, we're not leaving until we get this sorted out.'

As the day went on, Bank Street was packed with people wanting to be part of the protest. They brought us food and drinks, and signed the petition. The mission was accomplished at 11 a.m. the following day.

I ended up doing nearly four years at EON (now MMM). But I became frustrated with their restrictive playlist. The station refused to play my two favourite acts at the time, Prince and Madonna. But I would smuggle in their new releases and put them to air. I later heard there was a hole in the bedroom wall at program director Lee Simon's place—he would punch the wall when he'd wake up and hear me playing Prince or Madonna.

I aged ten years doing breakfast radio with Molly. But it was a wonderful ride.

Gavin Wood

Of course, *Countdown* remained my priority in the '80s. Many great artists appeared on the show, including the Divine Miss M, who I absolutely love. At the start of the '80s, New Zealand band Mi-Sex were one of the biggest bands in the land. Their success prompted this exchange on *Countdown*:

Molly: There you go, that was Mi-Sex.

Bette Midler: The band's called Mi-Sex?

Molly: They're from New Zealand.

Bette: Which sex is it?

Molly: I don't know.

Bette: You don't know? You, of all people, don't know! Sex that you've never experienced before? I find this very hard to believe. Your reputation precedes you, Mr Meldrum.

In October 1982, I interviewed Professor Rubik on *Countdown*. 'I can't work it [the Rubik's Cube] out,' I told the Professor. 'Can you do it? I have enough trouble driving my car. Can you drive your car properly?'

(Not long after, I drove my Rolls-Royce through the boom gates at the Jam Factory in South Yarra. Believe it or not, I also had some flying lessons in the '80s. But it wasn't for me—people were saying, 'Gosh, you're bad enough on the road, let alone in the air!')

On a cold Thursday night in June 1983, I drove a couple of kilometres from my Richmond home to The Jump Club in

Collingwood to see a band called Pseudo Echo. I fell in love with their electro-pop straight away. Even though they were yet to make a record, I invited the band to appear on *Countdown*.

On 26 June, 1983, I told viewers across the land:

> We're about to present a group, a local group, who have got no record contract. We saw them at a gig. I think they have loads of potential, so all you record companies out there, have a look at them, and the public, you judge for yourselves. We think they're pretty good. A young group, they go under the name of Pseudo Echo. Here they are with 'Listening'. Go, boys!

Pseudo Echo were the first unrecorded band to appear on *Countdown*. At the time, singer Brian Canham was a cabinet-maker in a factory, still living at home.

> Our manager, who was just one of our mates, rang me and said, 'I've got your next gig—*Countdown*.' It was such an event. The next day, I was walking down the street as a pop star. Girls were screaming, people were pointing, and the phone was ringing. It was really full-on and instant.
>
> I never asked any favours of Ian. He just took it on himself that he was going to make a big song-and-dance about our band. To this day, I'm really thankful.
>
> **Brian Canham, Pseudo Echo**

Before the end of the year, Pseudo Echo had signed to EMI and released 'Listening' as their debut single. Their cover of 'Funky Town' later hit the Top 10 in the US and UK and spent seven weeks at number one in Australia.

Countdown also helped make stars out of a band called Moving Pictures.

We went on the show with our first single, 'Bustin' Loose'. The show was hosted by Adam Ant and it was the height of Antmania. It was absolute chaos—screaming, fainting girls all over the place. But they weren't there for us. We were on and off, and that was it. But the next gig we did after *Countdown*, there was a line around the block. We returned to do 'What About Me?' on the show. We were staying at a hotel called the Diplomat on Acland Street in St Kilda. On the Monday morning, I couldn't get out the hotel door to get breakfast—that was the power of *Countdown*.

Alex Smith, Moving Pictures

In 1983, Australian artist Wes Walters painted my portrait and entered it in the Archibald Prize, which prompted this piece in *The Age*:

Unkind souls have pointed to the wording of Jules Francois Archibald's bequest stating that the winning portrait be 'preferably of some man or woman distinguished in art, letters, science or politics' and have cynically wondered if a portrait of pop music guru Molly Meldrum is thus eligible.

That was, indeed, a little unkind! The portrait didn't win the Archibald, but Elton bought the painting for me and it hangs in my house.

Also in 1983, I did a Desert Island Discs segment on radio. Journalists are always asking me to list my favourite songs and albums. It's an impossible task, but in 1983 I nominated these albums: Pink Floyd's *Dark Side Of The Moon*, David Bowie's *Ziggy Stardust*, Michael Jackson's *Off The Wall*, Human League's *Dare*, the Small Faces' *Itchycoo Park*, The Beatles' *White Album*, John Lennon's *Imagine*, and *Molly's Oz Evolution*.

I continued to DJ in the '80s, which was a great way of keeping in touch with what music was connecting with the fans. I had a lot of fun in the clubs, though occasionally I got into trouble.

In August 1984, I was arrested at a Perth disco and charged with disorderly conduct for using obscene language. I had been a guest DJ at Pinocchio's nightclub. When a woman requested a song, I claim that I said: 'If you want to funk, get up on the stage and have a funk.' But six police officers heard it differently.

Later, I testified, 'Unless you were trendy at that stage, you'd have no idea that I was meaning "funk", and, obviously, the cops had no idea.' Fortunately, the judge sided with me, and the charge was dismissed.

A bigger news event in 1984 was Culture Club's first Australian tour. I interviewed Boy George in London before the tour for an ABC special: *Boy George—Who's A Tart?* We had a good chat about make-up—George loves it, but it's never really worked for me—and we also talked about Culture Club's feud with Duran Duran. 'Oh,' George shrieked, 'they hate us!'

> We presented a gold record to Boy George on *Countdown*. Molly fell onto the stage with the gold record, flaring at all the cameras. The mike was under his arm, so you couldn't hear what he was saying. But he said, "Well, Culture Club, the whole thing—you've done us all a lot of proud.' Even though we weren't particularly proud—Virgin Records were—we all knew what he meant. It was just a great Meldrum way of saying it.
>
> **Stephen Jones, *Countdown* producer**

Another headline-grabber in 1984 was Billy Idol, who appeared at the Countdown Rock Awards to sing 'Rebel Yell'. He stood at the podium, bare-chested, except for a huge crucifix, with his arm around me.

> **Billy:** I've had some really heavy sex since I've come to Australia.
> I said I've had some really heavy sex.
> **Molly:** Well, welcome to Australia. Have you been a good boy?
> **Billy:** Don't ask that, Molly, don't ask that.

Billy was always up for a surprise. For one interview, I met Billy at his hotel room in San Francisco. He insisted on doing the interview in bed. When the cameras were rolling, he threw back the sheets and said, 'Molly, suck on this!' What do they say about Idol hands?

At the 1985 *TV Week* Logie Awards, I received a special Logie for Outstanding Contribution to the Australian Music Industry and Encouragement of Talent. I gave the Logie to the family of Wayne De Gruchy, John Paul Young's manager, who died the week of the awards.

The biggest event of 1985 was Live Aid.

I was in London when the show was announced. John Reid, Elton's manager, said to me: 'Look, I've got to go to Wembley today because Bob Geldof's making a big announcement. Do you want to come?' As Bob talked about his plans to have concerts at Wembley and in the US, with satellite links around the world, I turned to John and said, 'He's living in a dream world.' Even Elton looked a bit bewildered.

But then the dream started to become a reality.

Channel Nine was to telecast the event in Australia, but for some reason they pulled out. Bob Geldof somehow tracked me to the Rihga Royal Hotel in New York. 'Get your arse back to Australia,' he ordered. He said Live Aid needed the ABC in Australia. I told him I wasn't sure if they could be involved at such late notice.

'Just fucking do it,' he insisted.

It was three weeks out from Live Aid. I had a meeting with

Michael Shrimpton and Grant Rule. To my surprise, Michael was open to the idea. The next day he called me and said, 'Meldrum, we're going to do it. But you have to be the chairman and you have to take responsibility for every cent raised—every cent has to be accounted for.'

'No problem, that's cool,' I said, not knowing that this would be my nightmare for the following year.

You have to go back and realise what sort of technology was available. Today, you could do it easily, but in the mid-'80s, it was extraordinary. One half of me was saying, 'This is a great challenge, let's do it,' the other half was saying, 'This is nuts!' We agreed to do it eleven days out.

Grant Rule, *Countdown* executive producer

A big part of Live Aid was a Melbourne businessman named Bill Gordon. He sold his furniture company and dedicated himself to the African cause, organising the EAT Concert at Melbourne's Myer Music Bowl, which raised nearly $2 million—seven months before Live Aid. Bill then worked with Bob Geldof on Live Aid, convincing Bob that a worldwide telethon should be part of the event.

For the Australian leg of Live Aid, Bill teamed up with my old manager Brian de Courcy, and we decided to do a concert at the Sydney Entertainment Centre. Due to time differences, this was the first Live Aid concert anywhere in the world. The Oz For Africa bill included INXS—who were on the verge of breaking worldwide—Men At Work, Australian Crawl, the Uncanny X-Men, The Angels, and LRB with John Farnham. Ian Smith, who helped put the concert together, did a wonderful job. With 17 acts on the bill, it was a mammoth production. I nearly derailed the entire schedule when, at the end of LRB's set, I tried to coax John Farnham into performing his brilliant cover of 'Help', which I thought was appropriate. John was up for it and the crowd was going nuts, but unfortunately the roadies had already set up the stage for Mondo Rock. As many TV producers have said to me over the years: 'Stick to the rundown, Molly!'

Our headquarters was the Southern Cross Hotel in Sydney. We recorded the concert on Friday night and then launched the on-air telethon at 8 a.m. on Saturday. Channel Seven gave us access to their facilities, and I commandeered a ferry, the *Harbour Queen*, where I sat for sixteen hours, with Grant Rule and *Countdown* directors Walter Boston and Karl Steinberg. The public response was phenomenal. At one stage I said, 'It's a bit cold here.' Heaters started arriving from everywhere! People gave me money and gifts. Boats cruised past and people threw us watches and diamond rings. One guy donated an Arabian colt. Another person gave us a 1964 tour program signed by The Beatles. It was a powerful experience. And it continued for weeks. People would just walk up to me and give me money. I had to have a 'Live Aid pocket', so I wouldn't get it confused with my own money.

I hadn't slept for more than 48 hours when I did *Countdown* the day after Live Aid. But I was on a high. 'I thought when I attended the recording of "We Are The World", that was one of the highlights of my life in rock 'n' roll,' I said. 'This weekend exceeds all of that.'

I closed the show: 'Instead of saying, "Goodnight Australia", I'll simply say, God bless, Australia.'

I visited many schools that raised money for the cause. I particularly remember one Catholic boys' college, which presented me with a huge cheque. After the lunchtime presentation, I was mobbed by the kids. The principal, a priest, stepped in. 'Boys, Mr Meldrum will go to Room B, where you can all line up for autographs.' They sat me behind a desk, and I was still there at 4.30 p.m. My hand was killing me and I was nearly in tears. I told Lynne, my assistant, 'I can never do that again!'

But the response was fantastic. Bob Geldof did an incredible job, and it was a buzz being part of Live Aid. Australia raised nearly $10 million, which went to the starving millions in Africa.

> If someone had come to me with this idea, but without Ian being involved, I doubt I would have done it. People have great ideas, but Ian can make them happen. He has the capacity to enthuse people. I'll never forget the 'thank-you' lunch at the Southern Cross on the Monday after Live Aid for the event's corporate backers. It was a heap of corporate heavies and Molly just staggered up and kissed me. It was a magic moment.
>
> **Grant Rule**

Bob Geldof later gave me a copy of his autobiography, *Is That It?*, signing it: 'To Molly, Is That It? No. But it nearly was when you got involved. Love and thanks for everything you've done— Bob Geldof.'

Towards the end of 1985, charity also saw me return to the recording studio. My old friend Jim Keays asked if I would like to produce a version of John Lennon's 'Happy Xmas (War Is Over)' for a band called The Incredible Penguins, who wanted to raise money to protect Australia's fairy penguins.

> This recording is a book in itself. At first, he [Molly] wasn't going to do it. But when I told him we were going to do a John Lennon song, he went, 'Great, we'll do it.' The recording became a monster.
>
> **Jim Keays, The Masters Apprentices**

The single features eighteen voices—including John Farnham, Bob Geldof, Colin Hay, Brian Mannix, Brian Canham, Colleen Hewett, Angry Anderson, Scott Carne and Jim Keays—plus

The Peninsula Boys Choir and The Hare Krishna Chorus. The single also incorporated the voices of world leaders, including Margaret Thatcher, Mikhail Gorbachev and P.W. Botha.

It was a cast of thousands. There was so much on it that it didn't fit on 24 tracks. We had to get two 24-track machines and run them in tandem. Not many studios could do it.

One night, Molly wanted to do some phasing or something, like he'd done with 'The Real Thing'. The engineer said, 'We can't do that.' As soon as he said this, Molly went absolutely berserk. 'Whadooya mean, you can't do it? DJs at the fucking Chevron can do it!' He looked at me and said, 'Right, we're going to another studio!'

He ran to the machine and started to try to pull the two-inch tape off the machine. The tape's going around and around and he's trying to pull it off! The engineer is freaking out because it's very expensive equipment. Molly finally got the tapes and threw them at me and said, 'We're outta here.'

The only problem was there was no other studio in Melbourne that could do it. We had to go to Sydney. We filled the two 24-track machines and Molly wanted to go onto a third one. The problem was this was a Christmas record—we were running out of time!

Jim Keays

I remember the day they decided to shoot the video. I was looking pretty scruffy and needed to get home to change, so Molly offered me his wheels— his Rolls-Royce! I will never forget pulling up to my dumpy Grey Street St Kilda flat in his Roller, with everyone checking me out. I took about an hour to do the five-minute trip. First and last time I have ever driven a Roller— and Molly's Roller at that!

Scott Carne, Kids In The Kitchen

Mushroom Records ended up releasing the single two weeks before Christmas in 1985.

It was big for a week, but then, of course, it was all over.

Jim Keays

Believe it or not, I also had a couple of acting roles in the '80s. In 1983, I made my movie debut in a film called *At Last Bullamakanka: The Motion Picture*, about a corrupt politician. I played a priest who doubled as a Boy Scouts leader. The cast also featured John Farnham, Gordon Elliott, Angry Anderson, Derryn Hinch, Donnie Sutherland and Frank Thring. I never saw the end result. They called it 'Australia's answer to *Animal House* and *The Blues Brothers*'. It's meant to be one of the worst Australian movies of all time.

My next acting role had a much bigger audience.

In 1986, my good friend Brian Walsh, who was then at Channel Ten, convinced me to play myself on a show I had never seen—*Neighbours*. Little did I know that when I made my *Neighbours* debut in episode 351, I was following in the footsteps of other *Neighbours* guest stars, Warwick Capper and Leanne Edelsten.

The storyline was that Scott Robinson (played by Jason Donovan) and Mike Young (Guy Pearce) had a song called 'I Believe'. They seek my help after reading a piece in my *TV Week* column about songwriting. But the guys are the victim of a practical joke.

On the day of the filming, my assistant Lynne Randell and I decided to play a practical joke of our own. The guys turn up, Lynne tells them they don't have an appointment and then Lynne and I have a fight, throwing vases and ashtrays at each other. You should have seen the looks on Jason and Guy's faces. They didn't know that Lynne had bought cheap props for the stunt.

This is the take that *Neighbours* didn't show:

Lynne: Can I help you?

Scott: Is Molly Meldrum in?

Lynne: What's it about?

Mike: We've come to play him our tape.

Lynne: Look, he doesn't see anyone without an appointment.

Scott: Oh, but we've got an appointment.

Molly [walking into the room]: Lynne, are those records that Brian brought around here yet? Oh, hi fellas, how you doing?

Lynne: These guys are trying to con me into getting you to listen to their tape.

Scott: We're not trying to con you. We had a call from Molly's secretary, telling us to be here at nine.

Molly: Is that right?

Lynne: It certainly is not.

Molly: Well, fuck, Lynne. I mean, you're meant to be . . . *[smashes vase]*.

Lynne: Don't start at me, Meldrum. I'm sick to death of this bullshit. This is exactly why I'm going to live overseas, you stupid old poofter.

Of course, I get to hear the song. The storyline was that I didn't think much of the song, but I liked the singer—Charlene (played by Kylie Minogue). I arranged for her to meet 'Mr Big', a Michael Gudinski-like recording executive. I actually wanted Michael to play the part, but he wouldn't be in it.

'Me, you want *me*?' Charlene says to the record executive. 'I could be a singer!'

I didn't realise how big *Neighbours* was until I went to London about a year later. I was mobbed by a group of schoolkids at the House of Horrors on the banks of the Thames. 'What's Charlene like?' they screamed. 'What's Scott like?' I had no idea what was going on. A friend had to explain to me that my *Neighbours* episodes had just gone to air in the United Kingdom.

It's funny to think that less than a year after that *Neighbours* storyline, Kylie signed to Michael Gudinski's Mushroom Records and hit number one with her first single, 'Locomotion'. What do they say about art imitating life?

Locally, the biggest music event of the '80s was John Farnham's comeback.

At the start of the '80s, John and I talked about me producing an album for him. We actually worked on it for a while, but nothing eventuated, which was no doubt a good thing for John, because knowing my track record in the studio, we'd probably still be working on it!

John issued a great cover of The Beatles' 'Help', and also did three albums with LRB, but it was obvious that he needed the right song to really make his comeback. 'You're The Voice' was definitely that song. For me, it was love at first listen. I'll never forget a radio programmer friend of mine didn't like it at all. I went to play it for him, thinking that no one could be that stupid. Anyway, everyone else loved it, and *Whispering Jack* became the first local album to sell 1 million copies in Australia.

As it topped the charts, one image played over and over in my head. A couple of years before his resurgence, John was singing at a corporate function. Not many people in the crowd were listening as they talked amongst themselves. Jill Farnham jumped on the table and yelled, 'Shut up, my husband is singing!'

Jill has been a pillar of strength for John.

I, of course, was one of many critics who said that John should have spent more time and effort trying to make it overseas. But when you've got a loving family, great friends and a successful career at home, what more could you wish for?

Speaking of family, a big part of *Countdown* in the '80s was two sisters, who became known as 'The Countdown Sisters'.

Linda Freedman was ten when she first went to *Countdown*. She came along with a youth group in 1980 to see an episode that featured James Freud, Juice Newton and American actor Peter Gallagher. The next year, Linda returned to the Ripponlea studios, with her older sister, Karen, to see Adam and the Ants. Over the following six years, Linda and Karen rarely missed a taping of the show.

Linda's autograph books document the times, with inscriptions from her favourite acts—Duran Duran, Beargarden and The Little Heroes—plus artists such as Elton John, INXS, Boy George, Crowded House, Billy Idol, Julian Lennon, Pseudo Echo, Bucks Fizz, Bonnie Tyler, Laura Branigan, Corey Hart, Ben Elton, Rik Mayall and Marilyn.

Looking at those books brings back a flood of memories. Brian Mannix signed his name as 'Bwian' and wrote, 'Give us a boodge!' ['Boodge' being the Uncanny X-Men's term for 'root'.]

Dave Faulkner of the Hoodoo Gurus wrote, 'Dear Linda, give up Simon and Duran Duran and be my Guru.'

I even regularly signed the books. A 1983 message from me was: 'To Linda, I hope you are doing your homework. Keep studying.'

Karen got stars to sign Linda's book when Linda was home in bed, suffering from the measles. Goanna's Shane

Howard wrote, 'Oh Linda, get unmeasled and have a great Christmas,' adding, 'why do all our roadies have measles? Weird.'

The wait for *Countdown* tickets could run into months, but the ABC's security guard, Paddy, would always let Linda and Karen in, even if they didn't have tickets. He called Linda 'Nuts', and Karen 'Crackers'.

When Culture Club appeared on the show, the sisters' favourite crew member, Mervyn Magee, gave them twenty tickets. Karen thought she'd be a 'legend' in the eyes of her school friends, but the plan backfired when I caught her smoking in the ABC canteen. I ripped the Alpine menthol cigarette from her lips and demanded, 'Why are you smoking?' Karen no longer felt so cool. *Sorry, Karen.*

After another *Countdown* episode, Jeremy Healy from Haysi Fantayzee invited Karen to a nightclub.

> But I stupidly told my mum, who said, 'There's no way you're going, you're only thirteen!' I had to tell Jeremy, 'I'm sorry, my mum said I can't go.'
>
> **Karen Freedman, The Countdown Sisters**

But Karen could be cunning. When Billy Idol appeared at the Countdown Awards, she got some crutches and pretended to have a broken leg, knowing that this would help her get a better seat and improve her chances of meeting Billy. It worked.

Karen also shook Princess Diana's hand at Rocking With The Royals. And I introduced Linda to her idol, Duran Duran bass player John Taylor.

> We were outside the Hilton, where the band was staying, and then John and Andy drove off. I said, 'I bet they're going to Molly's', so we headed over to his house. Sure enough, they were there, and Molly introduced us. Molly and

Lynne Randell were always welcoming. Lynne was so lovely to us, and I was always so jealous of her raspy, sexy voice.

Linda Freedman, The Countdown Sisters

Countdown changed Linda and Karen's lives. They were meeting bands and forging lifelong friendships with other *Countdown* fans.

After I started going to the show, I didn't socialise as much with my school friends, it was all about my *Countdown* friends.

Linda Freedman

When the show was taped on a Friday, the sisters would race home from school, get changed and then walk to the show from their grandparents' house, which was just around the corner from the ABC. I would often drive them home, in my black Rolls-Royce. (Years later, Karen told me that occasionally she'd ride her bike to the studios, but she never wanted to miss a ride in my Roller, so she'd then have to walk back to the ABC to retrieve her bike.) Karen and Linda lived in Bailey Avenue, a dead-end street in East St Kilda. They were always amused by the sight of me trying to turn the Rolls-Royce around and manoeuvre my way back out of the street.

Linda and Karen say only one star was rude to them—Human League's Phil Oakey. He refused to sign anything and when Karen gave him a Cherry Ripe in the ABC canteen, he threw it back, saying, 'I don't want that!' Years later, Linda met Phil when she was working for EMI. He apologised for his behaviour, explaining that he had been suffering from a 'horrendous toothache' when he appeared on the show.

The Countdown Sisters were a big part of the show during the '80s. When they were invited to one of the *Countdown* parties, they decided they would do the right thing and ask their mother if they could attend. She said no.

Karen recalls another occasion when Sex Pistols manager Malcolm McLaren appeared on *Countdown* and then invited everyone back to his hotel room. Again, Mrs Freedman said, 'No way!'

The moral of this story is that often it is best to lie to your parents.

Karen Freedman

Since then, Karen and Linda have both enjoyed many jobs in the music industry, and I'm proud to say we're all still friends.

In the mid-'80s I brought Lauren Bacall to Australia to do a play called *Sweet Bird Of Youth*. She loved Bob Dylan, who happened to be touring at the same time with Tom Petty. Molly was having a big party at his place, so Lauren turned up. Molly had this wall, which he'd get people to sign. She always went by the name 'Betty', so she signed the wall 'Betty Bacall'.

About half an hour later she felt a tap on the shoulder. It was Molly: 'Excuse me, you've signed the wrong name.' She thought he was pretty strange.

Wilton Morley, theatre producer

19: WHEN THE RIVER RUNS DRY

1987: Countdown to extinction—Over the Hill—It takes a lot to laugh, it takes a train to cry—Rockin' the rails—Hair today, gone tomorrow.

> *W.C. Fields put it beautifully: It is funnier to bend things than to break them.*
> **Ian Buckland, TV presenter/magician**

1986 ended with an article in *TV Week*, 'Molly: Not Down For The Count!'

> Ian 'Molly' Meldrum has hit back at rumours that the ABC plans to axe the weekly rock show next year. 'It's absolute crap!' Molly says of rumours which had found their way into print in Sydney.

When the show returned in 1987, it had been renamed and reinvented as Countdown Pirate Television—CDPTV. The first song played for the year was by Swedish hard-rock band Europe. It was called 'The Final Countdown'.

The title of the opening song didn't go unnoticed in my mind, and the song proved prophetic. As much as I didn't want to admit it, I knew that this could be the last roll of the dice. I was totally disillusioned by this time, continually fighting the

ABC over budget cuts. This was the era of David Hill, who was out to make a name for himself.

And the show had slipped from favour.

> I think that towards the end it was hip to put shit on *Countdown*. I think the music business took it for granted and didn't realise what an important part of the whole process it was.
>
> **Michael Gudinski, Mushroom Records**

> A lot of bands resented us enormously. It was something I always found puzzling because fans are fans—why wouldn't you want to appear for your fans?
>
> **Grant Rule, *Countdown* executive producer**

I thought about success and fame when I interviewed Sting. In the mid-'80s, The Police were the biggest band in the world, but they stopped touring. 'I think we all became casualties of that success,' Sting explained. 'God, the pressure.'

When I asked Sting if the band would re-form, he replied:

> The head of our record company said something very interesting about this the other day. He was addressing the issue of what Sting will do next. He said, 'You know, it's like the 600-pound bear: Where does he sit? Where he likes.' And I'm the 600-pound bear.

By 1987, *Countdown* was no longer the 600-pound bear. Ironically, video helped kill *Countdown*. Without huge budgets, the show could not compete with the mega video productions of the '80s. Bands would spend thousands of dollars on a video, and then tell me: 'Why should we appear live? Just play the video.' And, if they did appear, after having spent so much money on their image, they refused to allow the *Countdown* crew to do their own thing.

As Billy Joel remarked to me in an interview in 1987, 'MTV used to say, "More music video to come," now they say, "More video music . . ." I don't like it.' The tail was starting to wag the dog.

Adopting the old 'if you can't beat 'em, join 'em' approach, executive producer Grant Rule actually banned live bands and audiences for a while. (The waving ban was instituted after things got a little out of hand when I hosted the show with Grace Jones. Hands clapping out of time during Grace's performance looked a bit messy on screen.) But without the live buzz, ratings dipped. After all, *Countdown* was always about colour and movement.

We also fell into our own trap because our directors were so good. We were re-creating album covers and the sets were so amazing, it looked like an expensive video clip. I was always like, 'Pull back, show the audience, show them waving, that's what *Countdown*'s always been about!'

Towards the end of 1986, Michael Shrimpton had called Grant Rule to inform him: 'The end is nigh.'

> I was never really told the reasons. I was just told to get out gracefully. To be honest, I knew a lot longer than I admitted. I included Ian very late in the process. It always troubled me that I lied to Ian and said everything was fine. I can look back now and regret it, but at the time it was my job. I couldn't disobey what I was instructed to do. But we were friends, and I'm not proud of what I did.
>
> **Grant Rule**

On a Friday, early in 1987, Michael Shrimpton—then the ABC's head of arts and entertainment—flew to Melbourne to see me. We went to Vogues, a restaurant in Church Street, Richmond. It's now a tile shop.

'We are in deep trouble,' Michael explained to me. 'The ratings . . . budgets . . .'

'I know the reality of all of this,' I replied. 'I can't fight it and no one else can fight it.'

I told Michael that I wanted out, but the show should continue in the same time slot with another host and perhaps a new name. But Michael insisted, 'No, if you go, no matter what time you do it, the show goes.'

'Well, what should we do?'

Michael suggested that the curtain could come down when the postponed Countdown Awards were held in July. He gave me the weekend to think about it. It was one of the worst weekends I've ever had. For a start, I had to go to the ABC studios to tape *Countdown*. I didn't know that Grant was aware the show was coming to an end, but I'm sure he thought it would last at least until the end of the year.

I pondered the decision all weekend and concluded that the Countdown Awards would be a fitting end. I had no idea what my television future would be, but it didn't seem to matter at the time. Michael rang me at 6 p.m. on Sunday—just as that week's episode of *Countdown* went to air.

'I've definitely made my mind up,' I sighed. 'This is when it should happen.'

David Hill endorsed the decision, but asked Michael and I to deny it until it could be announced. When members of the press started calling me, Michael cheekily contacted the ABC boss: 'Hey, Dave, why don't you issue a press release saying, "We're in it for the long haul"?'

I was angry that David Hill wouldn't allow us to announce the decision. I believe he just wanted to grandstand and make the announcement himself. It became ridiculous when the situation dragged on for a couple of weeks. I've always prided myself on being honest with the press, and it hurt me to have to say, 'No, the rumours are simply not true.'

Finally, I decided to carefully leak the story to media friends of mine, to force David Hill to go public. It annoyed me that he got to make the announcement, because he was the one who failed to realise the gap that would be left in the Australian music industry and within the ABC itself.

The *Countdown* axing was announced on 26 June, 1987. I called my former assistant Lynne Randell and asked if she could come to the house and field the calls.

> At one point the operator rang from Sydney to see if something was wrong with the phone because so many people were trying to get through. Molly didn't show a lot on the surface, but I think it was a difficult time for him. They were tearing down an institution, and he didn't know what he was going to do.
>
> **Lynne Randell, former personal assistant**

'It is a very sad time,' I told the press. 'I feel like the Grim Reaper.'

I just wanted to get out of town, go fishing and windsurfing, hire a 4WD and head to Queensland.

On the day the axing was announced, Richard Stubbs, then co-host of 3XY's breakfast show, said: 'I don't think it will have a big effect. It's been running for a while and it's about time for a change.' David Hill said the show was outdated. 'It had been evident for more than eighteen months that the style of the program needed to change significantly to keep step with audience demand.'

But the Opposition spokesman for education and youth affairs, Mr Peter Shack, said the decision showed a remarkable insensitivity to young audiences.

Karen Freedman, who spent much of her childhood at the ABC studios, watching the taping of *Countdown* as one-half of 'The Countdown Sisters', did an interview with *The Age*. 'Everyone's a bit depressed,' she said.

The *Countdown* crew was upset and angry.

I still am. I believe it was a very shortsighted decision. Just because you might be sick of the show, you shouldn't be contemptuous of the audience. Someone will always be growing up, going through that [pop music]. Testament to that is the fact that *Top Of The Pops* was still on air in the UK. And just because you're over it, doesn't mean the consumer is.

Stephen Jones, *Countdown* producer

It could have gone on, no doubt about it.

Grant Rule

But David Hill was a performance-oriented boss, and we were rating around 10, when the show had had a glorious 20 career. Halve the ratings and you have to face the brutal fact. Also, to me, what had happened was there was a new generation of kids who were fracturing in their tastes, saying, 'We don't want this mainstream thing.' An extraordinary kaleidoscope of tastes, and no one has been able to capture that to this day.

Michael Shrimpton, ABC executive

Sometimes I wonder what would have happened if we'd hung in there just a little bit longer. If we'd been able to tough it out, things might have turned around. Unfortunately, we'd been going through a bit of a pop drought, but great acts such as Kylie Minogue and Bon Jovi were about to break big.

But I guess, after thirteen long years, I was worn out.

Kylie Minogue actually co-hosted the second last episode of *Countdown* on 12 July.

It wasn't her first visit to the *Countdown* studio. She was part of the audience for an episode in 1981, when she was thirteen. She came to see The Swingers perform 'Counting The Beat'.

> They threw a drum stick into the audience and I didn't catch it. I was gutted.
>
> **Kylie Minogue**

Kylie hosted *Countdown* with radio DJ Mike Hammond, who was then a rising star on 2SM.

> I, like the rest of my generation, had grown up with *Countdown*. I never in my wildest dreams thought I'd ever be a part of this magical show, other than as a viewer. Two memories stick in my mind: Molly told me he thought I looked like Rick Springfield. I guess looking back at the '80s stonewash denim and white Reeboks, there was a similarity (just). And I'll never forget Kylie gave me a kiss and thanked me for supporting her song, 'Locomotion', on radio in Sydney. There were a lot of knockers of Kylie back then. Surprisingly, they've all been pretty quiet for the past 20 years or so.
>
> **Mike Hammond, DJ, TV presenter**

One more studio *Countdown* was broadcast the following week, at 6pm, preceding the Final Countdown Awards, at 7.30.

We taped the final studio show in Melbourne. I hosted with Carol Hitchcock and my old mate Jim Keays, who had recorded a new version of The Masters Apprentices' debut single, 'Undecided'. It was a strange feeling saying goodbye to the studio that had been my home for thirteen years. The music world—and *Countdown*—had changed so much. We started the show in 1974 with five live acts and screaming fans. Our final studio show was all music videos and no studio audience.

Countdown's final chart-topper was Mel & Kim's 'Respectable'. Sadly, the English duo's pop career was cut short when Mel Appleby was diagnosed with cancer. She died in 1990.

This was *Countdown*'s final Top 10:

10 Club Nouveau—'Lean On Me'
9 Billy Idol—'Sweet Sixteen'
8 Icehouse—'Crazy'
7 Dave Dobbyn—'Slice of Heaven'
6 Starship—'Nothing's Gonna Stop Us Now'
5 George Michael—'I Want Your Sex'
4 Breakfast Club—'Right On Track'
3 Whitney Houston—'I Wanna Dance With Somebody (Who Loves Me)'
2 The Party Boys—'He's Gonna Step On You Again'
1 Mel & Kim—'Respectable'

The producers played Frank Sinatra's 'My Way' as they showed some of my 'finest' *Countdown* moments. But what I remember most about the final studio show is the stunning looks of Carol Hitchcock, who was the first Aussie act to release a single produced by Stock Aitken and Waterman (a dance cover of The Temptations' 'Get Ready'). Carol had a completely bald head—which was a highly unusual look in 1987. And it probably sparked an idea in my own noggin . . .

For the final show—The Final Countdown awards ceremony, to be held in Sydney on 19 July—I was determined to have fun. I told Lynne I wanted to travel to Sydney on the train—with all of my friends.

Lynne called the train people, but they said, 'Sorry, but we don't have room for all those extra people.' I think Lynne was relieved, because she wasn't looking forward to the train trip. But when she told me the news, I said, 'You can fix it, Lynney.' And, of course, she did. They added an extra carriage and The Molly Express was bound for The Final Countdown.

Halfway through the journey, the train stopped, in the middle of nowhere. Lynne was woken by me pounding on her door. 'Lovey, let us in!'

'Go away,' she said, 'I haven't got any clothes on.'

'As if I care!'

Lynne opened the door to see me standing alongside two friends, looking like naughty schoolboys. 'No one can have breakfast in the morning,' I revealed.

'Why?'

'Because we're barred from that part of the train.'

A few of my friends had run amok. In fact, three friends had been thrown off the train. 'You'll have to find them tomorrow, Lynney, and get them to Sydney in time for the awards,' I added.

'Is that all?'

'Yeah, and you don't look very good without your clothes on.'

When my friends were thrown off the train, I tried to negotiate with the station attendants. I was not negotiating from a position of strength, as I was wearing only my underpants. Then the train took off without me. I've never run so fast in all my life. Fortunately, another passenger was able to drag me back onto the train.

One of the evicted passengers was a journalist, Peter Lalor, who is now one of the nation's best sportswriters.

The conductors kept warning Molly and his friends to 'Stop walking up and down the train.' So Molly said, 'All right, the party's over.' I fell asleep in another compartment and when I woke up, I went to get my bags. 'That's it,' the conductor said, 'you're off the train!' He threw me onto the platform at Cootamundra, where two cops dragged me away. Molly jumped off the train, screaming, 'Let him go!'

I woke up in the Cootamundra lock-up and had to catch the bus to Sydney— with a terrible hangover.

Peter Lalor, journalist

A press crew was waiting for The Molly Express when it pulled into Sydney.

When I saw the drama reported on the news, I was not surprised. Would you expect anything less?

Michael Shrimpton

The story made it into *The Truth*, in a piece by my old buddy Dave Dawson: 'Rowdy Riders Rock The Rails'. Dave didn't name Peter Lalor in his story, but cleverly alluded to his namesake, saying the train trip was 'worse than facing bullets at the Eureka Stockade'.

Nearly thirteen years after that fateful meeting with Michael Shrimpton and Robbie Weekes at the Botanical Hotel, it came to the final *Countdown*—19 July, 1987 at the Sydney Entertainment Centre. But Robbie didn't attend.

I wished them all the best, but I took the view that if I had been there for the reality, why would I be there for the parody?

Robbie Weekes

Countdown's first host, Grant Goldman, had proudly watched the show over the years. He also hosted a second *Countdown* episode, in April 1975. His only memory of that show was Michael and Robbie taking him out drinking afterwards, until 4 a.m.—when he was meant to be on the radio at 5 a.m. Grant was also *Countdown*'s first voiceover man, a role he had to relinquish when he moved to 2GB in Sydney in 1975.

Even though it was not my production, I felt like it was my baby and I watched it grow up.

Grant Goldman

Countdown's 40th anniversary coincides with Grant's 50th year on radio—he's been on the air since 1964, a remarkable record. He now does the breakfast show on 2SM.

He's also been the ground announcer at Brookvale Oval since 1978—the home of Melbourne Storm's arch rivals, Manly.

Grant's son, Mike, who was just three when *Countdown* went to air, found fame as a co-host of *Big Brother*. Sadly, Grant's *Countdown* work is lost. We were unable to show clips from the first *Countdown* on the final show because the ABC had recycled the tapes.

There are no copies of those early shows. They erased it. They erased our history. I never even saw that April episode go to air.

Grant Goldman

Executive producer Grant Rule made sure that 'The Countdown Sisters', Linda and Karen, got tickets to the final show.

It was Linda's first trip to Sydney. A security guard stopped them on the red carpet, but Grant spotted them and took them inside. They recall sitting in front of Kamahl, and meeting Cameron Daddo. Karen also pestered Split Enz's Eddie Rayner for Paul McCartney's address. He kindly wrote it down for her.

The final *Countdown* was a massive live show. James Reyne premiered his debut solo single, 'Fall of Rome'. Icehouse performed 'Crazy', Wa Wa Nee did 'Sugar Free', Mental As Anything did 'He's Just No Good For You' and Crowded House performed 'World Where You Live'.

One of *Countdown*'s original stars, John Paul Young, was also there. He appeared on stage and took a bite out of my corsage.

> He was bumbling away, so I thought I'd take a bite. It wasn't a good move because it was full of insecticide. I had to keep chewing until I could leave the stage and spit it out.
>
> **John Paul Young**

Kylie Minogue, Jason Donovan and their former *Neighbours* co-star Peter O'Brien presented the award for Most Popular Group. The nominees were INXS, Pseudo Echo, the Uncanny X-Men and Wa Wa Nee. One of *Countdown*'s biggest discoveries, Pseudo Echo, took the trophy. And Brian Canham won Most Popular Male Performer.

> Hutch [Michael Hutchence] came up to me later and said, 'It's yours, take it.' I really felt I had no right to that [award]. It still makes me laugh.
>
> **Brian Canham, Pseudo Echo**

On the day of the show, my good friend Heloise Pratt kindly allowed me to host a cocktail party at her family's Circular Quay apartment. One party-goer remembers that the event was memorable 'for Molly whipping out his dick', which may be true.

I left the cocktail party and returned to the Southern Cross Hotel, where I had my head shaved. I then had to gaffer-tape hair to my head, so it looked like I still had hair. I came up with this idea about a week before the show. I had some help, too, because my girlfriend at the time, Liz, was a hairdresser. TV shows often end on a bitter note, but I wanted *Countdown* to end on a happy note. I wanted everyone to have a good time because it had been thirteen good years. People had always been asking, 'What's under the hat?' And this was my way of saying, 'Well, we didn't have the bald man [Peter Garrett] on— but here he is anyway . . .'

Before the show, I handed an envelope to Michael Shrimpton, with the message: 'Not to be opened until the final segment.'

The envelope contained a lock of my hair.

Not for one second did I know that Molly had shaved his head. It was astonishing because he's such a blabberer, but this was one secret he kept perfectly. It was a wonderfully theatrical parting gesture, but I remember thinking, I wish he'd done that a month before—it would have been great for the ratings.

Michael Shrimpton

He's a true eccentric. I couldn't believe he shaved his head. At first I thought he had on one of those plastic things!

John Farnham

I revealed what was under my hat at the end of the show, thanking my hairdresser—'I never ever thought I'd give a credit to a hairdresser'—and addressing Peter Garrett, who of course wasn't there. 'Peter,' I said, 'I hope you don't mind me doing an impersonation of you.'

Michael Hutchence was the first member of the crowd to rush on stage to kiss me after I revealed my bald head.

I gave my hat to John Farnham, who had dominated the awards, winning Best Single, Best Album and the Outstanding Achievement Award. He wore it when he led the all-star jam that closed the show. It was fitting that John, who sang the first song on *Countdown*, 'One Minute Every Hour', also did the last, 'You're The Voice'. He's had a remarkable career.

John was joined on stage by his best mate and manager, Glenn Wheatley, who played bass, as well as the man John had replaced in LRB, Glenn Shorrock. It was a rousing finale.

My final words on *Countdown* were:

'Goodnight, Australia, and thank you for thirteen years, you've been bloody wonderful.'

> It was a great final show, but I regret not doing a tribute to Molly. He would have hated it, but we could have done a twenty-minute tribute to him. I've often thought afterwards, 'Hell, this guy is unique in the world.'
>
> **Grant Rule**

At the post-awards press conference, when the press asked me about my future, I said: 'I have no idea what is going to happen in my life now, but I do know my sex life is terrific.'

David Hill told the press: 'It went out with a bang and not with a whimper.' He said he suspected I would return to the ABC, 'as he is too much of an institution and an authority for him not to be back'.

At the party afterwards, at Sydney's Jamison Street Nightclub, I announced: 'I'm not finished yet!'

The party was noteworthy as the night that Michael Hutchence yelled across the room to Kylie Minogue: 'I want to fuck you!' The two later became a couple. *Countdown* had started another chapter in Australian music.

Later, at the Southern Cross Hotel with a few close friends, I declared, 'A weight has been lifted off my shoulders. I feel like a new man.'

I'll never forget waking up to a scratching sound the morning after the awards. It was my bald head rubbing on the pillow. Asked on the night if my hair would grow back, I replied, sadly: 'Do things grow back?' But already, my hair *was* growing back. It was like sandpaper. I remember thinking, 'What a weird life Peter Garrett must live.'

I spent that afternoon sailing around Sydney Harbour on Richard Pratt's boat, staying away from the public and the media, before flying home to Melbourne. Stopping at a 7-Eleven near my house, I saw that day's newspapers. Staring at me from the front of *The Age* and *The Sun* was my own bald head.

It was then I realised how much the show had meant to the country.

The demise of *Countdown* coincided with news that I was planning to produce a TV mini-series based on the true story of a Russian fighter pilot, who, after flying in World War I, moves to Java where the Australian Government commissions him to shuttle people threatened by Japanese advances in World War II. On his last flight out of Java he is given a package of diamonds to hand to a Commonwealth official in Australia. But the plane is shot down and the diamonds disappear.

On 3 August, Channel Ten's publicity department said talk of me doing a show with the network was 'pure speculation'. The rumour was that I would do a half-hour show, five nights a week, with a four-hour block at the weekend.

Really, I just wanted a break.

My whole life had changed. It was like I had to detox from *Countdown*. I tried to take a holiday to Queensland, but that was interrupted by a call from Channel Ten, wanting me to host a Madonna special.

Then Channel Nine wanted me to fly to Tokyo to interview Michael Jackson for *60 Minutes*.

A whole new life was beginning.

I remember Molly ripped up the pages of *RAM* magazine on *Countdown* to protest at a bad review of our debut album. That's passion. *RAM* were probably right in many respects, but Molly wasn't having any of it. The next issue of *RAM*, we got even worse treatment. Fans were siding with Molly or against. Boy, the kids took their pop seriously back then!

Paul Gray, Wa Wa Nee

20: WHATEVER HAPPENED TO THE REVOLUTION?

1987–2007: I start a record label—The Revolution starts here—
I heckle myself—Hey Hey, it's my next adventure.

A couple of times in the more recent years, he's said to me, 'I'm sick of being Molly.' And I say, 'Well, take off that stupid fucking hat and throw it away!' Don't give me this I'm sick of Molly shit. What's so bad about being Molly?
Michael Gudinski

The final *Countdown* was in 1987. But *Countdown* has never left my life. Not a day goes by when someone doesn't mention the show. And more often than not, they say:

'Why don't you bring *Countdown* back?'

But I've never wanted to live in the past. It can be fun to visit, every once in a while, but you don't want to live there.

Of course, if Molly did live in the past, he wouldn't be around now.
Keith Millar, *Kommotion*

After *Countdown* finished, I was free to start a record label, so I created Melodian with Michael Gudinski and Amanda Pelman. I had met Amanda during the *Countdown* years.

It was mid-1981 and I was working at Polygram as a runner while I was doing a media studies course. 'Stars On 45' was the number one song in the country, but there was no video for it. So we organised for all these dancers to go into the ABC studios and do a video for *Countdown*. But half the dancers didn't turn up, and Molly came up to me and said, 'If you don't dance, you will never work in this town again.' I was absolutely terrified. I had a friend with me, Linda Curtis, and we got up there with the real dancers and did this appallingly bad dance.

Unfortunately, the record was number one for six weeks, so I was on every Sunday night. It did nothing for my reputation.

Amanda Pelman, Melodian

Amanda and I became great friends, and she was actually my housemate for a while. She had signed Kylie Minogue to Mushroom Records, so she had an excellent pop pedigree.

Melodian's whole charter was to sign young pop acts—acts that otherwise would not get a go.

Amanda Pelman

I liked the name Melodian. It sounded musical and it managed to combine my two names—Meldrum and Ian. We had great success with Roxus, Indecent Obsession, Jo Beth Taylor and Peter Andre. Indeed, Indecent Obsession, Roxus and Peter all had Top 10 hits in Australia; the Indecents had a Top 40 single in the US ('Tell Me Something'), and Peter had three number one singles and a number one album in the UK.

I signed Indecent Obsession after hearing their demo tape. I met Juno Roxas at Daryl Somers' wedding. 'Hi, I'm Juno Roxas,' he said, shaking my hand. 'Someday you're going to make me a star.'

We became good friends and Molly also became the manager of Roxus. One day, we went to a Greek restaurant in Chapel Street for my birthday dinner. Molly and my dad were sitting together. Molly had everyone laughing. He told me, 'Me and your father are the two oldest people in the music business and don't you forget it.' Later, he did the old, 'Oh, shut up, you came here in a boat!' line.

I replied, 'Listen, lovey, I'd rather have come in a boat than some of the fucking things that you've come in.' That's my favourite Molly line of all time.

Juno Roxas, Roxus

I discovered Peter Andre when I was a judge on *New Faces*. He performed Bobby Brown's 'Don't Be Cruel' and I signed him on the spot. And Mark McGahan—Plucka Duck on *Hey Hey*—gave me Jo Beth Taylor's demo tape, saying, 'She is like a Perth Madonna.'

By 1989, I had almost forgiven David Hill for how he'd treated *Countdown*. And in the 3 July edition of *TV Week*, I wrote the ABC a letter.

Dear Aunty,
Well, the moment that I've dreamed about for a long time has arrived, and I'd just like to say: Thank you very much.
Just think of all the years we were so close . . . the ups and downs, not to mention the times when everything seemed impossible and, oh dear, all those tantrums! How long was it? If I count them down, it adds up to thirteen years! Frankly, Aunty, I thought I'd never see the day when we would put all that behind us and start afresh. That it is indeed happening is a bit like winning TattsLotto!

The chance to be reunited with you and all your wonderful
relatives is . . . well, I can't tell you how excited I am. Oh, all
right then, I'll try . . .
For the past two years, everyone has been saying the idea of
taking in a group of almost total strangers was idiotic. It would
never work. But I believe it will. In my own heart, I believe it.
And I hope for everyone's sake that it does work.
Okay, so they come from very different backgrounds and their
tastes are completely contrasting. And for most of them, this is
a completely new experience. But they will be a team—a great
team—and I'm sure everyone will love them.
Of course, it hasn't been an easy road. But, Aunty, I'm proud
of all that you have done for them—and me—already.
And as we head out on this new road together, I defy anyone
to say you're over the hill—in fact, there's one Hill I'd like to
thank for giving us the chance. I think you know who he is,
Aunty.
So I must sign off now—I've got a new TV show to produce.
I promise I'll drop in every weeknight at 6.30 p.m.—in spirit
if not in the flesh!

Yours truly,
Molly

I first revealed details of my new show in my *TV Week* column a
few months earlier, on 13 May, 1989. The coverline was: 'Molly
Reveals: TV's New Countdown!'

> The revolution is about to begin . . . Right, now that that's settled,
> maybe everyone will stop asking me when *Countdown* is coming
> back on TV!

'The guru is dead!' I declared. Instead of me fronting the
camera, the new *Countdown Revolution* would have three fresh

hosts—television newcomers Andy McLean, Lisa Collins and Daniel Woods, who were dubbed 'gurettes'.

I was back working with Michael Shrimpton, though he was now based in Sydney as the ABC's head of arts and entertainment.

> I was immensely involved. It was emotionally stimulating and terrifying at the same time. I heard the voice of Ken Watts over my shoulder, even though he had died a few years earlier . . . 'Find me the next generation of ABC watchers.'
>
> **Michael Shrimpton, ABC**

The ABC was struggling in the 6.30 p.m. time slot and, again, there were no music shows in prime time. Michael actually offered me the 6 o'clock slot on a Sunday night, but I said no. We also argued over whether using the word 'Countdown' would be a help or a hindrance.

My main motivation was to find some new TV talent. I was *Countdown Revolution*'s producer, not on-air talent. I was obsessed with getting kids off the street and making it work. Total unknowns. Michael had some doubts, but he gave me his full support. But can you just throw unknowns on television?

> I remember the first link for the show: 'Hi, I'm Andy . . . Hi, I'm Lisa . . . And I'm Dan, welcome to *Countdown Revolution.'* *The Comedy Company* took us off, which would have been pretty easy to do because we looked pretty stupid.

> I think the show struggled at the start, so Molly was always looking at ways to change it. He certainly came up with scheme after scheme. One day it would be 'The ABC is going to dress you—meet the wardrobe person,' then the next day it would be, 'No, we want you to be natural, wear what you would normally wear.' At first, it was: 'Introduce the band in your own way.' Then it

was like: 'Say this.' And then Molly would come in and say, 'Listen, I've got some more hosts.'

In the end it was like, 'Geez, what's going on?'

Andy McLean, co-host

The executive producer was Richard Reisz, who had worked on *The Meldrum Tapes*.

Molly? He's an angel with devil's wings.

Richard Reisz

Elton John appeared on the show towards the end of 1989. Everyone was on edge because Clark Forbes had just given his concert a caning in *The Sun*. The *Countdown Revolution* publicist, Debbie Withers, was worried about the catering. I told her to get 'some Champagne and some nice cups of tea', so she went out and got Moët and Twinings tea and shortbread, and asked one of the props guys to get some good china from the set of the drama *Embassy*.

When Elton arrived with Patti Mostyn, Deb asked if he would like a drink.

'Yes, thank you, I'll have a glass of wine.'

'Are you sure you wouldn't like a Champagne?'

'No, I'd like a glass of white wine.'

The only wine Deb had was cask wine from the ABC bar. In a panic, she grabbed two of the show's reporters, Robbie James and James 'The Hound Dog' Young—and got them to race to the Elsternwick Hotel to get a bottle of Houghton's White Burgundy.

Despite the panic, it was a really special time. Seeing Elton rehearse 'Sacrifice' in the studio was something I will never forget. And then Molly had a party for Elton at his house. His [Elton's] mum, Sheila, was telling us stories about how she would put Elton on the train to go to piano lessons on Saturday mornings and he would just ride the train around and around because he didn't want to go. Then she pushed Molly's friend Dennis into the pool. She was great value.

Deb Withers, publicist

Unfortunately, *Countdown Revolution* failed to find a big audience. Whereas *Countdown's* ratings peaked in the 20s, *Countdown Revolution* never got into double figures. Andy and Lisa left the show at the end of 1989, and Dan's role was reduced, with *Neighbours* star Mark Little and Tania Lacy becoming the show's main hosts in 1990.

I left during 1990, and the show finished at the end of that year.

What was I hoping to achieve? I guess I was hoping to find ten Molly Meldrums. But maybe there is only one. People have to find their own way of doing things.

I think the hosts did a good job, but I don't think we hit the music line. I think the kids were speaking to their own. The trouble was their own weren't listening, because in a family of three kids, you might have three separate music tastes. And it wasn't like that in the *Countdown* years. Back then, it was easy to pull the whole country together with ABBA. You can't do that anymore, it's so fractured.

Michael Shrimpton

Countdown's Stephen Jones directed the first two months of the show.

I don't know where it went wrong. It struggled right from the start. It replaced a program called *The Factory*, which was very popular with the ABC people in Melbourne. They weren't happy it was being replaced by what they saw as some pale imitation of *Countdown*. It never got the support of the Melbourne ABC. It had lip-service and professionalism, but no heart, no passion.

Stephen Jones, director

Sometimes you just can't go back. But I've had some fun revisiting *Countdown* over the years. In 2006 and 2007, I teamed up with Michael Gudinski to present the Countdown Spectacular tours, which gathered some of the biggest stars from the era and celebrated the show. Sherbet re-formed for the first tour, and the second year's bill included Rick Springfield, The Knack's Doug Fieger, Bay City Roller Les McKeown, Pilot's David Paton, and Plastic Bertrand.

I was amused by the list of backstage demands from The Motels' Martha Davis:

> David Bowie; assorted teas with a teapot that actually pours; a new drug that makes you horny, happy and skinny with no side effects; world peace; a fruit plate; and George Bush and friends relocated to janitorial positions.

With Renée Geyer on the road, it was almost like a return to *Countdown*'s 100th episode—I'm sure she wanted to hit me a couple of times. I wrote a note in the tour program:

> When you've got the likes of JPY, Wilbur Wilde and Renée Geyer, there's humour, there's drama, there's pathos . . . And there's tragedy. Maybe I'm the tragedy!

It was a buzz going on the road with many old friends, including the wonderfully cheeky Ignatius Jones from Jimmy And The Boys. Fortunately, we didn't re-enact one of his old stage moves—the Countdown Spectacular was a family show, after all.

As part of my onstage schtick, I would (a) perform mock-fellatio on my transvestite keyboard player Joylene Hairmouth, and (b) do a long and truly outrageous stand-up routine about Molly, every night.

The first time we performed at Bombay Rock was our first big tour of Melbourne and we'd sold the place out. I was onstage in full bondage gear doing the Molly-number. It was utterly over-the-top and particularly obscene that night. Then the audience kind of went all quiet and started pointing behind me.

There, onstage, was Molly himself.

Anything could have happened, but for some reason I counted the band into our S&M anthem 'Butchy Boys', picked Molly up, turned him upside down and did the mock headjob on him. Crowd went nuts, and Molly and I have been great mates ever since.

Ignatius Jones

Along for the ride on the first Countdown Spectacular was Uncanny X-Men's Brian Mannix, who back in the late '90s had also created a stage show called *Countdown The Musical Comedy*.

Brian is very clever. The X-Men were a big part of *Countdown* in the '80s, and Brian, with his razor-sharp wit, Rod Stewart hair, and black tights, became a national celebrity, hosting *Countdown* eight times. He started to write a book about the '80s pop scene. It was originally titled 'People Never Fail To Disappoint Me'. Then it became 'Pop Stars, Roadies And . . .' The opening line was: 'Benny always said there were three types of people in the music industry—pop stars, roadies and arseholes. Pop stars got the chicks, roadies got the drugs, and arseholes got the money.'

The press had a lot of fun when the stage show was being cast: who would play me? I suggested National Party leader Tim Fischer. 'Well, at least he's already got the hat.' Funnily enough, the casting director was my former housemate and Melodian partner Amanda Pelman, who had become a major agent and manager. The role of Molly ended up going to Michael Veitch.

> He is not easy to play, because I think there was so much in his mind at the one time. That's why he used to fumble. He's like someone carrying a lot of plates at a restaurant. He wants to get them all to your table, but he ends up dropping them all. I think he is very intelligent. But his brain was always far ahead of his mouth. He wanted to tell us six things at once. The way Molly spoke could give me a false sense of security, thinking that it's really loose. But the very lack of structure *is* its structure, if you can understand that in a metaphysical sense. I could easily trip myself up. I can't just blab anything. It's a big challenge.
>
> **Michael Veitch, actor**

The show opened at Melbourne's Comedy Club on 12 November, 1998, under a legal cloud. The musical was forced to point out it was 'not an ABC production and is not sponsored, authorised or approved of by the ABC'.

Peter Wilmoth wrote in *The Sunday Age*:

> Like archaeologists with their little brushes, Brian Mannix and his cast will unearth long-buried treasures which some believe should remain buried.

I decided not to attend the opening night. 'I wish them all the best of luck,' I told the press. 'But it's just too weird for me.' But about a month into the show, I put on a baseball cap and snuck in with some friends. No one noticed me until I decided to heckle myself. As Michael Veitch stumbled and bumbled and mumbled, I yelled, 'Listen, you little poof, just get on with the bloody show, won't you!'

'Listen, mate,' Michael shot back, 'if you want to get up here and do a better job, then you bloody well can.'

> Only Molly could pick a fight with himself.
>
> **Brian Mannix, Uncanny X-Men**

The crowd loved it, and I loved the show. Brian captured *Countdown*'s sense of humour, loading the script with stacks of 'Molly-isms' and double and single entendres:

> Not to say that Elton's Rod doesn't Sting . . . Christie Allen has got big things in front of her . . . Tonight we're going to Mount Eliza . . . The Bay City Rollers are in their pyjamas, they're ready for bed, Molly . . . 'Come On Eileen', I know it's a great song, but you wouldn't want to be Eileen, would you?
> Speaking of '80s new-wave stuff, which I wasn't, but now I am, so there you go . . .
> TMG—if this album is not number one in America, I'll retire . . . [*The following week*] The reason why it didn't hit number one is a couple of radio stations. I won't name them, EON and XY, all I want to say is if you don't wanna support Australian music, get out of the country.

The show also sent up INXS's non-attendance at award shows: 'We're in West Meadows recording, sorry we can't be there tonight,' said a Michael Hutchence impersonator.

And, of course, there was a send-up of my Prince Charles interview: 'One day, my mum told me my Prince would turn up and here you are.'

Molly: Is it a spin-out seeing all your rellies on stamps? I mean, everyone's licking the back of your Mum's head.

Prince Charles: The Queen . . .

Molly: Call me Ian, please.

Countdown The Musical Comedy also marked the major events in music history.

Molly: Welcome to a special, very sad edition of *Countdown*. This week the world lost a genius. More than a musician, he was a philosopher who taught us a lot about our lives. I don't see how music is going to be the same.

We'll hold a vigil this week. If you want to get the address, get a pen, it's very important that you don't forget it. Take time off school, whatever. The address is—the City Square.

I'm still in shock. The whole world is in shock. I still can't believe it happened.

I still can't believe that um, that um, Elton got married.

The show made me realise how *Countdown* had become part of the culture. And it was like thirteen years of my life flashing before my eyes.

Back in 1981, I was a judge on Channel Ten's *Search For A Star*, alongside my good friend Kenn Brodziak—the man who brought The Beatles to Australia—and singer Judy Stone. Judy said that to be a star, you had to have talent. But Kenn disagreed. 'You don't have to have talent to be a star,' he said. 'You've got a prime example right here at the table—Ian has no talent, but he's a big star.'

I know I have lived the most extraordinary life for an ordinary person, with no discernible talent.

When you think about it, the guy's been involved with successful artists in the '60s, '70s, '80s, '90s and 2000s. It's unbelievable.

Michael Gudinski

During the *Countdown* years, Grant Rule said to me, 'Ian, when you're 50, you'll still be doing music.'

'Bullshit,' I replied.

I was wrong.

I owe so much to all the people I have worked with, particularly Michael Shrimpton and Robbie Weekes. What would have happened to me if I'd not decided to buy that bottle of scotch on that cold Melbourne day in August 1974?

As I write this, I've had 48 years on television. Believe it or not, I don't really like being on television. In fact, I've always looked on television people as being different from myself. My TV career happened by accident, and it's still an accident.

I've met and got to know the biggest music stars of the past 50 years. It's been an enormous privilege. Many of them have become my good friends. But some of my best friends aren't . . . big stars. In fact, most of them are just 'normal' people.

When I was a little boy, with no idea what I wanted to be in this world, my grandmother told me:

'Son, all you have to remember is, no one is above you. But more importantly, no one is below you. Treat everyone the same.'

These are good words to live by.

After the end of the original *Countdown*, I spent the summer of 1987–88 in Noosa with Red Symons, my friend Jan and her two-year-old son, Morgan. It was a magical time, and I ended up adopting Morgan. But my holiday was interrupted by Gavan Disney, who was then the executive producer of *Hey Hey It's Saturday*.

I'd known Gavan since the '70s, when he was the general manager of *Go-Set*.

'Why don't you join *Hey Hey*?' Gavan proposed.

We had a few chats, but I was non-committal—after thirteen years on *Countdown*, I was enjoying my freedom and didn't want to be tied down to a weekly show.

When I returned to Melbourne, Gavan called again. 'Look, I'm taking you out to lunch. Be ready in ten minutes.'

He took me to a restaurant in Acland Street, St Kilda. It seemed like quite a gathering, with members of the *Hey Hey* cast and the press. Suddenly, Gavan decided to make a speech. 'I'd like to introduce the *Hey Hey* cast for 1988,' he announced.

Then he added: 'And I'd like to introduce a new member of the cast.'

Oooh, I thought, I wonder who this will be?

As I stood back, Gavan nudged me. 'Get into the shot, Molly.'

My new life had begun.

What is he? If your son or daughter came to you and said, 'I want to be what Molly is', what would you say? You can't go to the Molly school. Many have tried and they have been bad copies.

There will never be another Molly.

Gavan Disney, *Hey Hey It's Saturday*

SAY I LOVE YOU

Thank you for the music, the songs I'm singing
Thanks for all the joy they're bringing
Who can live without it, I ask in all honesty
What would life be?
Without a song or a dance what are we?
So I say thank you for the music
For giving it to me
ABBA, 'Thank You For The Music'

All the friends I have made over the years, both private and public, I have treasured like jewels unearthed from an Egyptian tomb.

Many I met in front of the camera, and we became mates after years of working together. It is both a curse and a blessing to have recorded footage of so many dearly departed friends: it can bring back so many wonderful memories, but also make your heart ache when they are right there in front of you.

Anubis was an Egyptian god whose domain was death. He ushered souls into the afterlife and presided over a ritual called the Weighing of the Heart, in which it was decided if a soul could enter the realm of the dead. These days, the media can weigh up someone's life when they die. If I am ever privileged to be asked to comment on the passing of a friend and prominent person, I like to remember the positive times, to ensure the weighing of the heart is all good.

Some of the souls that have touched me died decades ago; others just a few painful weeks. In the music world, all of them added to the fantastic soundscape that is the soundtrack of our lives, and—thanks to the wonders of technology and their amazing fans—they will never be forgotten. As the names roll through my head, so many stories flood my mind. And I'm grateful that my accident did not rob me of my past and these precious memories.

If what John Lennon said is true—*'Count your age by friends, not years. Count your life by smiles, not tears'*—then I am far older than I think. But age really is a state of mind. Ironically, I recall talking about age to *The Age* way back in 1980. I said: 'I always laugh at that line where Lois Lane says to Superman, "How old are you?" and he says, "I'm over 21." Well, I'm over 21.'

Our society can be age-obsessed, but age is irrelevant.

When I close my eyes, the faces of so many talented people leap onto an imaginary stage, stars that I have worked with, many who became friends and guests at my home.

Elsewhere in this book, I have written about the pain of losing superstars such as John Lennon (8 December, 1980), Michael Hutchence (22 November, 1997) and Michael Jackson (25 June, 2009). The King of Pop once told me: 'I love to create. I love to make magic. I love to create the unexpected.' He gave us such amazing music and powerful messages of peace.

When I heard that Michael Jackson had died, I was getting ready to go to a Sony lunch, which was fortunate, because Sony Australia's longtime chief Denis Handlin was also at the lunch and we were able to comfort each other. Denis, a driving force behind so many careers, was shattered. We both were. Later, as I spoke about Michael on Channel Seven with Melissa Doyle and David Koch, I remembered how he once said that he believed in being 'humble, and having true love in your heart for the world and really trying to help people through the love of music and dance'. And I do believe that's how he tried to live.

Whitney Houston (11 February, 2012) also spoke about the power of music in her final interview with me, for Channel Seven's *Sunday Night*. 'We all have our moments where we're going through something, one adversity or another, one tribulation or another,' she said. 'And there is always something—one song … where you hear something and you go, "Oh, I can get strength from that."'

I also had some fun, asking Whitney about her wardrobe malfunction on the UK's *The X Factor*. 'I was taught to perform,' she replied. 'When things go wrong, you have to outperform it … forget about it, keep moving and get stronger with it.'

Yep, the show must go on.

When I was writing this book, I was struck by the realisation that so many key members of the *Countdown* years are no longer with us: Dragon's Marc Hunter (17 July, 1998), Models' James Freud (4 November, 2010), Mi-Sex's Steve Gilpin (6 January, 1992), Sherbet's Harvey James (15 January, 2011) and Clive Shakespeare (15 February, 2012), Australian Crawl's Guy McDonough (26 June, 1984) and Brad Robinson (13 October, 1996), Cold Chisel's Steve Prestwich (16 January, 2011), William Shakespeare (5 October, 2010), Christie Allen (12 August, 2008), Crowded House's Paul Hester (26 March, 2005), and Men At Work's Greg Ham (19 April, 2012). And Rose Tattoo's Mick Cocks—part of *Countdown's* infamous 'chewing gum incident'—died of liver cancer on 22 December, 2009.

In one terrible week in 2001, we lost Shirley Strachan and Ted Mulry. Shirl was killed in a helicopter accident on 29 August. He was just 49. Three days later, Ted died of cancer, aged 53. Both were an enormous part of *Countdown*. And both had wicked senses of humour. Shirl loved telling people we'd slept together. It was true. He was also quick to add there was a woman between us in the bed. And that woman was Jan Pickett, the mother of my adopted son, Morgan. But it was very innocent—we were all just good friends.

Some *Countdown* episodes I will never forget. One was having to talk about Bon Scott's death (19 February, 1980). I was devastated. I remember the great Fifa Riccobono—who was a big part of the success of the Alberts label—telling me how she struggled to accept the news. 'I got a call from the UK saying he'd died and I found it incredibly hard to believe,' Fifa said. 'I had to hear it from three people to believe it.' I felt the same way. Bon was a great mate and one of our finest rock 'n' roll frontmen. His legacy lives on in the worldwide success of AC/DC, and he will always be the Aussie rock icon, a larrikin, with the tight jeans, the missing teeth, and a voice that personified pub rock: raw, loud and proud.

In 2012, Bon's old Valentines' bandmate Vince Lovegrove was killed in a car accident (24 March, 2012). Vince also managed Divinyls, fronted by the fantastic Chrissy Amphlett (21 April, 2013). She was feisty, sometimes ferocious, and a true trailblazer for women in Australian rock.

Another pub rock icon, The Angels' Doc Neeson checked out in 2014 (4 June). A gentleman off-stage, a menacing presence on-stage. Am I ever gonna see his face again? You bet I fucking will!

Doc actually suggested the name Zoot for an Adelaide band who then relocated to Melbourne. Zoot's singer Darryl Cotton (27 July, 2012) ended up working with some of my oldest and dearest friends in the business: Ronnie Burns, Russell Morris and Jim Keays (13 June, 2014). As Russell remarked at Jim's funeral, 'I love him, I miss him and I'll carry him in my heart forever.' I told the packed house that I liked to imagine my friend as a star in the night sky, keeping company with Bon

Scott, Chrissy Amphlett and John Lennon, adding, 'If only they could all get together and sing "Give Peace a Chance" for us.'

I also spoke at the funeral of the man who called me Molly— Stan 'The Man' Rofe (16 May, 2003). 'He was a big star with an open heart,' I said. 'No ego, no acting like a big shot. He was a true gentleman who had a great love for music and the people involved in it.'

Another industry figure I'll never forget is Peter 'Iris' Ikin, who was tragically murdered in Paris (12 November, 2008). And as I was writing this chapter, I was saddened to learn of the passing of manager Ian Smith (20 August, 2014), who was instrumental in the Australian Live Aid concert. Apologies for not sticking to the rundown, Smithy!

Of course, we have also said goodbye to many local legends who were stars before *Countdown* came along, including the pioneering Johnny O'Keefe (6 October, 1978), Billy Thorpe (28 February, 2007), Peter Allen (18 June, 1992), Slim Dusty (19 September, 2003), and the Bee Gees' Maurice Gibb (12 January, 2003) and his twin brother Robin (20 May, 2012). And we should never forget the youngest Gibb brother, Andy (10 March, 1988), who had three number one singles in the US.

A highlight of my life was meeting the great Dame Joan Sutherland (10 October, 2010). My mother loved opera and she absolutely idolised Dame Joan. On a trip back from London, I was lucky enough to be sitting in first class when the cheeky flight attendant said, 'Well, this is a privilege—we have two Dames aboard.' He then sat Dame Joan next to me. She was a delight. We had a long chat about music and then she fell asleep. I was so frightened I would snore, so I stayed awake all night. I kept thinking about my mother and how she would have killed me if I snored in front of Dame Joan.

On the world stage, I became friends with Queen's incomparable Freddie Mercury, (24 November, 1991), Paul

McCartney's lovely wife, the talented Linda McCartney (17 April, 1998), and the uniquely talented Amy Winehouse, who sadly became a member of rock's "27 Club" when she died on 23 July, 2011. I fondly remember my first chat with Amy, in 2006 in a tiny hotel room in New York. We had a few lazy vodkas. Later that night, I attended Amy's concert with New York's A-List, and Amy was a little under the weather. When she sang, she was note perfect, but when she spoke, she was a little, er, incoherent. I had a bit of a chuckle, and Amy later asked why I'd been laughing. I told her I was probably the only person in the room who could understand what she was saying. We spoke the same language—I understand vodka talk.

I tried to be on my best behaviour, however, whenever I was around Princess Diana. During the '70s, I was told that electricity usage in Australia peaked on a Sunday evening when *Countdown* was on; well, the world dimmed its lights the night Diana died (31 August, 1997). She was a positive force for change in this world. After attending a charity event in Melbourne with Diana, I mentioned that my house was nearby. Curious about my Egyptian décor, she asked if she could pop in for a look. We walked inside to find my personal assistant, Lynne Randell, doing the dishes. I did the introductions: 'Princess Diana, this is my assistant, Lynne Randell ... Lynne, I'd like you to meet the Princess of Wales.' Lynne was a little stunned, to say the least. All she could say was, 'You've got to be fucking joking.'

It's not every day that a Princess drops in for a cup of tea.

Then there was a memorable party at my place in 1986. Dire Straits and Tom Petty were there. Cyndi Lauper was comforting Stevie Nicks, who was having a problem with the musicians union. And then someone told me that Bob Dylan had arrived. I sprinted down the hall to greet him, to find that Lauren Bacall was on his arm. I dropped the glass I was holding. When

Ms Bacall died on 12 August, 2014, my mind raced back to that night: how she graciously answered all my questions about Humphrey Bogart and stayed at the party for a few hours. I forgot trying to be cool and I asked for an autograph. When I couldn't find a piece of paper, I said, 'Please, just sign the wall.' And she did.

Sometimes, amazing memories flood my mind. 'Did that really happen?' I think. 'It's too wild a dream.'

I met Nelson Mandela (5 December, 2013) at a reception in London when he was involved with the Live 8 event in 2005. It was an honour to be in his presence. I eagerly shook his hand. I was also fortunate to spend time with Mother Teresa (5 September, 1997), seeing her twice in India, and once in London with Princess Diana. Mother Teresa looked at me and said, 'You have been with me in India.'

'Yes,' I replied.

'You were not wearing your cowboy hat.'

'No,' I said quietly. Mother Teresa had that effect on me—she was capable of making me quiet. No mean feat.

Of course, I wasn't so quiet when I had lunch at The Lodge with Charles and Diana, Bob and Hazel Hawke (23 May, 2013) and the cheeky Jack Newton. When I sent my peas flying, Hazel laughed and said, 'If one of those peas hits my dress, you're dead!' I tried to get everything back on my plate, but the gravy left a terrible skid mark on the white linen tablecloth. 'I'm so sorry,' I said to Hazel.

'That's okay, Molly,' she replied. 'We love you.'

I guess I've gotten used to interviewing rock stars over the years, but I'm totally in awe of sportspeople. I dearly miss a couple of St Kilda legends: Trevor Barker (25 April, 1996) and Darrel Baldock (2 February, 2011). Darrel was captain of St Kilda's one and only premiership team, in 1966. R.I.P. The Doc and Barks—and I won't rest until the Saints win another flag.

Also very close to my heart is Lynne Randell, who died on 8 June, 2007. Lynne led a remarkable life. She was a child star in Melbourne and later went on the road with The Monkees and Jimi Hendrix. Then things got a little more challenging—she became my personal assistant. 'Do I love Molly?' Lynne once pondered. 'By love, do you mean he's the sort of person I would lay down on the train tracks for? Yes, I would. He gave me back a reason to be.'

I miss Lynne every day.

Strangely, at the end of this never-ending story, I find the need to say that I don't enjoy talking about myself. Maybe I'm still a country boy at heart. Country people don't like to talk about their achievements, preferring actions to words. Also, even though I've just written a book celebrating a golden era in Australian music, I don't live in the past. I find it silly when people live in the past. Move on! People often say, 'Ah, the good old days.' Forget the good old days—we're living now.

Perhaps I am reticent to reflect on some of my harder times, my childhood spent shifting from my mother to my grandmother, and then those long tram rides to visit my ailing mother in the mental hospital Larundel, with only a thermos of homemade tomato soup and the view of Melbourne out the window to keep me company.

When I arrived in Melbourne, I knew I had to prove myself. I was searching for direction, working at the Bank of New South Wales in St Kilda, the Titles Office, Myer, and as a roadie. And then Go-Set brought me into the recording and music world.

I had found my place.

Did I know then all the amazing people I would meet? All the places I would go and the opportunities that would be afforded me? Of course not, but I knew two things: I always go where the music is—always have and always will—and if you go the extra mile for someone, or something important, only good can come from it.

Of course, my accident forced me to think about my own mortality. Death doesn't scare me. And I want my funeral to be the silliest, happiest thing on earth. I've even told my friend Crystal, *Hey Hey*'s props guru, to work with the undertakers and rig it so the lid of my coffin flies off. I'll pop up and say:

'Just one more thing—"Can I have another drink, please?"'

Would I have traded my life to be a pop star? A footballer for St Kilda? A cricketer for Australia?

No. I wouldn't trade my life for anything. It's been the most extraordinary, fortunate life.

Can I say there is anything different about me that brought me here? Yes and no. I do believe I was in the right place at the right time, and I have always changed with the times and tried to do my own thing. You can only be yourself. And you've got to be true to yourself.

I like to see things through, to be involved in the creative process, even when I'm working with a team. And sometimes things take a little time, like this book and 'The Real Thing'.

And so that brings us to the end of this never, um, ever, er, ending story. Or this instalment, at least. And I have to say I've had more than enough of talking about myself. It's time I started talking to some other people again. That's the part of my life I love the most. If I was forced to describe it, I'd say my interviewing style is more like a conversation. I just want the subject to be relaxed. I want to know about their passions and interests. I want to learn from them.

And I still have so much to learn.

I would like to thank my great friends Michael Gudinski and his lovely wife Sue, and their two children, Matt and Kate. Michael and I have sometimes been called the 'Odd Couple'; he is the odd one and I am straight!

AFTERWORD

By Lawrie Masterson

I started writing this book about 1979, when Molly was still Ian and didn't wear hats. So, you can imagine how delighted I am that it is finally being published 35 years and at least two other ghost-writers later.

Originally, the idea was for me to sit around with Molly and a tape recorder, going over his various adventures and misadventures and translating them into a first-person account of his life, from his childhood in regional Victoria to his brushes and genuine friendships with some of the world's biggest stars.

It sounded easy, but it wasn't. At our first 'book meeting', no one thought to bring a tape recorder. We tried using a telephone answering machine, but, of course, it didn't work. Later sessions were more productive, but, for many reasons I did not understand at the time, the book did not happen back then.

I now understand the main reason perfectly—it just wasn't meant to happen then because Molly's story was still evolving. There were still too many unwritten chapters, so to speak.

I have been lucky enough to experience some of them with Molly or to hear his unedited versions of others. He is actually a great storyteller . . . he just can't write!

Molly's story (so far) should be told now. For someone who can't sing, tap dance or, to my knowledge, play the spoons, his influence on Australian music and television is indelible and he remains a larger-than-life character, a genuine one-off. He just forgets appointments and has a lousy football team, which is why he has needed people such as Allan Webster, Chrissie Camp, Jeff Jenkins and me in his life over the years.

I don't think it is an accident that it has been left to Jeff to—finally—come up with a manuscript. The best man for the job usually gets it done. So, Molly, when can we start work on the sequel?

THE COUNTDOWN YEARS

1974

Top singles: Paper Lace, 'Billy Don't Be A Hero'—Paper Lace, 'The Night Chicago Died'—Alvin Stardust, 'My Coo Ca Choo'—Stevie Wright, 'Evie'—Suzi Quatro, 'Devil Gate Drive'

Top albums: Elton John, *Caribou*—Paul McCartney & Wings, *Band On The Run*—Suzi Quatro, *Quatro*—Mike Oldfield, *Tubular Bells*—Elton John, *Goodbye Yellow Brick Road*

Milestones: Sister Janet Mead's 'The Lord's Prayer' hits number four in the US, where it is the first Australian-produced single to sell 1 million copies—Olivia Newton-John represents the UK in Eurovision, singing 'Long Live Love'; she comes fourth. ABBA win, performing 'Waterloo'—*Go-Set* ceases publication, after eight years—Bon Scott replaces Dave Evans as AC/DC singer—Skyhooks release *Living In The 70's*

1975

Top singles: ABBA, 'Mamma Mia'—Pilot, 'January'—Sweet, 'Fox On The Run'—The Carpenters, 'Please Mr Postman'—Captain & Tennille, 'Love Will Keep Us Together'

Top albums: Skyhooks, *Living In The 70's*—Skyhooks, *Ego Is Not A Dirty Word*—ABBA, *ABBA*—Elton John, *Captain Fantastic and the Brown Dirt Cowboy*—Pink Floyd, *Wish You Were Here*

Milestones: 2JJ starts broadcasting. Its first song is Skyhooks' 'You Just Like Me Cos I'm Good In Bed'—The final Sunbury Music Festival is headlined by Deep Purple—AC/DC release their debut album, *High Voltage*—Two new music papers start: *RAM* and *Juke*—Daddy Cool play their final shows

1976

Top singles: ABBA, 'Fernando'—ABBA, 'Dancing Queen'—ABBA, 'Money, Money, Money'—Ted Mulry Gang, 'Jump In My Car'—Sherbet, 'Howzat'

Top albums: ABBA, *The Best of ABBA*—Rod Stewart, *A Night On The Town*—ABBA, *Arrival*—Queen, *A Night At The Opera*—Sherbet, *Howzat*

Milestones: John Farnham splits with his manager of nine years, Darryl Sambell—AC/DC release 'It's A Long Way To The Top'—Skyhooks tour the US—Sherbet's 'Howzat' hits number four in the UK—The Saints release '(I'm) Stranded'

1977

Top singles: Wings, 'Mull of Kintyre'—Julie Covington 'Don't Cry For Me Argentina'—Pussyfoot, 'The Way You

Do It'—Andy Gibb, 'I Just Want To Be Your Everything'—
Peter Allen, 'I Go To Rio'

Top albums: Boz Scaggs, *Silk Degrees*—Eagles, *Hotel California*—Fleetwood Mac, *Rumours*—Rod Stewart, *Foot Loose & Fancy Free*—ELO, *A New World Record*

Milestones: Red Symons quits Skyhooks—Little River Band's *Diamantina Cocktail* goes gold in the US, the first Australian-produced album to do so—Neil Finn joins Split Enz—INXS play their first gig, as The Farriss Brothers—*Saturday Night Fever* hits cinemas

1978

Top singles: John Travolta & Olivia Newton-John, 'You're The One That I Want'—Bee Gees, 'Stayin' Alive'—Boney M., 'Rivers of Babylon'—Commodores, 'Three Times A Lady'—Village People, 'YMCA'

Top albums: *Saturday Night Fever* soundtrack—*Grease* soundtrack—Meat Loaf, *Bat Out Of Hell*—Jeff Wayne, *War Of The Worlds*—Billy Joel, *52nd Street*

Milestones: Five Gibb songs are in the US in the one week: 'Love Is Thicker Than Water', 'Stayin' Alive', 'Emotion', 'Night Fever' and 'How Deep Is Your Love'—Cold Chisel release their self-titled debut album, featuring 'Khe Sanh'—*Grease*, starring Olivia Newton-John, hits cinemas—John Paul Young's 'Love Is In The Air' hits number seven in the US—Johnny O'Keefe dies of a heart attack, aged 43

1979

Top singles: Racey, 'Lay Your Love On Me'—The Buggles, 'Video Killed The Radio Star'—The Knack, 'My Sharona'—

Blondie, 'Heart of Glass'—Patrick Hernandez, 'Born To Be Alive'

Top albums: Supertramp, *Breakfast In America*—ELO, *Discovery*—Rod Stewart, *Blondes Have More Fun*—Rickie Lee Jones, *Rickie Lee Jones*—Bee Gees, *Spirits Having Flown*

Milestones: Shirley Strachan leaves Skyhooks and is replaced by Tony Williams—The Bee Gees win four Grammy Awards for *Saturday Night Fever*—Sherbet become known as Highway in the US—Silverchair singer Daniel Johns is born—James Reyne makes his *Countdown* debut, singing Australian Crawl's 'Beautiful People', with both arms in plaster, after being hit by a car

1980

Top singles: Split Enz, 'I Got You'—Joe Dolce, 'Shaddap You Face'—Queen, 'Crazy Little Thing Called Love'—Genghis Khan, 'Moscow'—Village People, 'Can't Stop The Music'

Top albums: Split Enz, *True Colours*—Village People, *Can't Stop The Music*—Barbra Streisand, *Guilty*—ELO & Olivia Newton-John, *Xanadu* soundtrack—John Lennon & Yoko Ono, *Double Fantasy*

Milestones: Bon Scott dies—Skyhooks break up—2JJ moves to FM, becoming 2JJJ, and commercial FM radio launches in Australia—AC/DC's *Back In Black* tops the UK charts—Norman Gunston's 'Kiss Army' enters the charts

1981

Top singles: Men At Work, 'Down Under'—Olivia Newton-John, 'Physical'—Kim Carnes, 'Bette Davis Eyes'—John

Lennon, '(Just Like) Starting Over'—Roxy Music, 'Jealous Guy'

Top albums: Rolling Stones, *Tattoo You*—Men At Work, *Business As Usual*—Australian Crawl, *Sirocco*—Dr Hook & The Medicine Show, *Greatest Hits*—Cold Chisel, *Swingshift*

Milestones: Joe Dolce's 'Shaddap You Face' knocks off John Lennon's 'Woman' to hit number one on the UK charts—Cold Chisel tour the US—Air Supply's 'The One That You Love' hits number one in the US, one of seven consecutive Top 5 hits in the US for the duo—Rick Springfield's 'Jessie's Girl' hits number one in the US—MTV starts in the US

1982

Top singles: Moving Pictures, 'What About Me'—Charlene, 'I've Never Been To Me'—Survivor, 'Eye Of The Tiger'—Dexys Midnight Runners, 'Come On Eileen'—Joan Jett & The Blackhearts, 'I Love Rock 'n' Roll'

Top albums: Dire Straits, *Love Over Gold*—Moving Pictures, *Days of Innocence*—Australian Crawl, *Sons of Beaches*—Roxy Music, *Avalon*—Cold Chisel, *Circus Animals*

Milestones: John Farnham replaces Glenn Shorrock as the singer in LRB—Hunters & Collectors release their self-titled debut album—Men At Work's 'Who Can It Be Now' and *Business As Usual* top the US charts—Goanna release 'Solid Rock'—Midnight Oil release *10, 9, 8, 7, 6, 5, 4, 3, 2, 1*

1983

Top singles: Austen Tayshus, 'Australiana'—Laura Branigan 'Gloria'—Irene Cara, 'Flashdance . . . What A Feeling'—

Culture Club, 'Do You Really Want To Hurt Me'—Bonnie Tyler, 'Total Eclipse Of The Heart'

Top albums: Michael Jackson, *Thriller*—Culture Club, *Colour By Numbers*—The Police, *Synchronicity*—*Flashdance* soundtrack—Men At Work, *Cargo*

Milestones: Men At Work have the number one single and album in the US and UK in the same week; they also win a Grammy for Best New Artist and become the first Australian-based band to appear on the cover of *Rolling Stone* in the US—INXS play their first US show, at a club in San Diego—Skyhooks re-form for a national tour—Cold Chisel break up—James Reyne stars in *Return To Eden*

1984

Top singles: Stevie Wonder, 'I Just Called To Say I Love You'—Wham!, 'Wake Me Up Before You Go-Go'—Pat Benatar, 'Love Is A Battlefield'—Nena, '99 Luft Balloons'—Madonna, 'Like A Virgin'

Top albums: Bruce Springsteen, *Born In The USA*—INXS, *The Swing*—Midnight Oil, *Red Sails In The Sunset*—Lionel Richie, *Can't Slow Down*—Prince, *Purple Rain*

Milestones: *Hey Hey It's Saturday* moves to Saturday nights—Australian Crawl's Guy McDonough dies of viral pneumonia—Delta Goodrem is born—Split Enz split, doing the 'Enz With A Bang' tour—Peter Garrett is nearly elected as a senator for the Nuclear Disarmament Party

1985

Top singles: USA For Africa, 'We Are The World'—Foreigner, 'I Want To Know What Love Is'—Madonna,

'Crazy For You'—Tina Turner, 'We Don't Need Another Hero'—Models, 'Out Of Mind Out Of Sight'

Top albums: Dire Straits, *Brothers In Arms*—Jimmy Barnes, *For The Working Class Man*—INXS, *Listen Like Thieves*—Phil Collins, *No Jacket Required*—Eurythmics, *Be Yourself Tonight*

Milestones: *Neighbours* starts—Paul Kelly releases his debut solo album, *Post*—Men At Work release their third and final album, *Two Hearts*—Hey Hey It's Saturday moves from 9.30 p.m. to 6.30 p.m.—Live Aid

1986

Top singles: John Farnham, 'You're The Voice'—Bananarama, 'Venus'—Pseudo Echo, 'Funky Town'—Billy Ocean, 'When The Going Gets Tough, The Tough Get Going'—Madonna, 'Papa Don't Preach'

Top albums: John Farnham, *Whispering Jack*—Whitney Houston, *Whitney Houston*—Paul Simon, *Graceland*—Cyndi Lauper, *True Colors*—Madonna, *True Blue*

Milestones: Australian Crawl play their final shows—Hunters & Collectors release their *Human Frailty* album—the Models' 'Out Of Mind Out Of Sight' enters the US charts, where it peaks at number 37—John Farnham releases his *Whispering Jack* album, which goes on to become the first local album to sell more than 1 million copies in Australia—The Easybeats re-form for an Australian tour

1987

Top singles: Kylie Minogue, 'Locomotion'—Rick Astley, 'Never Gonna Give You Up'—Los Lobos, 'La Bamba'—

Whitney Houston, 'I Wanna Dance With Somebody (Who Loves Me)'—Dave Dobbyn, 'Slice Of Heaven'

Top albums: Icehouse, *Man Of Colours*—Bon Jovi, *Slippery When Wet*—Midnight Oil, *Diesel And Dust*—Jimmy Barnes, *Freight Train Heart*—Whitney Houston, *Whitney*

Milestones: The Australian Made festival tours the country, with an all-Australian line-up, including Jimmy Barnes, INXS, Mental As Anything, Models, Divinyls and The Triffids—The first ARIA Awards are held, hosted by Elton John; John Farnham wins Single and Album of the Year; Crowded House win Best New Talent—John Farnham's 'You're The Voice' hits number six in the UK—INXS release *Kick*—The final *Countdown*

ACKNOWLEDGEMENTS

Eternal gratitude to Lawrie Masterson. A fine writer, a magnificent boss and a great friend.

Lawrie once wrote:

Perhaps someone such as James A. Michener, with teams of researchers delving into the prehistoric origins of rock—musical, not alluvial or abyssal—and an uncanny power of perception might wind up somewhere in the proximity of *The Story So Far*. By the time they'd arrived, though, it would have moved.

Ian 'Molly' Meldrum's life is like that.

Where would Molly's life be without Yael Cohn, his long-suffering assistant? Without Yael, this book would not have been finished. Big love to Yael and her wonderful partner, Edan Gill.

Molly is also blessed to have a great manager, Mark Klemens. Without Mark, this book would not exist. Molly and I take our hats off to Mark, Claire McLennan and everyone at Profile Talent Management.

A big thank you to all at Allen & Unwin, particularly Tom Gilliatt, Mark Lewis, Siobhán Cantrill, Katri Hilden and Jane Palfreyman.

One of my best mates, Patrick Delves, used to call this book 'Chinese Democracy'. But then Axl Rose managed to release that Guns N' Roses album before we finished this book.

The great American writer Tom Wolfe once said:

> I can tell you, taking eleven years to write one book is a killer
> financially, a blow to the base of the skull mentally and physically,
> hell for your family, a slovenly imposition upon all concerned—
> in short, an inexcusable performance verging on shameful.

I couldn't have done it without the love and support of these people:

Phil Burke and Sam Goodwin, Lucy Mariani, Cory & Heidi O'Bryan, Deb Withers, Luke Wallis, Christopher 'Hoops' Hollow, Patrick Delves, John Cain, Nelly Phelan & Oscar Righele, Darren Sanicki, Billy Pinnell, Kate Duncan & Julian Tovey, Mara Blazic, Marisa Stella, Jessie Malignaggi, Sticko & Paula Whitson, Mick & Tiffany Bunworth, Marg Renwick & Matty Foulsham, Andrew McUtchen, Miranda & James Young, Craig Kamber, Matty 'Harem' Arundell, Phil Lawrence, Bill Page, Andrew Murfett, Jamie Berry, Matty Renwick, George Megalogenis, Fiona Hando, Ally Sloan, Bruce Eva, Scotty 'Pop' Thurling, Kelly Reynolds, Therese Cloonan, Chris Howell, Donna Bishop & Gaynor Simpson, Darren Devlyn, Tim Prince, Daniela Masci, Cryss Plummer & Patrick Lauwers, Narelle Graefe, Michael Witheford, Marisa Paolone and Scott Stewart.

Much gratitude to all the fine journalists who have written about Molly over the years, chiefly Ed Nimmervoll, Peter

Wilmoth, Dave Dawson, Cameron Adams, Christie Eliezer and the great Ian McFarlane.

Special thanks to my friends and colleagues, including Neil Rogers & Aaron Jones, Jonathan Alley, Lindy Burns, Trevor Chappell, Marty Jones, Bryget Chrisfield, Lee-Roy Stancliffe, Lauri Wearne, Barry Bissell, Graham Simpson, Ian Strachan, Andrew Tanner, Steve Woods, Sonja Simunkovic, Shellie Murton, Dave Carter, Dean McLachlan, Josie Parrelli, Frankie Palermo, Adrian Prosen, Christian Ryan, Vicki Poupounaki, Paul Cashmere, Jason Stephens, Peter Bain-Hogg, Sue Williams, Jan Sardi, Jim Murphy, Nick Place, Chrissie Camp, Allan Webster, Serge Thomann, and Headley Gritter & Darren 'DD' Brown (the book is out for Christmas!).

And big thanks to John Molloy, Michael Gudinski, Bethany Jones, Gemma Crofts, Matt Cameron, Liz Doran, Andrew Anastasios and all at Mushroom Pictures.

For their sound advice and input, thank you to everyone who has contributed to this book, especially Brian & Gill Meldrum, Michael Shrimpton & Robbie Weekes, Brian de Courcy, John Hoffman, Ted Emery, Grant Rule, Stephen Jones, Mark Opitz, Joe Galjar, Georgina McKay, Sandy Breen, Rui Mac, David Tonner, Billy Miller, Garry Williams, Brian Mannix, Andy McLean & Scotty Kingman, Darren Danielson, Gavin Wood, Graeme Stephen, Mark Hartley, Carmel Nunan, Lizzie Joyce and the wonderful Countdown Sisters—Linda & Karen Freedman.

Thanks to my favourite radio station, SEN, for keeping me company, particularly the exemplary work of Stephen J Peak and Rohan Connolly.

Thanks always to Peter, Amanda & Geraldine Jenkins; John, Imogen & Hugh Bishop; John & Barbara Barnes, Lachlan Vendy and William O'Neil-Shaw. And I'll always remember watching *Countdown* with my cousins Jenni, Julie and Sandra Barnes.

To our dear friends who are sadly no longer with us: Lynne Randell, Stan Rofe, Jim Keays, Rob Austen, Darryl Sambell, Kenn Brodziak, Peter 'Iris' Ikin, Shirley Strachan, James Freud and Zoran Romic.

And, finally, how can I thank Molly? He's unpredictable, emotional, irrational and illogical—and they're just his good points.

Thanks for all the fun.

PERMISSIONS

JEFF JENKINS is the author of several music books, including *50 Years Of Rock In Australia* and *Ego Is Not A Dirty Word, The Skyhooks Story*, and co-author of *Sophisto-punk, The Story of Mark Opitz & Oz Rock*. He writes the weekly Australian music column 'Howzat!' for *The Music*, and is a regular on ABC radio. Jeff's all-time favourite band is Horsehead, and he barracks for Essendon and the Melbourne Storm.

INDEX

Uptight 36
Upton, Andy 90

Van Halen 297
The Vapors 164
Vaughan, Sarah 5
Veitch, Michael 404–5
Versace, Gianni 190
Vicious, Sid 125, 127–8
Visali, Ross 64
Viscount Linley 336–7
volunteer fireman 331
Vuat, Tony 88, 223

Wa Wa Nee 388, 393
The Waggles 211
Walker, Don 282–3
Walker, Robbie 53
Wallis, Jim 20
Walsh, Brian 367
Walters, Wes 360
Waltham, Peter 228
Ward, Frank 91
Warner Music 272, 283, 298
Watson, John 41
Watts, Ken 3, 6–7, 50
Wayne, Jeff 257
'We Are The World' 223–6, 364
WEA 68, 113, 173
Webb, Marius 48, 90, 94–5
Webster, Allan 422
Weekes, Robbie 1, 73, 407
   0–10 Network 4
   Countdown 3–6, 11, 45, 47,
   75–6, 78–9, 86–8, 99, 152–3,
   270, 279–80, 386–7
   Happening series 4, 6
   Kommotion 4, 6, 29
   The Real Thing clip 4
Wendt, George 238

Wendt, Jana 230, 234
Wendy & The Rocketts 100
Wham! 164
Wheatley, Glenn 390
Wheeler, David 179–80
White, Patrick 42
Whitlam, Gough 43, 94, 143
Whitlam Government 41–2
The Wiggles 211
Wilde, Kim 148
Wilde, Wilbur 267, 402
Wilkins (Wilde), Richard 159,
   240, 245, 247–8
Williams, Garry 194–5
Williams, Keith 158
Williams, Kevin 179
Williams, Robbie 54
Williams, Tony 268
Williamson, David 42
Williamson, Dawn 19–20
Williamson, John 18–19, 22, 36
Willis, Rod 281
Willison, Lorraine 184–5, 187
Wilmoth, Peter 230, 232, 404
Wilson, Caroline 62
Wilson, Ian 62
Wilson, Jo 68–9
Wilson, Ross 65, 103, 149
Withers, Debbie 400–1
The Wiz 218
The Wombats 204
Wonder, Stevie 121–2, 225
Wood, Gavin 192, 327, 341–2,
   354–8
Woods, Danielle 295, 399,
   401
Woods, Rodney 271, 295
Wright, Darren 338
Wright, Stevie 34, 45
Wyllie, Ross D. 36